MANAGING PERFORMING ARTS COLLECTIONS IN ACADEMIC AND PUBLIC LIBRARIES

Recent Titles in
The Greenwood Library Management Collection

Time Management Handbook for Librarians
J. Wesley Cochran

Academic Libraries in Urban and Metropolitan Areas:
A Management Handbook
Gerard B. McCabe, editor

Managing Institutional Archives:
Foundational Principles and Practices
Richard J. Cox

Automated Information Retrieval in Libraries
Vicki Anders

Circulation Services in a Small Academic Library
Connie Battaile

Using Consultants in Libraries and Information Centers:
A Management Handbook
Edward D. Garten, editor

Automation in Library Reference Services: A Handbook
Robert Carande

Planning Second Generation Automated Library Systems
Edwin M. Cortez and Tom Smorch

Strategic Management for Academic Libraries: A Handbook
Robert M. Hayes

News Media Libraries: A Management Handbook
Barbara P. Semonche, editor

Reaching a Multicultural Student Community:
A Handbook for Academic Librarians
Karen E. Downing, Barbara MacAdam, and Darlene P. Nichols

Library Records: A Retention and Confidentiality Guide
Shirley A. Wiegand

Managing Performing Arts Collections in Academic and Public Libraries

EDITED BY

Carolyn A. Sheehy

THE GREENWOOD LIBRARY MANAGEMENT COLLECTION

Gerard B. McCabe, Series Adviser

Greenwood Press
WESTPORT, CONNECTICUT • LONDON

Library of Congress Cataloging-in-Publication Data

Managing performing arts collections in academic and public
   libraries / edited by Carolyn A. Sheehy.
      p.   cm. — (The Greenwood library management collection, ISSN
   0894–2986)
      Includes bibliographical references and index.
      ISBN 0–313–27976–4 (alk. paper)
      1. Libraries—United States—Special collections—Performing arts.
   2. Public libraries—United States—Administration.   3. Academic
   libraries—United States—Administration.   I. Sheehy, Carolyn A.
   II. Series.
   Z688.P38M36   1994   93–35837

British Library Cataloguing in Publication Data is available.

Library of Congress Catalog Card Number: 93–35837
ISBN: 0–313–27976–4
ISSN: 0894–2986

First published in 1994

Greenwood Press, 88 Post Road West, Westport, CT 06881
An imprint of Greenwood Publishing Group, Inc.

Printed in the United States of America

The paper used in this book complies with the
Permanent Paper Standard issued by the National
Information Standards Organization (Z39.48–1984).

10 9 8 7 6 5 4 3 2 1

To Harry L. Sheehy,
for his loving and invaluable support

Contents

Introduction

Carolyn A. Sheehy

Managing Performing Arts Collections in Academic and Public Libraries attempts to provide a practical perspective on managing performing arts collections in academic and public libraries that are not solely devoted to the performing arts. The aim of this book is to assist academic and public librarians working with performing arts materials, library students considering a career in performing arts librarianship, and those members of the community interested in conducting performing arts research. Although performing arts can be defined in a variety of ways, for the purposes of this book, performing arts will be interpreted as those arts that can be publicly performed. The performing arts collections described in this book are dance, film studies, music, and theater.

Performing arts collections have been a part of academic and public libraries in the United States for over 150 years. For a few libraries, like the Performing Arts Research Center of the New York Public Library, performing arts collections form the core of their holdings. For most academic and public libraries, performing arts collections are only one part of the materials collected. In many large academic and public libraries, performing arts collections may be independent units or may be part of a larger section. For example, performing arts collections may be found in any one of the following departments or divisions: special collections, the art and music department, the fine arts division, the fine arts and recreation department, the audio-visual center, the music and performing arts department, and the film and video center. In smaller academic and public libraries, performing arts materials may constitute independent collections or may be dispersed among a variety of subject collections. For instance, dance materials may be found in physical education, theater, or music collections.

The demands on librarians managing performing arts collections have increased dramatically in recent years. As public interest in the performing arts has risen and more courses in the performing arts have entered the curricula, these collections have been facing new management challenges. In the past, many performing arts collections were solo operations. If a librarian had subject expertise and met users' demands, their lack of management skills was often overlooked. Today, not only increased interest in the collections but also the emergence of more complex technological environments, ever-increasing budgetary and space constraints, and new developments in areas such as conservation and preservation require that performing arts librarians possess greater management skills.

Performing arts collections offer some unique management concerns. Such collections frequently consist of a variety of formats (for example, scores, recordings, clippings, notebooks, programs, scrapbooks, films, videotapes, audiotapes, compact discs–read only memory [CD-ROMs], and slides). Many of these formats are not easily acquired through commercial vendors and publishers. Once acquired, cataloging, storing, and making these materials accessible to the public may present unusual challenges. Issues of copyright may also be more complex than in a collection consisting of only print materials.

Users of performing arts materials may have special needs. Patrons may be professionals working in a performing art or students, scholars, and enthusiasts learning about a performing art. They may want to "try out" materials in viewing rooms, practice rooms, soundproof spaces, or rooms large enough in which to move. They may want to play a score, reconstruct a dance, see a variety of scenes from a film, or act out the role of a character in a play. In developing facilities and services to meet patron needs, librarians can face particularly creative challenges in managing performing arts collections.

Managing Performing Arts Collections in Academic and Public Libraries consists of six chapters. Chapters One and Six (written by the editor) provide, respectively, a historical overview of the field and an annotated bibliography. Chapters Two through Five, written by librarians managing performing arts collections in both academic and public libraries in the United States, are devoted to the management of specific performing arts collections: dance, film studies, music, and theater. These chapters cover in the same order eight specific management issues (personnel, collection development, technical services, public services, new technologies, facilities, budget and finance, and politics), as well as pertinent subtopics. When relevant, contrasts between managing performing arts collections in academic libraries and in public libraries are noted by the chapter authors.

The book has been designed by the editor to meet readers' specific interests:

1. A reader interested in managing different types of performing arts collections—dance, film studies, music, and theater—is encouraged to read the book in its entirety. The similarities and differences among the four fields will quickly become apparent.

2. A reader interested in managing only one kind of performing arts collection will find information on that area by going directly to the appropriate chapter. Chapters Two through Five were each designed to stand alone to accommodate this need.

3. A reader interested in only one of the eight basic management issues covered in the book (personnel, collection development, technical services, public services, new technologies, facilities, budget and finance, or politics) will find that subject covered in the same order in Chapters Two through Five.

4. A reader interested in only one aspect of one of the eight management issues described in the book will find particular subtopics covered, also in the same order, in each of the four chapters on collections. For example, if the reader is concerned about conservation and preservation of performing arts collections, that issue is always covered under "Technical Services" in Chapters Two through Five.

It is the editor's hope that this approach will provide easy access to information for anyone interested in the management of performing arts collections in academic and public libraries.

The editor wishes to acknowledge the contributions of each of the chapter authors and the editor of the series, Gerard B. McCabe.

1

Historical Overview

Carolyn A. Sheehy

PROLOGUE

Why would an academic or public library begin collecting materials in the performing arts? The answers vary. For some libraries, the reason is fortuitous—a sizable donation of performing arts materials becomes available to them. For other repositories, the motivation is to respond to patron requests for performing arts materials for research, study, or pleasure. For still other libraries, the basis for the collection is a desire to expose present and future generations to the performing arts.

Academic and public libraries in the United States did not begin collecting performing arts materials at the same time or at the same rate. Dance, film studies, music, and theater collections each have a unique chronology in the history of U.S. libraries. Yet, all performing arts collections followed similar developmental stages—acquiring materials, providing access to them, promoting their use, and preserving them for future generations. This historical overview is an attempt to briefly delineate these phases. It does not purport to be an exhaustive study of the topic.

Particular attention is given in the overview to a cadre of performing arts library leaders and to the library organizations and associations that they helped to establish. Although many names in this pantheon are unknown to those outside of performing arts librarianship, it is dubious whether performing arts collections in academic and public libraries in the United States could have prospered without their foresight, dedication, and commitment.

ACT ONE: LAUNCHING PERFORMING
ARTS COLLECTIONS

Of all the performing arts, music collections in academic and public libraries in the United States have the longest and best documented history. When H.G.T. Cannons's *Bibliography of Library Economy* (reflecting library literature from 1876 to 1920) was published by the American Library Association (ALA) in 1927, there were no entries for "performing arts collections," "performing arts libraries," or "performing arts librarians." The index did contain thirteen entries for music, seven for motion pictures, and three for theater; there were no entries for dance.

In the nineteenth century, public and special libraries were faced with exceptional opportunities to purchase or receive as gifts significant private music collections. The Boston Public Library became the first public library to collect music when in 1859 it purchased for $750 the collection of Baron de Koudelka, "a very valuable collection of works on the theory of music, and music of the fifteenth and sixteenth century" (Caldwell 1928: 395). The New York Public Library received in 1888, as a bequest, the music collection of Philadelphian Joseph W. Drexel, one of America's first collectors. The Allen A. Brown Collection of music and musical literature was deposited in 1894 in the Boston Public Library, and Italian Count Pio Resse's unique music collection of 751 titles was purchased in 1889 by The Newberry Library in Chicago. According to James M. Wells, Custodian Emeritus of the John W. Wing Foundation on the History of Printing at The Newberry Library, Pio Resse's collection "contained works on the history and theory of music, mostly Italian, including a copy of the first published opera, Jacobo Peri's *Euridice* printed at Florence in 1600, one of two known copies and the first in the United States" (Wells 1987: 28).

Music collections in public libraries far outnumbered those in academic libraries at the beginning of the twentieth century. The Boston Public Library developed the first departmental music collection in a public library in 1895. The same year that the Library of Congress formed a separate music library—1897—so, too, did the Brooklyn Public Library, Buffalo Public Library, and Milwaukee Public Library (Bradley 1990: 5). By 1915, music collections had been created in public libraries across the United States. A "Symposium on Music in Libraries" in the August 1915 issue of *Library Journal* contained articles on music collections in California, Connecticut, Illinois, Indiana, Massachusetts, Missouri, and Tennessee. Most of the librarians who authored the symposium articles felt, as did John G. Moulton of the Haverhill Public Library, that "[t]he music collection is one of the most popular features of the library, and has helped to advertise it" ("Symposium on Music in Libraries" 1915: 566).

The growth of music collections in academic libraries paralleled the development of music courses in the curriculum. Some of the earliest academic music collections were established at conservatories responsible for training serious students of performance, such as Oberlin Conservatory (ca. 1865), New England Conservatory (1867), Cincinnati Conservatory (1867), and Peabody Conservatory (1868). Tufts College, Harvard University, and the University of Oregon were among the first colleges and universities to provide music collections in support of the historical study of music (Bradley 1990: 5). When numerous European musicologists immigrated to the United States during World War II, music courses in colleges and universities increased exponentially. As music historian Carol June Bradley notes, "in the decades since 1940, the number of academic music libraries has tripled from 74 in 1939 to 230 at the end of the 1970s" (1990: 5).

Although today performing arts libraries circulate information in a variety of formats, this was not always the case. For example, the circulation of music scores and books was not initiated until 1882, beginning with the Brooklyn Public Library. As W. A. Bardwell, acting librarian there, reported, "The idea of a circulating library of music is, I think, a novel one with libraries, although it has long been the practice of some of the large dealers in music, Messrs. Schirmer & Co. of New York, among others, to loan as well as sell it" (1887: 159).

Music librarians were quickly influenced by patrons' positive response to the circulation of music scores and books. The St. Paul Public Library launched circulation of another format, sound recordings, in 1915 (Smiraglia 1989: 15). By 1920, Amy Meyer of the Detroit Public Library observed that "[t]he tradition that the library function should confine itself to an accumulation and judicious circulation of the 'printed word' did not include in its neat and positive boundaries any intention of admitting printed music. But the number of people who know the musical alphabet, which unlocks and opens to them the realm of sound, is growing rapidly" (1920: 182). Thirty-three years after the Brooklyn Public Library began circulating music materials, Charles E. Farrington, branch librarian, reported that use of the library's circulating music collection "since the beginning shows that we have a large music-loving public among our borrowers and that many of our members are music students who recognize the advantages offered by the library through its large collection for home use" ("Symposium" 1915: 564).

The development of theater collections in academic and public libraries in the United States took a more circuitous route than did music collections.

Theater materials entered libraries through many different departments and divisions. For example, information on theatrical productions was scattered among a number of library units. Works on the costumes used in a particular play might be found in the fine arts department, while materials relating to the lighting design for that same play might be located in the science and technology division. Moreover, drama was collected as literature and classified and housed according to nationality.

As Gladys Walker White of Cornell University wrote in the October 15, 1957, issue of *Library Journal*, the creation of theater collections in the United States may be attributed to "the decline of puritanism and the increasing prestige of the theater as a respectable cultural medium" (1957: 2484). While the Library of Congress began collecting plays from all periods and countries in 1870, the collections of noted actors Edwin Booth and John Gilbert helped establish two formidable theater collections. Booth, the celebrated Shakespearean actor, gave his personal collection to the Players Club in New York in 1888. The widow of Gilbert left his collection to the Boston Public Library in 1889. Gilbert's collection consisted of "plays annotated by the actor, notes on the 1,150 roles which he played, souvenirs of his association with Lester Wallack, Joseph Jefferson, Charlotte Cushman and all the principal actors of the era, as well as a large body of more general material" (International Federation of Library Associations 1960: 230).

Other important theater collections and archives formed before the first half of the twentieth century included those at Harvard University, the Shubert Theatre, Yale University, and the New York Public Library. The Harvard Theatre Collection was founded in 1901 with a gift in memory of Harvard librarian Justin Winsor; Professor George Pierce Baker (teacher of many eminent U.S. dramatists) donated portraits of actor and producer David Garrick. The archive of the Shubert Theatre, one of the world's largest theatrical collections in a single institution, was begun in 1903. Yale University's theater collection was inaugurated in 1920 with Professor J. R. Crawford's gift of his collection of programs, engravings, and photographs, covering both dramatic and musical theater. The Theater Collection of the New York Public Library was launched in 1931 with two important bequests: the David Belasco Collection, which included the noted U.S. theatrical producer and playwright's scrapbooks, photographs, designs, and promptbooks; and the Robinson Locke Collection of dramatic scrapbooks.

When Rosamond Gilder (drama critic and associate editor of *Theatre Arts*) began a national survey of theater collections in the United States in 1932, she first consulted the Special Libraries Section at the Library of

Congress. Only six theater libraries were listed there. However, Gilder's survey discovered that over sixty—rather than six—theater collections existed in museums and libraries in forty-three states. "Thirty-two had rooms or sections devoted to the theatre, twenty-five had librarians on full or part-time schedules" (Gross 1941: P-177). These collections represented "the growing need for library facilities on the part of the steadily increasing numbers of directors, actors, and staff involved in a variety of theatre programs in the United States" (Rachow 1981: 4).

Many theater collections initiated in academic and public libraries during the first half of the twentieth century attempted to meet the needs of local theater communities. For example, in a paper on "The Library Needs of a Little Theater" presented at the 1926 American Library Association annual conference, Blanche K. S. Wappat of the Carnegie Institute of Technology Library described the work of that institute's Arts Branch Library, which was located near a little theater and had close ties to the theater community. Books needed by the community for theater research were used in the library. Wappat pointed out that "Libraries far distant from the theater using their resources, may wish to have more generous lending rules. One of the largest public libraries, I understand, sends material to the theater for reference use. This would be done, I suppose only when the theater staff members are known to the library" (Wilcox 1926: 482).

The increase in theater collections also represented the growing respectability of the study of theater as an academic discipline. Theater courses entered college and university curriculum after World War I and continued to increase after World War II. At Princeton University, the William Seymour Theatre Collection, documenting the activities of the scenic director of the Empire Theater in New York, was inaugurated in 1936. Brown University, Columbia University, Dartmouth College, the Folger Shakespeare Library (administered by the Board of Trustees of Amherst College), Ohio State University, and the University of Texas at Austin were among those American institutions whose theater collections were listed in the 1960 edition of *Bibliothèques et Musées des Arts du Spectacle dans le Monde/Performing Arts Libraries and Museums of the World* (International Federation of Library Associations 1967). (Public libraries whose theater collections were noted in that same edition included Chicago, Cleveland, Detroit, Los Angeles, Philadelphia, and San Francisco.)

While music and theater collections in U.S. libraries matured during the beginning of the twentieth century, dance collections remained in the earliest stages of development. Reflecting perhaps the most ephemeral of the performing arts, dance collections struggled to grow beyond infancy.

Unlike the other performing arts, "the art of dance has limitations in that it possesses no easy means of recording itself. Dance has no equivalent of the musical score or the written text" (Oswald 1991: 80). Moreover, the puritanical constraints and lack of cultural respectability that had plagued theater in the United States also hampered dance. Until the second half of the twentieth century, "dance," "dance collections," "dance libraries," or "dance librarians" were not indexed in *Library Literature*. The first entry for "dance" appeared in the 1952–1954 edition of *Library Literature*, and the first entry for "dance libraries and collections" in the 1955–1957 edition.

Four institutions played—and continue to play—essential roles in the history of dance collections in the United States: Harvard Theatre Collection (founded 1901), Dance Collection of the New York Public Library (1944), San Francisco Performing Arts Library and Museum (1947), and the Library of Congress's Performing Arts Library at the Kennedy Center (1979). Representatives from these four repositories formed the first Core Administrative Committee of the Dance Heritage Coalition, dedicated to preserving and disseminating information about dance materials in the United States.

The largest and best known dance collection in the United States is at the New York Public Library's Performing Arts Research Center. The collection began at the 58th Street Music Library, when Dorothy Lawton, who was hired to develop the music collection, began to systematically collect dance materials in 1927 (Bradley 1990: 149). Subsequently, the collection was transferred to the public library at 42nd Street and Fifth Avenue, where it became a special collection within the Reference Department's Music Division. In the mid-1940s, Genevieve Oswald, who worked at the Music Division, noticed the frequency of dance inquiries and persuaded Dr. Carleton Sprague Smith, the division chief, to "set off a small corner of the already overcrowded Music Room for an embryonic collection on dance. Dr. Smith naturally put her in charge as full-time curator" (Rosen 1975–1976: 23).

The Dance Collection of the New York Public Library became a division of the library in 1964. As dance historian Lillian Moore noted in *Images of the Dance*, "[t]his extraordinary development would have been impossible without the tireless enthusiasm of its Curator, Genevieve Oswald, the generosity of its many donors, and the encouragement of the Library's farsighted Administration" (1965: 5). Oswald's abilities to expand the collection and to discern the role that technology would play in disseminating information about performing arts collections were remarkable. As early as 1978, Oswald was calling the advent of home video systems and video formats such as the videodisc " 'a tremendous leap forward,' in the accessibility and lendability of dance resources" (Sneed 1978: 683).

Starting in the 1960s, there was a great surge in the popularity of dance in the United States and in the collection of dance materials in American libraries. Oswald observes: "In the United States, according to a conservative estimate made by *Variety*, six million people in 1956 attended the ballet. . . . During the last two weeks in April 1967 half a million people attended ballet performances at Lincoln Center alone" (Oswald 1968: 147). Diana Reische wrote in *The Performing Arts in America* that in the 1970s "[d]ance is enjoying a wave of unprecedented popularity, with new companies and schools forming every year" (1973: 107). Significant dance collections were created at large academic institutions with strong dance programs (e.g., Ohio State University, University of California at Los Angeles, and University of Hawaii) and at special libraries with particular historical interests in dance (such as the Dance Notation Bureau and The Newberry Library). Smaller dance collections were established at public libraries, some responding to the increasing popularity of dance, others benefiting from donor generosity. For example, the Bryan (Texas) Public Library received a special ballet collection in 1974 from Mrs. Howard Gee, professionally known as Ana Ludmilla, the former premier danseuse of the Chicago Opera. When the collection opened, the *Texas Library Journal* reported that "The special collection is housed in an antique oak bookcase with glass doors. . . . Mrs. Richardson and the staff of the Bryan Public Library are quite proud of their fascinating collection and hope to receive many visitors" (McCarty 1974: 34).

Film studies collections made their entry into academic and public libraries in the United States later than music, theater, and dance collections. Librarians were even more reluctant to acquire films than they were to collect and circulate sheet music. Not until film studies entered the curriculum of colleges and universities in the 1960s and 1970s did most librarians begin to perceive film as a performing art form.

Initially, librarians were concerned about the safety of collecting film. Although motion pictures had been introduced in 1896 with Thomas Armat's vitascope at Koster and Bial's Music Hall in New York, the possibility of fire limited the use of films in libraries (Rehrauer 1975: 14). "It was not until 1923 that technicians produced a practical 16mm camera, projector, and compatible nonflammable film" (Rehrauer 1975: 15).

In the first half of the twentieth century, librarians, particularly in public libraries, also hesitated to collect or circulate films because of questions they had about the educational or moral value of film. Many public librarians viewed film primarily as a medium by which to spur patrons to read books. In the 1920s, the Children's Librarians Section of the American Library Association expressed concern about the unsuitability of some films for children. Mrs. Adele Henry Maze, librarian at the South Branch of the Oak Park (Illinois) Public Library, presented a resolution adopted at the section's 1923 meeting "[t]hat children's librarians express an interest in more direct and neighborly cooperation with the motion picture theatres in the encouragement of programs primarily for children with films of greater educational and artistic value, especially those that will lead to the reading of good literature" (Ayres 1923: 226).

By 1924, the American Library Association's Committee to Investigate the Proposed Distribution of Educational Films through Libraries, charged with studying library activities as they related to moving pictures, lantern slides, stereopticon reproduction, microscopic equipment, educational exhibits and museum material, still "had not yet been completely organized" ("Committee" 1924: 224). The reluctance of librarians to collect or circulate films prompted the chair of the ALA's Committee on Moving Pictures and the Library, J. Ritchie Patterson (director of Visual Materials and Binderies at the Chicago Public Library), to express his frustration with the situation at the committee's 1928 meeting. Angry with the committee's reluctance to deal with the problem, Patterson stated that "[t]his year's Committee is going to try some plans that will shed some light on the above queries. The A.L.A. Headquarters office has cooperated generously in the proposed program and it will not be its fault if a dent is not made in the library mind in the matter of the duty, desirability and feasibility of public libraries interesting themselves in this latest child of the arts" (Patterson 1928: 437).

Yet, even in the 1930s, many public librarians continued their resistance to collecting films. The May 1936 issue of the *Bulletin of the American Library Association* reported the findings of the chair of the ALA's Visual Methods Committee, George T. Bowerman (librarian at the Public Library of the District of Columbia). Bowerman notes, "So far as the committee has been able to ascertain, no library, at least no municipal public library, has thus far undertaken to collect and make available to its public motion picture film" (1936: 416).

Two of the earliest institutions to recognize the importance of film and to collect film were the Library of Congress and the Museum of Modern Art in New York. The Library of Congress collected over 3,000 films from 1894 to 1912, and "moving-picture shows" first appeared in its classification in 1915. The Museum of Modern Art's Art Film Library was established in 1935 to acquire, catalog, preserve, and circulate as complete a record as possible of all types of motion pictures made in the United States or abroad from 1893 to the present (White 1957: 2487). (The Museum of Modern Art published a major source book on the history of film, *Circulating Film Library Catalog*, in 1984.)

The use of films as training and educational tools during World War II helped to increase librarians' interest in collecting and circulating films. "Bertha Landers (who founded *Landers Film & Video Reviews* in 1956) created an audiovisual division at the Dallas Public Library in 1942; her example was followed by Cleveland in 1943, Boston and Cincinnati in 1947, Rochester, New York, in 1948, Los Angeles in 1951, and Brooklyn in 1952" (Slide 1992: 60). With a grant of $5,500 from the Rockefeller Foundation, the ALA published Gerald Doan McDonald's *Educational Motion Pictures and Libraries* in 1942. The Carnegie Corporation of America gave the association a grant in 1945 to encourage audiovisual services in libraries and to establish a film advisory service at its head-quarters (Rehrauer 1975: 17). In the service's first annual report in 1948, Patricia Blair, the ALA's library film adviser, revealed that many librarians wanted to establish some type of film service and that "[t]he most phenomenal growth which has occurred in the past year has been in the public library field" (1948: 474).

According to George Rehrauer, author of *The Film User's Handbook*, "During the fifties the increased use of films in education institutions and training programs—supplemented by the visual experiences provided by television—constituted the final argument for placing films in libraries" (1975: 18). Film services grew in public libraries across the country. Grace Stevenson explored public library film catalogs in 1951 and five years later Patricia Blair Cory and Violet F. Myer wrote *Cooperative Film Services in Public Libraries*. Reflective of this change in the attitude of public librarians toward film, *Public Library Service: A Guide to Evaluation with Minimum Standards*, issued by the ALA in 1956, included guidelines not only for print collections but also for nonprint collections.

The first entry for "film libraries" (as contrasted to "motion picture libraries" or "moving picture research libraries") appeared in *Library Literature 1964–1966* and coincided with the introduction of film studies courses into college and university curricula. In the 1940s, only 5 universities—University of Southern California, University of California at Los Angeles, City College of New York, New York University, and Boston University—had film departments (Grant 1989: 7). By the late 1970s, over 1,000 colleges and universities in the United States offered courses in film and/or television (Grant 1989: 17). The growth of these courses, and as a corollary of film studies collections in libraries, may be attributed to a number of factors: the popularity of European "art" films, the writings of new film critics and scholars, a reexamination of American film, and new developments in technology. The burgeoning independent film movement in the 1970s also helped provide "a wider variety of films and better films available to libraries at a time when many libraries have faced serious disruptions in their funding" (Sloan 1978: 128).

The development of video technology significantly impacted the growth of film studies collections in libraries in the 1980s. The American Film Festival, sponsored by the Educational Film Library Association, included a video competition, for the first time, in 1981. As William Sloan, film librarian at the New York Public Library, notes, "One of the dominant questions facing film librarians and library administrators during 1986 was, 'how shall we shape our 16mm film collection in the light of the growth and popularity of videocassette collections?' With videocassettes of some Hollywood entertainment films selling for as little as $10 and averaging abut $30, there has been a move by some libraries to consider giving up films entirely for video" (1987: 130).

While librarians long debated the issue of collecting and circulating 16mm film, their acceptance of video was almost immediate. As Barry Keith Grant states in his essay "Film Study in the Undergraduate Curriculum," "The introduction of relatively inexpensive, widespread video technology in recent years, and the large number of classic films now available in video format, offers still another possible direction for film programs" (1989: 15). As a result of this surge in video collections in libraries, many academic film libraries that formerly rented 16mm films to off-campus clients ceased operations in the 1990s. For example, the Film and Video Library at The University of Michigan ended its operations to external clients in 1992, after fifty-five years of serving institutions across the country.

ACT TWO: ORGANIZING PERFORMING ARTS LIBRARIANS

Librarians have formed professional associations to exchange ideas, establish and maintain standards, honor excellence, and recruit individuals to the profession. To reflect librarians' particular subject strengths or functions, specialized library organizations have been created. Among the latter, associations for performing arts librarians have been unique. These associations have succeeded in being inclusive rather than exclusive, welcoming not only librarians working in other subject areas but also teachers, publishers, administrators, performers, enthusiasts, and others interested in the performing arts as a vocation or as an avocation. As a result, today many librarians working in or interested in the performing arts belong to more than one professional association. On local, regional, national, and international levels, these professional organizations have been critical in establishing access to and promoting use of performing arts collections in academic and public libraries.

One particular event in the history of the American Library Association had a profound effect on the organization of performing arts librarians and performing arts collections. The March 2, 1924, *Bulletin of the American Library Association* reported that at its annual conference Antoinette Douglas (chief of the Art Department at the St. Louis Public Library) initiated an Art Reference Round Table to bring together librarians working not only in the visual arts but also in the performing arts. "The meeting was attended by 63 persons, representing art departments of public libraries, libraries of art schools and museums and other organizations concerned with the handling of books, plates, clippings and lantern slides" (Wappat 1924: 293).

Until it became part of the Specialized Libraries Division of the American Library Association in 1956, the Art Reference Round Table actively encouraged librarians to develop performing arts collections. For example, Barbara Duncan (librarian at the Sibley Musical Library of the Eastman School of Music) presented a paper in 1927 to the Art Reference Round Table on "Music from the Library Point of View," in which she urged librarians to collect all material possible pertaining to local music history (Wilcox 1927: 331). At the Art Reference Round Table meeting in 1932, Leon R. Maxwell (director of the Newcomb School of Music) made a more specific plea "for the preservation of folk music of the south, the Creole, and the Negro and said that it was essential to record accurately the music as well as the words" (Breen 1932: 520).

The Art Reference Round Table offered crucial support to performing arts librarians long before librarians in these disciplines formed their own associations. For example, before the founding of the Music Library Association and the Theatre Library Association, the Art Reference Round Table was instrumental in offering music and theater librarians advice and encouragement. As chair of the Art Reference Round Table in 1928, Gladys Caldwell (head of the Art and Music Department of the Los Angeles Public Library) reported that Mr. Julius Mattfeld (librarian at the National Broadcasting Library) accepted the position of chair of the Art Reference Round Table's new music committee "which should assist smaller libraries in building up and maintaining adequate music collections" (1928: 396). The Art Reference Round Table offered programs and other forms of support to music librarians until 1944. At that time, the group recommended that "[a]rt librarians whose departments include music libraries will wish to have membership in the Music Library Association which now handles all music library activities" ("Art Reference" 1944: H-50). However, it was not until 1950 that the Art Reference Round Table formally stated that "[t]he subject of music is, by agreement with the Music Library Association, excluded from discussion" ("Art Reference" 1950: 427).

The Music Library Association (MLA) was launched in 1931 by Eva Judd O'Meara (librarian of the Yale University School of Music Library) and a small coterie of her colleagues "to promote the establishment, growth, and use of music libraries; to encourage the collection of music and musical literature in libraries; to further studies in musical bibliography; and to increase efficiency in music library service and administration" (Steuermann 1976: 237). According to former MLA president Donald Krummel, "The nucleus of a dozen members met regularly and grew slowly over the early years. They established a precedent for small-scale, high-quality, personalized activities and began an occasional mimeographed journal called *Notes*" (1982: 180). The irregularly issued, typewritten first series of *Notes* was succeeded in 1943 by a quarterly, printed, second series. *Notes* contributors have included such illustrious composers as Marc Blitzstein, Aaron Copland, Henry Cowell, Mitch Miller, Gunter Schuller, and Charles Seeger (Krummel 1982: 180). (Currently, the MLA also publishes a monthly *Music Cataloging Bulletin*, a quarterly newsletter, technical reports, and index and bibliography series.)

The growth in collections of sound recordings in libraries helped the MLA increase its membership. As president of the MLA in 1947, H. Dorothy Tilly (chief of the Music and Drama Department of the Detroit Public Library) spoke at the annual meeting on the need for giving better publicity to the association's activities. She noted that

It did not appear to be clearly understood that the Music Library Association's main objective was service to *all* libraries, large or small, not only to the special library. It might have been true at one time that the larger libraries were the principal beneficiaries of the association's activities, but the advent of record service into public, as well as school libraries, has changed the picture. No library is now too small to install records service, and it is in this field particularly that the Music Library Association, through its record committees, can be of help (Tilly 1947: P-97).

Not long after music librarians formed the MLA, theater librarians also organized their own association. Initially, the American Library Association

attempted to organize theater librarians by creating a Round Table on
Theater and the Library in 1934 and appointing a joint committee to foster
coordination with the National Theatre Conference, which had been
founded in 1932 (White 1957: 2484). Affiliation with this latter group did
not materialize. Instead, the Theatre Library Association (TLA) was
initiated in June 1937 when Harry M. Lydenberg (director of the New
York Public Library) convened a meeting "to bring together librarians and
individuals interested in the collection and preservation of material
relating to the theatre, and to stimulate general interest in the making and
use of theatre collections" (*Broadside* 1940: 1). George Freedley (curator
of the New York Public Library's Theatre Collection) was elected chair.
(In honor of Freedley, the TLA established an award in 1968 for a
distinguished publication on theater.) The initial membership of the TLA
numbered ninety and included European as well as American librarians
and theater people (Nemchek 1980: 59). A newsletter, *Broadside*, was
begun in 1940 when A. J. Wall of the New York Historical Society
"contributed a hundred dollars to print the fourfold broadside designed in
circus red, white, and black by Warren Chappell, the artist and book
illustrator" (Freedley 1967: 354).

The two new associations, the Music Library Association and the
Theatre Library Association, both dealt with some of the unique problems
confronting performing arts librarians. For example, at early meetings of
the TLA, librarians discussed the multitude of formats in their collections
and the need to create indexes to those collections. Speaking on "The
Library's Point of View in Theater Research" at the annual meeting in
1940, Kurtz Myers (from the Music and Drama Division of the Detroit
Public Library) cautioned members to remember that "theater has not
characteristically expressed itself in books—but in such ephemeral things
as performances upon a stage which exist for a matter of minutes or hours,
and in playbills, photographs, and the pipe-dreams of press agents which
endure a little longer but will wither less there is a theater-minded librarian
at hand to gather them lovingly and lay them away" (Gross 1940: P-235).
Moreover, he decried the scarcity and the quality of available theater
reference tools. He pointed out the need for "elaborate subject indexes to
plays and indexes to theater literature which will organize according to trends,
periods, theories, forms, nationalities, and the like" (Gross 1940: P-235).

After World War II, both the MLA and the TLA worked not only to
serve members locally but also to pursue international connections. Of the
two associations, the TLA was the first to join the International Federation
of Library Associations (IFLA). United Nations Educational, Scientific,
and Cultural Organization (UNESCO) charted the International Theatre

Institute (ITI) in 1948, and Rosamond Gilder was selected the first president of the International Theatre Institute/United States (ITI/US) in 1949. An International Section of Theatre Collections and Libraries, later called the International Section on Libraries and Museums of the Performing Arts (SIBMAS) was established in the International Federation of Library Associations in 1954 (Johnston 1979: 56). At an international conference on theater history in London in July 1955, the International Federation of Societies for Theatre Research was founded, and the first World Conference on Theatre (with three delegates from the United States in attendance) was held in 1956 in Bombay (White 1957: 2488). ITI/US became an independent, nonprofit organization in 1968.

The MLA passed a motion in 1947 sanctioning the association's application for membership in the International Federation of Library Associations (Tilly 1947: P-97). However, not all association members considered this international outreach advisable. As president of the MLA in 1948, W. Scott Goldwaite (head of the Music Library at the University of Chicago) read a letter at the annual meeting from Edward N. Waters, former MLA president and current chair of the Liaison Committee. The letter stated that Waters was "not so sanguine about international liaison at the present time, since international relations were excessively complicated. If anything was to be attempted along these lines, it should be handled through the National Music Council and UNESCO. This would be the logical and proper channel" (Campbell and Rogers 1948: P-90).

The International Association of Music Libraries, Archives and Documentation Centers (IAML) was founded under UNESCO's auspices in Paris in 1950. The MLA finally became a member of the International Federation of Library Associations in 1975 and created a joint committee with the U.S. branch of the IAML. Membership in the IFLA became increasingly important "as IFLA considered formats for music [ISBD (M)] and nonbook materials including sound recordings [ISBD (NBM)]. MLA had participated in the formulation of ISBD (M) through a special committee set up by the International Association of Music Libraries, but no similar vehicle has been available for nonbook materials" (Epstein 1977: 210).

During the 1960s, new associations for librarians working with sound archives were established. The Association for Recorded Sound Collections (ARSC) was launched in 1966 for private collectors, scholars, librarians, and archivists. The *ARSC Journal* brought new material on recorded sound to library literature (Stevenson 1975: 298). The International Association of Sound Archives (IASA) was begun in 1969, and the IASA *Phonographic*

Bulletin provided "indispensable intelligence from the international scene" (Stevenson 1975: 303).

Just as music and theater collections entered academic and public libraries in the United States earlier than dance and film studies collections, music and theater librarians organized professional associations before film studies and dance librarians. However, many different organizations, including those of music and theater librarians, welcomed the participation of dance and film studies librarians before these librarians formed their own associations.

Librarians involved with or interested in film met as early as 1924, with the founding of the American Library Association's Committee on Moving Pictures and the Library. Four years after its establishment, the scope of the committee was enlarged and its name changed to the Committee on Visual Methods. By the following year, "[t]he meeting of the Committee on Visual Methods was held on May 14 and proved to be of such drawing power that scores were unable to get into the crowded hall" (Patterson and Freeman 1929: 361). The committee's name was again changed in 1940, when, with the advent of television, it was decided that it would be advantageous for the Visual Methods Committee and the Library Radio Broadcasting Committee to merge. This new committee, the Audio-Visual Committee, achieved board status in 1948. Among its reasons for seeking board status were the committee's need to appoint subcommittees. "The problems of organizing and using collections of music records, group use of transcriptions, selection of 16mm films, are so very diverse that separate subcommittees need to be appointed to give them individual and continuing attention" (Graham and Blair 1948: 459).

In addition to the ALA, numerous national and international organizations provided assistance to librarians interested in collecting or circulating film. The International Federation of Film Archives (FIAF) was founded in 1938 to promote the preservation of film as art and historical document and to bring together all organizations devoted to this end. The American Film Center, established in 1938 by a Rockefeller Foundation grant and discontinued in 1946 after funding was withdrawn, assisted anyone involved with film, including film libraries. The center sought to promote and develop the distribution and use of motion pictures for educational and cultural goals (Rehrauer 1975: 16). Originally housed in the American Film Center, the Educational Film Library Association (EFLA) was founded in 1943 as a clearinghouse for information about 16mm film selection, evaluation, production, and distribution. (In 1967, EFLA began publishing *Sightlines* and issued its first *Manual on Film Evaluation*.) The

ALA formed a joint committee with EFLA in 1945 to work on common problems. That year the chair of the Audio-Visual Committee, Mary V. Rothrock (specialist with the Library Service of the Tennessee Valley Authority), reported that "[n]o other committee objective is as important as is the need for funds to make possible an immediate film advisory services and field service from A.L.A. headquarters" (Rothrock and Batchelder 1945: 396).

Since the 1960s, associations of interest to film librarians have continued to multiply. Two such organizations were founded in 1967. The American Film Institute sought to preserve American films made since 1896, and the Film Library Information Council (FLIC) brought together film librarians from public libraries. (FLIC began publishing *Film Library Quarterly*, under the editorship of William Sloan, in 1967.) The Consortium of University Film Centers (CUFC), a cooperative organization of universities maintaining 16mm film rental libraries, was established in 1971 and began publishing an educational film locator in 1977. While the ALA's Audio-Visual Committee disbanded in 1975, the inclusion of film studies programs in the curriculum of colleges and universities prompted the founding in 1977 of the Cinema Librarians Discussion Group in the Art Section of the Association of College and Research Libraries. Under the leadership of film librarian Nancy Allen, the group met until 1986 and published a *Cinema Librarians Newsletter* from 1977 to 1986. (Recently, there has been discussion in the Arts Section of the Association of College and Research Libraries of reviving this group.)

The growth in academic film studies programs has affected associations whose primary constituency was film librarians in public libraries. In 1984 FLIC merged with EFLA; that same year, FLIC's *Film Library Quarterly* joined with EFLA's *Sightlines*.

In recent years FLIC found it increasingly difficult to fulfill its mandate to effectively promote film and video in libraries. FLIC was, for instance, finding that the seminars it once held regularly were becoming too costly to maintain. At the same time it was losing members as public libraries abolished or neglected to fill film librarians positions. New subscribers came more and more from colleges and universities so that it became increasingly difficult for the magazine to hold on to its public library image (Sloan 1985: 119).

The increase of videos in library collections during the 1980s impacted the formation of associations of film studies librarians. EFLA moved its headquarters from New York City to LaGrange Park, Illinois, in 1987 and changed its name to the American Film and Video Association (AFVA), which began publishing the former *EFLA Evaluations* as *AFVA Evaluations*.

The Association for Library Service to Children created a Film and Video Evaluation Committee, and the Young Adult Services Association formed a Selected Films and Videos for Young Adults Committee. An ALA membership initiative helped form a video interest group in 1989 to bring together "ALA members who have an interest in and/or responsibility for video collections, and providing a unified voice for video advocacy in the areas of legislation, professional guidelines for collections, and other issues specifically related to video and libraries" (*ALA Handbook of Organization* 1989: 169). The group became the Video Round Table (VRT) in 1991 and today publishes the *Video Round Table News*. The chair of the interest group, Mary Patricia Lora (Visual Services Librarian at Toledo-Lucas County Public Library), became the first chair of the VRT. As a reflection of library interest in video, within one year of its founding the membership in the VRT increased from 62 to 181 (*ALA Handbook of Organization* 1992: 98).

The increased use of technology in all performing arts collections led to the creation in 1987 of the Technology in the Arts Discussion Group (now a committee) in the Art Section of the Association of College and Research Libraries. Dance, film studies, music, and theater librarians came together "[t]o keep informed of the uses of technology applicable to libraries and archives of the visual and performing arts; to act as a resource and information-sharing vehicle for those involved in the uses of technology for arts-related library and information service" (*ALA Handbook of Organization* 1987: 58–59). The committee is currently seeking an affiliation with the Library Information and Technology Association (LITA) of the ALA.

Of all performing arts librarians, dance librarians were the latest to organize. For many years, dance librarians participated in a variety of groups outside of the ALA, such as the Society of Dance History Scholars, the Congress on Research in Dance, and the Society of American Archivists. Dance librarians also joined the TLA, MLA, and Special Libraries Association. However, until recently, there was no single organization dedicated solely to dance librarians or to librarians interested in or involved with dance collections.

The impetus for launching an organization devoted to dance librarians began in 1989 when Madeleine Nichols (curator of the Dance Collection of the New York Public Library) and Carolyn A. Sheehy (then administrative head of the Chicago Dance Collection at The Newberry Library) discussed the problems of networking among dance librarians. "They agreed that they would actively attempt to join with their colleagues to improve this situation by seeking affiliation with the ALA for dance librarians" (Sheehy 1990: 4). The idea received support from Paula Murphy (then chair of the Art Section of the Association of College and Research Libraries) and was presented at the section's 1989 general membership meeting. The membership endorsed not only the idea of encouraging dance librarians to become a part of the Art Section, but also voted to change the name of the section from "Art" to "Arts" in order to indicate the section's commitment to librarians working in both the visual and the performing arts. (The section had been founded in 1972 to represent those working in the visual arts.)

The Arts Section's executive committee voted at its January 1990 meeting to send invitations to dance librarians to join the section. The Dance Librarians Discussion Group (DLDG) was initiated the following year to provide "a forum for dance librarians and others working in or interested in dance to discuss issues and exchange ideas; to encourage, develop, and support projects which will improve access to and the organization of dance materials in libraries and archives; to inform, educate, and encourage cooperation through activities and programs on dance" ("Mission and Goals Statement" 1993: 1). Under the leadership of chair Mary Bopp of Indiana University, the DLDG has grown to over 100 members, representing public, academic, and special libraries. At its 1993 annual meeting, the membership of the Arts Section voted to also form a Dance Librarians Committee, while retaining the DLDG. (The Arts Section's recently compiled directory, Arts Librarianship: Human Resources and Consultants List [1992], includes listings for dance librarians.)

Education, copyright, and censorship are three issues that have piqued the interest of all performing arts librarians and have been continual topics for discussion at performing arts librarians' association meetings. The debate on education—whether subject expertise alone or a combination of library training plus subject expertise is essential for a performing arts librarian—has been ongoing. Should an individual first be well-versed in one of the performing arts and then learn the necessary library skills on the job? Should an individual first be trained as a librarian and then acquire the necessary specialized information? Should an individual be acquainted with a performing art and then receive an advanced degree in librarianship? Should an individual receive graduate degrees in both library and information studies and a performing art?

Although courses in the management of performing arts collections have occasionally been conducted (e.g., The Management of Performing Arts Collections at New York University), today no graduate degree is offered in performing arts librarianship by any ALA-accredited graduate program. There are special library courses in some of the performing arts—with courses in music librarianship being the most prevalent. (The first entry for training related to a librarian in any of the performing arts was for "Music librarians—training" in *Library Literature 1936–1939*.) The resolution in music librarianship of the issue of library education and subject expertise may, in fact, serve as a model for other performing arts areas.

Otto Kinkeldey (University Librarian at Cornell University and the first Professor of Musicology in the United States) analyzed the training of music librarians in the 1937 *Bulletin of the American Library Association*. Among the criteria he listed were a general knowledge of library organization and procedure; a basic knowledge of music history and theory; familiarity with the bibliography distinctive to the field; a working knowledge of French, German, and Italian; and other languages desirable (Bradley 1966: 9). Music librarianship entered the academic curriculum at Columbia University School of Library Service that same year with a course in Bibliography of Music and Music Literature and the following year with a course in Music Library Administration—both taught by Richard Angell (music librarian at Columbia University Library) (Bradley 1990: 122, 124). Almost thirty years later, at the January 1966 midwinter meeting of the MLA, noted music librarian Guy Marco read a paper on "Educational Standards for Music Librarians." He advocated a B.A. in music with a double language minor and a year of graduate library school that "has some solid course work in music bibliography and music library administration, and which will allow some individual research in the field" (Bradley 1966: 10).

The MLA's Committee on Professional Education attempted to define the term "qualified music librarian" in 1974. For a person preparing for a career in music librarianship, the committee identified the following as appropriate: a strong background in music; a master's degree in library science from a library school with an ALA-accredited program; courses in music librarianship; previous work experience, in-service training, and formal internships; familiarity with foreign languages; and participation in the work of specialized professional organizations ("Qualifications" 1974: 58–59). The controversy over education—at least for music librarianship—appears to have been resolved in 1982. The Committee on Education and Training of the International Association of Music Libraries, Archives and Documentation Centers concluded (as had the MLA) that the educational program for preparing music librarians must include: a master's degree, or its equivalent, from a nationally accredited library school;

specific courses in music librarianship; and work experience, in-service training, and/or a formal internship in a music library (Deetman and Roberts 1982: 67).

During the last three decades, the other two issues that have engaged all performing arts librarians have been copyright and censorship. As a result, professional library associations in these disciplines have become involved with legislative issues. In the area of copyright, the MLA has been especially proactive. Music librarians began dealing with copyright issues in 1975, when the pending bill for the revision of copyright excluded music from the copying privileges granted other types of library materials (Steuermann 1977: 238). Due in part to their efforts, Section 102 of the Copyright Revision Act of 1976 includes, among the categories of authored work covered by copyright, sound recordings, dramatic works, choreographic works, musical works, motion pictures, and other audio-visual works. Librarians continue to struggle to interpret Section 110 of the act, which provides that certain performances and displays of copyrighted materials are not infringements of copyright.

Performing arts librarians remain at the forefront in the struggle against censorship. The MLA has dealt with a variety of conflicts among music librarians and music publishers and the public. Music librarians received support from the American Library Association Council in the mid-1980s when the labeling of music videocassettes became a censorship issue. The council reaffirmed the association's position against the labeling of books, motion pictures, and videos, as stated in its *Intellectual Freedom Manual* (Sloan 1988: 132). Published in 1974, the manual includes the "Library Bill of Rights" and "Statement on Labeling." Also in response to censorship issues, the American Film and Video Association in 1989 published its "Freedom to View" declaration that stated that the freedom to view "along with the freedom to speak, hear, and to read, is protected by the First Amendment to the Constitution of the United States" ("Freedom to View" 1991: 386).

In recent censorship cases involving National Endowment for the Arts (NEA) grants, performing arts librarians, individually and collectively, have been among the most vigorous supporters of the First Amendment. One of the leaders in the struggle for an unrestricted NEA was Richard Buck (secretary-treasurer of the Theatre Library Association and assistant to the executive director, The New York Public Library of the Performing Arts). However, Buck cautions that "[i]n the minds of many potential grant recipients, the appropriate purposes and uses of government funds in support of the arts and the humanities have been defined and the debate is lessened. But the experiences of 1990 strongly suggest that the issue has

not been put permanently to rest and that the struggle will continue"
(1991: 10).

ACT THREE: PROVIDING ACCESS TO
PERFORMING ARTS COLLECTIONS

Performing arts librarians are responsible not only for acquiring and
organizing performing arts materials but also for disseminating information
about and encouraging use of those materials. The four activities are
intertwined. To accomplish these goals, performing arts librarians need
cataloging standards and guidelines for bibliographic control, while
patrons need access to general information on performing arts collections
and specific information on items in those collections.

The earliest endeavors at creating cataloging schemes for performing
arts materials began at two institutions, the Library of Congress and the
New York Public Library. Music librarians were the vanguard of the
movement, and Oscar Sonneck was at the forefront. Sonneck (appointed
the first Chief of the Music Division of the Library of Congress in 1902)
wrote the first recognized code of practices for cataloging printed music.
He prepared the appendix for the fourth edition of Charles Ammi Cutter's
Rules for a Dictionary Catalog, which was published by the U.S.
Government Printing Office in 1904 (Bradley 1990: 2). Cutter had
included a single rule for music; Sonneck's appendix addressed author,
title, imprint, and notes for music. Sonneck also wrote the first edition of
the Library of Congress's *Classification: Class M, Music; Class ML,
Literature of Music; Class MT, Musical Instruction*, published in 1904.

Printed catalogs initially helped to disseminate information about
materials in music collections. For example, the printed catalog of the
Allen P. Browne collection at the Boston Public Library was issued
between 1910 and 1915, while the catalog of the Library of Congress's
music holdings appeared between 1908 and 1914. According to Richard Smiraglia (author of *Music Cataloging: The Bibliographic Control
of Printed and Recorded Music in Libraries*) "These catalogs, together
with the 1869 catalog of Joseph Drexel's Philadelphia music collection
(since moved to the New York Public) were only the beginnings of
attempts to disseminate widely bibliographic data about North American
music holdings" (1989: 179).

Although Sonneck was the first prominent librarian in the United States
in the field of music cataloging, other music librarians devised important
cataloging and classification systems for music. For example, George
Sherman Dickinson (music librarian at Vassar from 1927 to 1953) wrote

Classification of Musical Compositions in 1938. The MLA compiled a report on the maintenance and cataloging practices of major collections in 1937 and issued drafts in 1941 and 1942 of its *Code for Cataloging Music* and its *Code for Cataloging Phonograph Records*. As Smiraglia indicates, "These drafts taken together represented nearly a decade of effort at standardizing the principles and procedures for cataloging music materials" (1989: 16). In order to have these rules in a single volume, the MLA and the ALA jointly published *Code for Cataloging Music and Phonorecords* in 1958. The first volume of an international code for cataloging materials, *Der Autoren-Katalog de Musikdrucke/Author Catalog of Published Music*, was issued in 1957 by the International Association of Music Libraries, Archives and Documentation Centers.

In addition to the Library of Congress, the New York Public Library was one of the leading institutions in promoting the accessibility of performing arts materials, particularly in dance and theater. As early as 1919, "The Development of Scenic Art and Stage Machinery, A List of References in the New York Public Library" appeared in the library's monthly bulletin, listing more than 2,471 entries arranged under 21 headings with author and subject indices. Later, in 1960, since existing subject heading lists and authority files were still inadequate for nonbook materials, the New York Public Library published *Theatre Subject Headings Authorized for Use in the Catalog of the Theatre Collection*.

The New York Public Library was a pioneer in the cataloging of dance materials. Genevieve Oswald states that "there were no rules for cataloging any of this kind of material when the collection was begun in 1944" (1968: 150). The Dance Collection created a list of 8,000 subject headings with cross-references and an authority file of 45,000 names and cross-references (Oswald 1968: 151). Since the Dance Collection's attempts at automation preceded those at the Library of Congress, it also devised its own coding system, which Oswald notes was "remarkably similar in many aspects to that which the Library of Congress developed later in their MARC [Machine Readable Cataloging] format" (1968: 151). The *Dictionary Catalog of the Dance Collection* of the New York Public Library began in 1964 with an initial grant of $72,000 from the Ford Foundation and included both book and nonbook materials (Oswald 1968: 150). (Since 1974, G. K. Hall has regularly published supplements and bibliographic guides to the catalog and in 1992 issued the complete catalog on CD-ROM.)

As with music collections, not all dance and theater collections followed the cataloging schemes of the Library of Congress or the New York Public Library. There were exceptions. For example, the Juilliard School created its own dance classification. As Juilliard librarian Bennet Ludden wrote in 1968, the numbers that the Library of Congress assigned to dance (GV1580–GV1799) "were not laid out with the scope necessary to accommodate the materials now documenting an art which has blossomed into one of the typical theatrical expressions of the twentieth century" (Ludden 1968: 21). Juilliard moved dance from its former association with recreation to juxtaposition with the visual and theatrical arts. As Juilliard modified the Library of Congress classification system, so did the Museum of Modern Art alter the Dewey schedule for film, theater, and dance. The Museum of Modern Art placed dance by theater ("Museum of Modern Art's Film" 1972: 13).

Other attempts at establishing cataloging schemes for performing arts materials have included Mary Ambler's *Classification System for Theatre Libraries* (1939), Anthony Croghan's *A Faceted Classification for an Essay on the Literature of the Performing Arts* (1968), and Simon Trussler's *Classification of the Performing Arts* (1974). However, as Lee Nemchek remarked about these three proposals in her essay "Problems of Cataloging and Classification in Theater Librarianship," "None has ever been used in a library" (1981: 377).

Cataloging schemes for film collections were not developed until the middle of this century. The U.S. Copyright Office in 1946 drafted cataloging rules that were applied to motion pictures and filmstrips registered for copyright, titled *Catalog of Copyright Entries: Motion Pictures and Filmstrips* (Olson 1985: 145). Although the Library of Congress published *Rules for Descriptive Cataloging in the Library of Congress* in 1949, this work did not include rules for nonbook materials, like film. Based on those rules drafted in 1946 by the Copyright Office, the Library of Congress Film Cataloging Committee did draft cataloging rules for motion pictures and filmstrips in 1951. From 1952 to 1965, the Library of Congress issued supplements to its *Rules for Descriptive Cataloging in the Library of Congress* on the cataloging of nonbook materials, such as phonorecords (1952), motion pictures and filmstrips (1953), and pictures, designs, and other two-dimensional representations (1959).

One attempt at an alternative cataloging scheme for film was proposed in the 1960s by a nonlibrarian. Film teacher Robert Steele was frustrated by not being able to find cinema literature in libraries and recognized that "cinema is not an adjunct to show business, that its literature is becoming comparable to that of other art forms and communication media, and that it is now a field of knowledge" (Steele 1967: 9). Thus, he wrote *The Cataloging and Classification of Cinema Literature* in 1967. In his book, Steele argues that "[f]ilm specialists should make it their responsibility to be consultants to librarians concerning classification and reclassification" (1967: 25).

Three events—all taking place around the year 1967, in which Steele's book was published—significantly impacted the cataloging and classification of performing arts materials. These milestones included the publication of *Anglo-American Cataloging Rules* (AACR); the launching by the Library of Congress of a series of guides on the MARC format for books, music, manuscripts and films; and the chartering by the state of Ohio of the Ohio College Library Center (OCLC), which later became the Online Computer Library Center, Inc. Since most performing arts collections consist of information in a variety of formats, the inclusion in *Anglo-American Cataloging Rules* of nonbook materials was pivotal. Further, making this information available in machine-readable form provided a common system for describing library catalog records that was essential for their manipulation and dissemination. Finally, although not all performing arts collections joined OCLC (e.g., the Harvard Theatre Collection became part of the Research Libraries Information Network [RLIN]), the development of OCLC as an interactive online bibliographic network utilizing MARC records assured users access to information previously unavailable to them and enhanced the formation of national and international information links.

The second edition of *Anglo-American Cataloguing Rules* (AACR2), published in 1978, also had a profound effect on improving access to performing arts materials. This edition contributed detailed rules for the cataloging of nonprint material and incorporated the International Conference on Cataloging Principles (ICCP) and the International Standard Bibliographic Description (ISBD) framework for bibliographic description. Since entries were based on universal principles of attribution of creativity, AACR2 has integrated the cataloging of all types of materials.

To help performing arts librarians further understand the cataloging of motion pictures and video, a number of manuals and guides have been written since the publication of AACR2 and its 1988 revision. Among these have been the International Federation of Film Archives Cataloging Commission's *Film Cataloging* (1979), Nancy Olson and Jean Aichele's *A Manual of AACR2 Examples for Motion Pictures and Videorecordings* (1981), Wendy White-Hensen's *Archival Moving Image Materials: A Cataloging Manual* (1984), and Nancy Olson's *Cataloging Motion Pictures and Videorecordings* (1991).

Of all performing arts librarians, music librarians have most strongly affected the activities of both OCLC and the Library of Congress. By 1978, music librarians utilizing OCLC had organized into a powerful users' lobby, the Music OCLC Users Group (Smiraglia 1989: 185). Music librarians, through the publications program of the MLA, have also influenced the Library of Congress. For example, two technical reports published by the MLA—Judith Kaufman's *Recordings of Non-Western Music: Subject and Added Entry Access* (1977) and *Library of Congress Subject Headings for Recordings of Western Non-Classical Music* (1983)— have resulted in the Library of Congress adopting the principles espoused in those works for their "non-Western art music" and "Western non-art music" headings (Davidson 1984: 204).

While the history of cataloging and classifying performing arts materials has centered on the activities of a few individuals and institutions, the number involved in the creation of research tools for performing arts collections has been much larger. Scholars, students, and enthusiasts have generated a growing need for guides to performing arts collections and the materials in those collections. Those needs have not yet been fully met.

While printed guides to an individual institution's performing arts collection existed at the beginning of the twentieth century, surveys of collections were not as prevalent. For example, one of the earliest hand-books of theater collections, *Theatre Collections in Libraries and Museums*, compiled by Rosamond Gilder and George Freedley, was published in 1936 by Theatre Arts, Inc., under the auspices of the New York Public Library and the National Theatre Conference in cooperation with the American Library Association.

General directories containing information on performing arts collections in national and international repositories began appearing during the middle of this century. Information on performing arts collections in the United States and Canada can be found in Lee Ash's *Subject Collections*, which was inaugurated in 1958. This directory offers easy access to performing arts materials in academic, public, and special libraries, as well as museums and historical societies. Among the performing arts subjects included in the first edition are "Acting," "Ballet," "Drama," and "Theatre." Many performing arts materials held in academic and public repositories in the United States were also made known to the public for the first time when the Library of Congress published the *National Union Catalog of Manuscripts* in 1959/1961.

Since the 1960s, performing arts materials held in libraries and museums throughout the world have been described in directories. The Section for Performing Arts Libraries and Museums of the International Federation of Library Associations in 1960 published *Bibliothèques et Musées des Arts du Spectacle dans le Monde/Performing Arts Libraries and Museums of the World*. The work was revised and expanded by Andre Veinstein and

Rosamond Gilder in 1967. (A fourth edition was published in 1992.) The American Library Association published William C. Young's *American Theatrical Arts: A Guide to Manuscripts and Special Collections in the United States and Canada* in 1971. Under "theatrical arts," Young includes dancers, motion-picture pioneers, and musicians. The directory includes information on materials held in 357 public, academic, and special libraries and archives in the United States and Canada, and it includes a person and subject index.

Guides to specific types of performing arts libraries also increased during this period. A directory of film libraries in North America was published by the Film Library Information Council in 1971. One of the first dance handbooks, Nancy Reynolds's *The Dance Catalog*, was published in 1974 and includes a list of both public and private dance libraries and archives in the United States and Canada. Nancy Allen's classic *Film Study Collections: A Guide to Their Development and Use* was released in 1979. The work lists 103 of the 194 institutions from the 1978 edition of the American Film Institute's guide to college courses in film and television. Allen's descriptions of these institutions include not only the size of the film studies collection, including unpublished scripts, but also a summary of each library's interlibrary loan policy.

Increasing access to and interest in performing arts materials has varied among performing art disciplines. Theater librarians have been particularly active in this area. The Theatre Library Association initiated the *Theatre Annual* in 1942 to dispense research information, essays, and articles on dramatic arts and theater history. In cooperation with the Theatre Section of the International Federation of Library Associations and the International Theatre Studies Center of the University of Kansas, the TLA introduced *Theatre Documentation*, which provided information on new theater archives and collections from 1968 until 1972. It was succeeded by *Performing Arts Resources*, which first appeared in 1975 and continues to the present.

The ambiguous use of the terms "theatrical" and "performing arts" in describing research sources is apparent in the titles of two publications from the 1970s. Carl J. Stratman, C.S.V., visited 51 libraries in the United States and compiled a bibliography titled *American Theatrical Periodicals, 1798–1967: A Bibliographical Guide*, which was published by Duke University Press in 1970. The bibliography includes some 685 theatrical periodicals. However, Stratman uses the term "theatrical" to include dance, ballet, and music when these touched on the stage in some way. Although Marion K. Whalon's *Performing Arts Research: A Guide to Information Sources*, published in 1976 as the first volume of Gale's

Performing Arts Information Guide Series, is titled "performing arts," it is primarily a guide to theater arts research. Organized into seven sections, the work includes "Play Indexes and Finding Lists" and "Sources of Reviews of Plays and Motion Pictures."

Another interesting information resource conceived for theater researchers during the late 1960s and early 1970s is the *London Stage Information Bank* (LSIB) by Ben Ross Schneider, Jr. (English professor at Lawrence University). This full-text database and service offers information on the London stage from 1660 to 1800 to scholars in history, theater, economics, linguistics, and social history. Schneider's aim "was to permit access to all the information implicit in the database, such as careers of individual actors, their association with certain types of parts, their financial successes, and audience size at each performance" (Raben and Burton 1981: 253). His *Travels in Computerland: or, Incompatibilities and Interfaces* (1974) relates the vicissitudes of producing a theater database on a limited budget.

Theater departments within the "Big Ten" Midwestern universities formed a consortium in 1974 for the purposes of coordinating activities and sharing resources. Alfred S. Golding, director of Ohio State University Theatre Research Institute, developed a proposal for a national theater database, which, although unfunded, led to "A Thesaurus for the Big Ten Performing Arts Document Inventory Project" (1978), which sought to serve "as a model to fill the still existing void in nonbook theatrical document taxonomy" (Rachow 1981: 95).

Like theater librarians, music librarians have a long history of organizing and encouraging use of materials in their collections. *The Music Index*, first published in 1949, provides a subject-author guide to music articles in a variety of international publications and is available on CD-ROM. The first international effort at bibliographic control of scholarly literature has also been in music. *Répertoire International de Littérature Musicale/International Inventory of Music Literature* (RILM) was initially presented at the 1965 meeting of the International Association of Music Libraries, Archives and Documentation Centers (Lowens 1965: 1264). The first volume, published in 1967, indexed literature published from January to April 1967. (A RILM retrospective series was begun in 1972, and the first five-year cumulation was published in 1975 and is now available online and on CD-ROM.) A U.S. RILM office was established at Cornell University in 1984.

The International Association of Music Libraries and the International Musicological Society began in the 1950s a project to locate rare music sources, and in 1985 a U.S. RISM (*Répertoire International des Sources Musicales/International Inventory of Musical Sources*) center was

founded at Harvard University with funding provided by the National
Endowment for the Arts. The center was charged with gathering data and
creating bibliographic records for music manuscripts written between 1600
and 1800 and held in American collections (Ostrove 1986: 208). In
addition, a project for gathering data on libretti holdings was initiated.

Film studies librarians have also engaged in compiling international
reference resources. The Documentation Commission of the Federation
International des Archives du Film/International Federation of Film
Archives (FIAF) published *International Index to Film Periodicals* in
1972 and issued *Guidelines for Describing Unpublished Script Materials*
in 1974 (Bowser 1974). The latter publication is "a preliminary step
toward a proposed international listing of script holdings in the archives"
(Bowser 1976: 1). *Film Literature Index*, which indexes American and
British film periodical articles, was launched in 1973.

Despite the growth in dance collections and the popularity of dance,
access to information in dance has been more limited. Daniel Clenott, an
indexer at Business Research Corporation, did a study published in *RQ* in
1983 that found that of the more than 300 dance journals published
internationally, only 9 were indexed by the 12 major arts and humanities
indexes studied (1983: 89). Other than the University of Florida's guide
to dance periodicals, which indexes materials from 1931 to 1956, specific
dance reference tools have been woefully lacking. The development since
1985 of the University of California at Los Angeles's Dance Database
Project, the publication of Doris Robinson's *Music and Dance Periodicals:
An International Directory & Guidebook* in 1989, and the publication of
the Dance Collection of the New York Public Library's *Index to Dance
Periodicals* in 1992 appear to be correcting this situation.

Another exciting new development in dance librarianship is a possible
project of the Dance Heritage Coalition: the creation of a national union
catalog of dance materials. In mid-1990 the Andrew W. Mellon Foundation
and the Dance Program of the National Endowment for the Arts initiated
a study "to learn what comprises the existing system of dance documentation and preservation, how transactions are conducted within the system,
and to what extent the needs of the dance community are being met"
(Keens, Hansen, and Levine 1991: 3). The Dance Heritage Coalition's first
Core Administrative Committee consisted of Jeanne T. Newlin, curator of
the Harvard Theatre Collection; Madeleine M. Nichols, curator of the
Dance Collection of the New York Public Library; Margaret K. Norton,
executive director of the San Francisco Performing Arts Library and
Museum; and Vicky J. Wulff, dance specialist of the Library of Congress.

The effect of computer technology on providing access to all performing arts collections cannot be underestimated. As Jeffrey Rehbach stated in his essay on "Computer Technology in the Music Library," "[t]he possibility of storing, retrieving, and sorting vast quantities of data by computer offers libraries totally new dimensions in function and services. . . . access to a broad range of bibliographic data beyond those of the local library's holdings is possible through computer systems and tele-communications networks that promote the sharing of library information on regional, national and international levels" (1989: 123).

Parallel to the efforts made by performing arts librarians in providing access to and promoting the use of performing arts collections have been the steps taken toward preserving these collections. Performing arts librarians have been concerned not only with the proper storage and handling of materials but also with their duplication (especially through film or electronic means). Professional associations have provided support for this focus, with interest in the preservation of paper records preceding that of materials in other formats.

As early as 1930, a Committee on Preservation of Film was formed by the Society of Motion Picture Engineers to study the storage of film. Under the joint sponsorship of the National Archives and the Carnegie Corporation of New York, the U.S. Bureau of Standards (under an advisory committee of the National Research Council) in 1936 performed a comprehensive research study of film storage problems. Within a decade, these and similar efforts "brought the science of storage of motion picture film abreast with that of book and document storage" (Pickett and Lemcoe 1959: 1).

Ralph Sargent (who left the University of California Motion Pictures Division in 1971 to form Film Technology Company) was commissioned by the Corporation for Public Broadcasting and the NEA in 1974 to identify problems associated with film preservation and to propose solutions. According to Joel Zuker, instructor in the Department of Theatre and Cinema at Hunter College, Sargent's *Preserving the Moving Image* was the definitive study on the subject, and "Certainly one of the most important problems identified in Sargent's introductory comments is the need for greater standardization of existing videotape systems" (Zuker 1976: 28). The National Film Preservation Act of 1992 authorized a national study of film preservation activities (Pelzman 1993: 21).

Music librarians have also been working for decades on questions related to conservation and preservation of materials. Harold Spivacke, chief of the Music Division at the Library of Congress, received a grant from the Carnegie Corporation in 1940 to install a sound laboratory in the Music Division to duplicate fragile recordings (Bradley 1990: 60). He also supervised in 1959 a Rockefeller-sponsored study on the storage deterioration of sound recordings, which sought to "establish the optimum storage environments and techniques for library use" (Pickett and Lemcoe 1959: iv).

Theater librarians have shown concern not only for the preservation of theater materials but also for the preservation of all performing arts materials. Theater librarian Louis Rachow wrote on "Care and Preservation of Theatre Library Materials" in *Special Libraries* in 1972. Ten years later the TLA held a conference in Washington, DC (sponsored by a grant from the National Endowment for the Humanities), on preservation management of performing arts collections. The conference was "devoted to the care and handling of deteriorating ephemera in all forms" (Buck 1983: 267). Papers from that conference were transcribed and updated for *Preserving America's Performing Arts*, which was edited by Barbara Cohen-Stratyner and Brigitte Kueppers in 1985. The book addresses preservation problems unique to performing arts collections.

A year after the conference sponsored by the TLA, the MLA sponsored a workshop on the preservation of music and sound recordings. In 1988, music librarians met with music publishers on the issue of preservation and, as a result of that meeting, the Music Publishers' Association agreed to start printing scores for libraries on durable acid-free paper (Sommer 1989: 163).

Interest in the preservation of performing arts materials continues. PRESERVE: The Coalition for Performing Arts Archives was created in 1987 by Leslie Hansen Kopp (then chair of the Society of American Archivists' Performing Arts Roundtable) and the late Michael Scherker (then archivist of the Dance Theatre of Harlem). PRESERVE conducted a series of workshops (sponsored by the Andrew W. Mellon Foundation) around the country in 1990 on "Performing Arts Archives: The Basics and Beyond." Representatives from dance companies were taught how to organize and preserve the documents of their history. PRESERVE seeks "to educate the performing arts community as to the value of its documentary heritage, and to provide the means for preservation of these archives" (Kopp 1990: 13).

EPILOGUE

Within a relatively short period of time, performing arts collections in academic and public libraries in the United States have grown and prospered. Librarians working in these areas have created both informal networks and formal organizations, nationally and internationally. Collections have been acquired, cataloged, and publicized through print and electronic guides. Outreach efforts have been made to collect performing arts materials that represent a diversity of cultures. Performing arts librarians have been quick to applaud the benefits of technology and have used technology as an exciting means for furthering the study of the performing arts.

For all the exciting growth in performing arts collections since the 1927 publication of Cannons's *Bibliography of Library Economy*, coverage in library literature of performing arts collections, performing arts librarians, and performing arts librarianship continues to be sparse. Whether or not this is due to some continuing reluctance to regard the field as one for serious academic study—to look askance at the performing arts as somehow less serious or scholarly—remains to be seen. The rich developments in performing arts collections in academic and public libraries in the United States call for further research, documentation, and exploration. Hopefully, the future will see expanded efforts in these directions.

REFERENCES

AFVA Evaluations (Formerly *EFLA Evaluations*). 1987– . Niles, IL: American Film and Video Association.

ALA Handbook of Organization 1987/1988. 1987. Chicago: American Library Association.

ALA Handbook of Organization 1989/1990. 1989. Chicago: American Library Association.

ALA Handbook of Organization 1992/1993. 1992. Chicago: American Library Association.

Allen, Nancy. 1979. *Film Study Collections: A Guide to Their Development and Use*. New York: Friedrich Ungar.

Ambler, Mary. 1939. *Classification System for Theatre Libraries*. Chicago: University of Chicago.

American Library Association, Office for Intellectual Freedom. 1988. *Intellectual Freedom Manual*, 3rd ed. Chicago: American Library Association.

American Library Association, Public Libraries Division, Coordinating Committee on Revision of Public Library Standards. 1956. *Public Library Service: A Guide to Evaluation with Minimum Standards*. Chicago: American Library Association.

Anglo-American Cataloging Rules. 1967. Prepared by the American Library Association, Library of Congress, the Library Association, and the Canadian Library Association. North American text edited by C. Sumner Spalding. Chicago: American Library Association.

Anglo-American Cataloguing Rules, 2nd ed. 1978. Prepared by the American Library Association, British Library, Canadian Committee on Cataloging, the Library Association, and the Library of Congress. Edited by Michael Gorman and Paul W. Winkler. Chicago: American Library Association.

Anglo-American Cataloguing Rules, 2nd ed., revised. 1988. Prepared under the direction of the Joint Steering Committee for the Revision of AACR, a committee of the American Library Association, the Australian Committee on Cataloguing, the British Library, the Canadian Committee on Cataloguing, the Library Association, and the Library of Congress. Edited by Michael Gorman and Paul W. Winkler. Chicago: American Library Association.

ARSC Journal. 1968– . Silver Spring, MD: Association for Recorded Sound Collections.

"Art Reference." 1944. *ALA Bulletin* 38.13 (December 15): H-50.

"Art Reference." 1950. *ALA Bulletin* 44.10 (November): 427.

Arts Librarianship: Human Resources and Consultants List. 1992. Chicago: Arts Section, Association of College and Research Libraries.

Ash, Lee, comp. 1958. *Subject Collections*. New York: Bowker.

Ayres, Mary Armstrong. 1923. "Children's Librarians Sections." *Bulletin of the American Library Association* 17.4 (July): 222–227.

Bardwell, W. A. 1887. "A Library of Music." *Library Journal* 12 (April): 159.

Blair, Patricia. 1948. "Library Film Adviser." *ALA Bulletin* 42.11 (October 15): 474–477.

Bowerman, George T. 1936. "Visual Methods." *Bulletin of the American Library Association* 30.5 (May): 416–417.

Bowser, Eileen. 1974. *Guidelines for Describing Unpublished Script Materials*. Brussels: International Federation of Film Archives.

———. 1976. "Guidelines for Describing Unpublished Script Materials." In *Performing Arts Resources*, vol. 2, edited by Ted Perry, pp. 1–7. New York: Drama Book Specialists and Theatre Library Association.

Bradley, Carol June. 1990. *American Music Librarianship: A Biographical and Historical Survey*. Westport, CT: Greenwood Press.

———, ed. 1966. *Manual of Music Librarianship*. Ann Arbor, MI: Music Library Association.

Breen, Dorothy. 1932. "Art Reference Round Table." *Bulletin of the American Library Association* 26.8 (August): 517–524.

Broadside. 1940– . New York: Theatre Library Association.

Buck, Richard M. 1983. "Theatre Library Association." In *ALA Yearbook: A Review of Library Events 1982*, edited by Robert Wedgeworth, pp. 267–268. Chicago: American Library Association.

———. 1991. "Whither the NEA? The 1990 Legislation Does Not End the Dilemma." In *Libraries and Information Services Today: The Yearly Chronicle*, edited by June Lester, pp. 3–11. Chicago: American Library Association.

Caldwell, Gladys. 1928. "Art Reference Round Table." *Bulletin of the American Library Association* 22.9 (September): 392–396.

Campbell, Frank C., and Mary R. Rogers. 1948. "Music Library Association." *ALA Bulletin* 42.9 (September 15): P-90–P-95.

Cannons, H.G.T. 1927. *Bibliography of Library Economy: A Classified Index to the Professional Periodical Literature in the English Language Relating to Library Economy, Methods of Publishing, Copyright, Bibliography, Etc., from 1876 to 1920.* Chicago: American Library Association.

Cinema Librarians Newsletter. 1977–1986. Chicago: Cinema Librarians Discussion Group, Art Section, Association of College and Research Libraries.

Clennot, Daniel. 1983. "The Need for a Dance Periodical Index." *RQ* 23 (Fall): 87–90.

Cohen-Stratyner, Barbara, and Brigitte Kueppers, eds. 1985. *Preserving America's Performing Arts: Papers from the Conference on Preservation Management for Performing Arts Collection, April 28–May 1, 1982, Washington, D.C.* New York: Theatre Library Association.

"Committee to Investigate the Proposed Distribution of Educational Films Through Libraries." 1924. *Bulletin of the American Library Association* 18.4-A (August): 224.

Coral, Lenore. 1988. "Music Library Association." In *The ALA Yearbook of Library and Information Services: A Review of Library Events in 1987,* edited by Roger Parent, pp. 214–215. Chicago: American Library Association.

Cory, Patricia Blair, and Violet F. Myer. 1956. *Cooperative Film Services in Public Libraries.* Chicago: American Library Association.

Croghan, Anthony. 1968. *A Faceted Classification for an Essay on the Literature of the Performing Arts.* London: Croghan.

Cutter, Charles Ammi. 1904. *Rules for a Dictionary Catalog,* 4th ed. Washington, DC: U.S. Government Printing Office.

Davidson, Mary Wallace. 1984. "Music Library Association." In *The ALA Yearbook of Library and Information Services: A Review of Library Events 1983,* edited by Robert Wedgeworth, pp. 203–204. Chicago: American Library Association.

Deetman, Hulb, and Don L. Roberts. 1982. "Statement of Qualifications for Music Librarians." *Fontes Artis Musicae* 29.1/2 (January–June): 66–67.

Dickinson, George Sherman. 1938. *Classification of Musical Compositions; A Decimal-Symbol System.* Poughkeepsie, NY: Vassar College.

Epstein, Dena J. 1977. "Music Library Association." In *The ALA Yearbook: A Review of Library Events 1976,* edited by Robert Wedgeworth, p. 210. Chicago: American Library Association.

Federation International des Archives du Film/International Federation of Film Archives. 1972– . *International Index to Film Periodicals.* New York: Bowker.

Federation International des Archives du Film/International Federation of Film Archives, Cataloging Commission. 1979. *Film Cataloging.* New York: B. Franklin.

Film Library Information Council (FLIC). 1971. *Directory of Film Libraries in North America.* New York: Film Library Information Council.

Film Library Quarterly. 1967–1984. New York: Film Library Information Council.

Film Literature Index. 1973– . Albany, NY: Filmdex.

Freedley, George. 1967. "The Theatre Library Association: 1937–1967." *Special Libraries* 58.5 (May–June): 354–355.

"Freedom to View." 1991. In *Whole Library Handbook: Current Data, Professional Advice, and Curiosa about Libraries and Library Services.* Compiled by George M. Eberhart, p. 386. Chicago: American Library Association.

Gilder, Rosamond, and George Freedley. 1936. *Theatre Collections in Libraries and Museums.* New York: Theatre Arts.

Golding, Alfred S. 1978. "A Thesaurus for the Big Ten Performing Arts Document Inventory Project." Photocopy. Columbus: The Ohio State University.

Graham, Aubry Lee, and Patricia Blair. 1948. "Audio-Visual Committee." *ALA Bulletin* 42.1 (October 15): 459–460.

Grant, Barry Keith. 1989. "Film Study in the Undergraduate Curriculum." In *Film History*, edited by Erik S. Lunde and Douglas A. Noverr, pp. 7–20. New York: Markus Wiener.

Gross, Sarah Chokla. 1940. "Theatre Library Association." *ALA Bulletin* 34.7 (August): P-232–P-240.

———. 1941. "Theatre Library Association." *ALA Bulletin* 35.8 (September): P-174–P-179.

International Association of Music Libraries, Archives and Documentation Centers, International Cataloging Code Commission. 1957. *Der Autoren-Katalog de Musikdrucke/Author Catalog of Published Music.* Frankfurt: Peters.

International Federation of Library Associations, Section for Theatrical Libraries and Museums. 1960. *Bibliothèques et Musées des Arts du Spectacle dans le Monde/Performing Arts Libraries and Museums of the World*, 2nd ed. Under the direction of Andre Veinstein with the collaboration of Rosamond Gilder et al. Paris: Éditions du Centre National de la Recherche Scientifique.

International Federation of Library Associations, Section for Theatrical Libraries and Museums. 1967. *Bibliothèques et Musées des Arts du Spectacle dans le Monde/Performing Arts Libraries and Museums of the World*, 2nd ed., revised. Under the direction of Andre Veinstein with the collaboration of Rosamond Gilder et al. Paris: Éditions du Centre National de la Recherche Scientifique.

Johnston, A. M. 1979. *Theatre Librarianship.* Occasional Publications Series no. 10. Sheffield, England: University of Sheffield Postgraduate School of Librarianship and Information Science.

Jones, Emily S. 1967. *Manual on Film Evaluation.* New York: Educational Film Library Association.

Kaufman, Judith. 1977. *Recordings of Non-Western Music: Subject and Added*

Entry Access. MLA Technical Report no. 5. Ann Arbor, MI: Music Library Association.

————. 1983. *Library of Congress Subject Headings for Recordings of Western Non-Classical Music*. MLA Technical Report no. 14. Philadelphia: Music Library Association.

Keens, William, Leslie Hansen Kopp, and Mindy N. Levine. 1991. *Images of American Dance: Documenting and Preserving a Cultural Heritage*. Report on a study sponsored by the National Endowment for the Arts and the Andrew W. Mellon Foundation. Washington, DC: National Endowment for the Humanities and Andrew W. Mellon Foundation.

Kinkeldey, Otto. 1937. "Training for Music Librarianship: Aims and Opportunities." *Bulletin of the American Library Association* 31 (August): 459–463.

Kopp, Leslie Hansen. 1990. "PRESERVE: Assuring Dance a Life Beyond Performance." In *Arts and Access: Management Issues for Performing Arts Collections*, edited by Barbara Cohen-Stratyner, pp. 7–18. Performing Arts Resources, vol. 15. New York: Theatre Library Association.

Krummel, Donald W. 1982. "Music Library Association." In *The ALA Yearbook: A Review of Library Events 1981*, edited by Robert Wedgeworth, pp. 180–181. Chicago: American Library Association.

Lansdale, Nelson. 1954. "At Harvard the Interest Is Historical." *Dance Magazine* 28 (January): 21–22.

Library Literature. 1921– . New York: H. W. Wilson.

Library of Congress. 1904. *Classification: Class M, Music; Class ML, Literature of Music; Class MT, Musical Instruction*. Washington, DC: U.S. Government Printing Office.

————. 1949. *Rules for Descriptive Cataloging in the Library of Congress*. Washington, DC: Library of Congress.

————. 1959/1961– . *National Union Catalog of Manuscript Collections*. Washington, DC: Library of Congress.

Lowens, Irving. 1965. "The Future of Music Librarianship." *Library Journal* 90: 1264.

Ludden, Bennet. 1968. "The Dance Classification System of the Juilliard School Library." *Theatre Documentation* 1.1 (Fall): 21–29.

McCarty, Trudy E. 1974. "A Ballet Collection at the Bryan Public Library." *Texas Library Journal* 50 (March): 33–34.

McDonald, Gerald Doan. 1942. *Educational Motion Pictures and Libraries*. Chicago: American Library Association.

Meyer, Amy. 1920. "Development and Use of a Circulating Music Collection." *Bulletin of the American Library Association* 14.3: 182–186.

"Mission and Goals Statement. Dance Librarians Discussion Group." 1993. Chicago: Arts Section, Association of College and Research Libraries.

Moore, Lillian. 1965. *Images of the Dance: Historical Treasures of the Dance Collection 1581–1861*. New York: The New York Public Library.

Museum of Modern Art. 1984. *Circulating Film Library Catalog*. New York: Museum of Modern Art.

"Museum of Modern Art's Film and Theater and Dance Classification System." 1972. *The U*N*A*B*A*S*H*E*D Librarian* 4: 11–13.

Music Cataloging Bulletin. 1970– . Canton, MA: Music Library Association.

The Music Index: A Subject-Author Guide to Music Periodical Literature. 1949– . Detroit: Information Coordinators.

Music Library Association, Cataloging Committee. 1941–1942. *Code for Cataloging Music*. Preliminary version.

Music Library Association, Cataloging Committee. 1942. *Code for Cataloging Phonograph Records*. Preliminary version.

Music Library Association and American Library Association, Joint Committee on Music Cataloging. 1958. *Code for Cataloging Music and Phonorecords*. Chicago: American Library Association.

Nemchek, Lee. R. 1980. "Education for Theater Librarianship." *Journal of Education for Librarianship* 21 (Summer): 49–62.

———. 1981. "Problems of Cataloging and Classification in Theater Librarianship." *Library Resources & Technical Services* 25 (October/December): 374–385.

New York Public Library, Dance Collection. 1975– . *Bibliographic Guide to Dance*. Boston: G. K. Hall.

———. 1964– . *Dictionary Catalog of the Dance Collection*. Boston: G. K. Hall.

———. 1992– . *Index to Dance Periodicals*. Boston: G. K. Hall.

New York Public Library, Reference Department. 1960. *Theatre Subject Headings Authorized for Use in the Theatre Collection*. Boston: G. K. Hall.

Notes: The Quarterly Journal of the Music Library Association. Series 1, 1934–1942. Series 2, 1943– . Canton, MA: Music Library Association.

Olson, Nancy B. 1985. *Cataloging of Audiovisual Materials: A Manual Based on AACR2*. Mankato: Minnesota Scholarly Press.

———. 1991. *Cataloging Motion Pictures and Videorecordings*. Minnesota AACR2 Trainers Series no. 1. Lake Crystal, MN: Soldier Creek Press.

Olson, Nancy B., and Jean Aichele. 1981. *A Manual of AACR2 Examples for Motion Pictures and Videorecordings*. Lake Crystal, MN: Soldier Creek Press.

Ostrove, Geraldine. 1986. "Music Library Association." In *The ALA Yearbook of Library and Information Services: A Review of Library Events 1985*, edited by Roger Parent, pp. 208–209. Chicago: American Library Association.

Oswald, Genevieve. 1968. "Creating Tangible Records for an Intangible Art." *Special Libraries* 59 (March): 146–151.

———. 1991. "The Development of a Dance Archive." In *Libraries, History, Diplomacy, and the Performing Arts: Essays in Honor of Carleton*

Sprague Smith, edited by Israel J. Katz, pp. 77–84. Festschrift Series no. 9. Stuyvesant, NY: Pendragon Press.

Patterson, J. R. 1928. "Moving Pictures and the Library." *Bulletin of the American Library Association* 22.9 (September): 434–439.

Patterson, J. R., and Marilla W. Freeman. 1929. "Visual Methods Round Table." *Bulletin of the American Library Association* 23.8 (August): 361–367.

Pelzman, F. 1993. "Film Preservation." *Wilson Library Bulletin* 67 (January): 21.

Performing Arts Resources. 1974– . New York: Theatre Library Association.

Phonographic Bulletin. 1971– . Stockholm: International Association of Sound Archives.

Pickett, A. G., and M. M. Lemcoe. 1959. *Preservation and Storage of Sound Recordings*. Washington, DC: Library of Congress.

"Qualifications of a Music Librarian." 1974. *Journal of Education for Librarianship* 15.1 (Summer): 53–59.

Raben, Joseph, and Sarah K. Burton. 1981. "Information Systems and Services in the Arts and Humanities." In *Annual Review of Information Science and Technology*, vol. 16, edited by Martha E. Williams, pp. 247–266. White Plains, NY: Knowledge Industry.

Rachow, Louis A. 1972. "Care and Preservation of Theatre Library Materials." *Special Libraries* 63 (January): 25–30.

———, ed. 1981. *Theatre & Performing Arts Collections*. New York: Haworth Press.

Rehbach, Jeffrey. 1989. "Computer Technology in the Music Library." In *Modern Music Librarianship: Essays in Honor of Ruth Watanabe*, edited by Alfred Mann, pp. 123–132. Festschrift Series no. 8. New York: Pendragon Press.

Rehrauer, George. 1975. *The Film User's Handbook: A Basic Manual for Managing Library Film Services*. New York: Bowker.

Reische, Diana, ed. 1973. *The Performing Arts in America*. The Reference Shelf, vol. 45, no. 2. New York: H. W. Wilson.

Répertoire International de Littérature Musicale/International Inventory of Music Literature. 1967– . New York: International RILM Center.

Répertoire International des Sources Musicales/International Inventory of Musical Sources. 1960– . Munich: Henle.

Reynolds, Nancy, ed. 1974. *The Dance Catalog*. New York: Harmony Books.

Robinson, Doris. 1989. *Music and Dance Periodicals: An International Directory & Guidebook*. Voorheesville, NY: Peri Press.

Rosen, Lillie F. 1975–1976. "Dream and Fruition: The Lincoln Center Dance Collection." *Dancescope* 10 (Fall–Winter): 22–30.

Rothrock, Mary U., and Mildred L. Batchelder. 1945. "Audio-Visual." *ALA Bulletin* 39.10 (October 15): 395–396.

Sargent, Ralph N. 1974. *Preserving the Moving Image*. Washington, DC: National Endowment for the Arts.

Schneider, Ben Ross, Jr. 1974. *Travels in Computerland: or, Incompatibilities and Interfaces: A Complete Account of the Implementation of the London Stage Information Bank.* Reading, MA: Addison-Wesley.

Schoolcraft, Ralph Newman. 1973. *Performing Arts Books in Print: Annotated Bibliography.* New York: Drama Book Specialists.

Sheehy, Carolyn A. 1990. "Invitation to the Dance." *Arts Newsletter* 5.2 (Spring): 4.

Sightlines. 1967– . Niles, IL: American Film and Video Association.

Slide, Anthony. 1992. *Before Video: A History of the Non-Theatrical Film.* Contributions to the Study of Mass Media and Communications no. 35. Westport, CT: Greenwood Press.

Sloan, William. 1978. "Films." In *The ALA Yearbook: A Review of Library Events 1977,* edited by Robert Wedgeworth, pp. 128–130. Chicago: American Library Association.

———. 1985. "Films." In *The ALA Yearbook of Library and Information Services: A Review of Library Events 1984,* edited by Robert Wedgeworth, pp. 118–121. Chicago: American Library Association.

———. 1987. "Films." In *The ALA Yearbook of Library and Information Services: A Review of Library Events 1986,* edited by Roger Parent, pp. 130–132. Chicago: American Library Association.

———. 1988. "Film and Video." In *The ALA Yearbook of Library and Information Services: A Review of Library Events 1987,* edited by Roger Parent, pp. 131–133. Chicago: American Library Association.

———. 1990. "Film and Video." In *The ALA Yearbook of Library and Information Services: A Review of Library Events 1989,* edited by Roger Parent, pp. 114–115. Chicago: American Library Association.

Smiraglia, Richard P. 1989. *Music Cataloging: The Bibliographic Control of Printed and Recorded Music in Libraries.* Englewood, CO: Libraries Unlimited.

Sneed, Laurel. 1978. "Recorded Dance: A New Era." *American Libraries* 9 (December): 682–684.

Sommer, Susan T. 1989. "Music Library Association." In *The ALA Yearbook of Library and Information Services: A Review of Library Events 1988,* edited by Roger Parent, pp. 162–163. Chicago: American Library Association.

Sperber, Ann. 1972. "Arts and the Community—A New Ecology: The Library and Museum for the Performing Arts at Lincoln Center." *Library Journal* 97 (April 15): 1493–1499.

Steele, Robert. 1967. *The Cataloging and Classification of Cinema Literature.* Metuchen, NJ: Scarecrow Press.

Steuermann, Clara. 1976. "Music Library Association." In *The ALA Yearbook: A Review of Library Events 1975,* edited by Robert Wedgeworth, pp. 237–238. Chicago: American Library Association.

Stevenson, Gordon. 1975. "Sound Recordings." In *Advances in Librarianship,* vol. 5, edited by Melvin J. Voight, pp. 279–320. New York: Academic Press.

Stevenson, Grace T. 1951. "Library Film Service." *Library Journal* 76 (January 15): 128–130.

Stratman, Carl J., C.S.V. 1970. *American Theatrical Periodicals, 1798–1967: A Bibliographical Guide.* Durham, NC: Duke University Press.

"Symposium on Music in Libraries." 1915. *Library Journal* 40 (August): 563–574.

Theatre Annual. 1942– . Akron, OH: College of Fine Arts, University of Akron.

Theatre Documentation. 1968–1972. New York: Theatre Section, International Federation of Library Associations; Theatre Library Association; International Theatre Studies Center, University of Kansas.

Tilly, H. Dorothy. 1947. "Music Library Association." *ALA Bulletin* 41.9 (September 15): P-91–P-97.

Trussler, Simon. 1974. *Classification of the Performing Arts.* London: Commission for a British Theatre Institute.

U.S. Copyright Office. 1946. *Catalog of Copyright Entities: Motion Pictures and Filmstrips.* Washington, DC: U.S. Government Printing Office.

Video Round Table News. 1991/1992– . Chicago: Video Round Table, American Library Association.

Wappat, Blanche K. S. 1924. "Art Reference Round Table." *Bulletin of the American Library Association* 18.4-A (August): 293–298.

Wells, James. 1987. "Building the Collection." In *Humanities' Mirror: Reading at the Newberry, 1887–1987*, edited by Rolf Achilles, pp. 27–35. Chicago: The Newberry Library.

Whalon, Marion K. 1976. *Performing Arts Research: A Guide to Information Sources.* Performing Arts Information Guide Series, vol. 1. Detroit: Gale.

White, Gladys Walker. 1957. "The Theatre Library Association Matures." *Library Journal* 82.19 (October 15): 2483–2489.

White-Hensen, Wendy. 1984. *Archival Moving Image Materials: A Cataloging Manual.* Washington, DC: Library of Congress.

Wilcox, Ruth. 1926. "Art Reference Round Table." *Bulletin of the American Library Association* 20.10 (October): 479–483.

———. 1927. "Art Reference Round Table." *Bulletin of the American Library Association* 21.20 (October): 329–334.

Young, William C. 1971. *American Theatrical Arts: A Guide to Manuscripts and Special Collections in the United States and Canada.* Chicago: American Library Association.

Zuker, Joel. 1976. "Ralph Sargent's *Preserving the Moving Image*: A Summary Review." In *Performing Arts Resources*, vol. 2, edited by Ted Perry, pp. 15–29. New York: Drama Book Specialists and Theatre Library Association.

2

Dance Collections

Nena Couch

INTRODUCTION

Dance librarianship has not been a well-defined field because dance scholarship has not been well established or well represented in the scholarly community. Many of those who have written about dance have come from other fields to do so. In fact, much of the important work in the twentieth century on historical dance was begun by musicologists rather than dancers or dance scholars. Because of this lack of scholars working in the field, dance has not had the great quantity of materials created for its study as have the related musical, theatrical, cinema, and visual arts.

As long-established disciplines, other performing arts have tended to exist in the academic setting in departments with relatively uniform structures. Dance, on the other hand, has not developed a typical college or university profile. There are certainly strong independent departments of dance with emphases in various areas in schools across the United States. Dance units may exist within an arts department or college or as part of a specific department, such as music. There are also schools that offer dance as a recreational program only. And there are colleges and universities that offer dance as part of the physical education program, a decision which surely has major implications for the philosophical approach to teaching dance held by that faculty and for the supporting library collection.

Because of the ephemeral and highly visual nature of the dance form, primary source documentation has been scarce. In recent years the field of dance scholarship has started to blossom, and work has begun on the sorts of standard tools that have been desperately needed, including bibliographies, dictionaries, encyclopedias, indexes, and guides (in addition to critical and analytical studies, authoritative biographies, and histories). Other forms of documentation are also being produced that, while not necessarily unique to dance, are intimately related to the comprehensiveness and vitality of dance scholarship, such as moving visual image formats, still photographic formats, and notation systems (both print and computerized) for movement.

Not only are studies in dance being undertaken, but also studies of the state of dance scholarship. An Andrew W. Mellon Foundation and National Endowment for the Arts (NEA) project was done "to learn what comprises the existing system of dance documentation and preservation, how transactions are conducted within the system, and to what extent the needs of the dance community are being met" (Keens, Kopp, and Levine 1991: 3). In response to the needs identified in that project, the Dance Heritage Coalition was created by a grant from the Mellon Foundation. Therefore, it seems that dance scholarship and dance librarianship will be developing and changing dramatically. For those librarians who have done the work and despaired of the lack of resources over the years and for librarians who are still to come, the future of dance librarianship should be exciting indeed. While this chapter must necessarily discuss the profession in its current state, it will also consider issues for the future.

PERSONNEL

Staffing Levels

Because of the many physical formats of materials in dance collections, the work can be both diverse and labor intensive. Materials may require special handling for preservation needs and cataloging. For materials with controlled access, greater staffing in public services may be needed. These jobs may be parceled out to a number of different people, many of whom are not actually "dance" librarians or staff but in fact may be part of the library system's preservation, acquisitions, and cataloging departments.

The behind-the-scenes labor required for the adequate running of a dance collection may be quite extensive and not at all apparent to the patron. Staffing levels for public services are visible to the patron and obviously must be adequate to assist patrons with collection use and reference questions. However, without the necessary technical work accomplished in advance, the patron will inevitably find that the dance collection, or access to it, will not adequately provide for his or her needs.

Due to the great diversity in the nature of dance collections, the institutions in which they exist, and the clientele they serve, it is impossible to generalize about ideal staffing levels. Some libraries have centralized technical services that serve all units including the dance collection and may or may not include librarians and staff who specialize in dance, whereas other libraries may have technical services staff within the dance collection. Depending on the organization of the library and the size of the dance collection, both public and technical services staff may be generalists, may specialize in a group of disciplines, or may serve specifically as dance librarians. The major consideration for staffing levels should be the accomplishment of the particular mission of a dance collection within the overall mission for the institution in which it exists.

Professionals

The number of librarians who actually hold the title "dance librarian" or even "performing arts librarian" is very small in relation to the number of working librarians in this country. However, it is clear that many librarians, without holding the title, do the job of handling dance materials and assisting patrons in their use.

The basic standard for librarians in the United States is the American Library Association certified master's program. For librarians focusing on certain disciplines, it is possible to obtain specialized training in those areas, both while working toward the master's as well as afterwards, through strong professional organizations that provide other educational opportunities. Unfortunately for the dance librarian, not only do library schools not provide course work in dance librarianship (and only occasionally in the performing arts—with the exception of music), but no strong organization exists that can provide extracurricular training.

For the librarian who is handed the job of acquiring dance materials and providing patron assistance in that area (in addition to the other disciplines for which he or she is responsible), self-education plays a significant role in how effective that librarian can be. At the very least, the librarian should attempt to gain a knowledge of the history of dance and dance terminology and should determine what use the dance patrons for that library make of the collection and in what way they can be best served.

In the performing arts, in particular for those library jobs that are so titled, the positions are frequently occupied by librarians who have a subject area interest. In academic libraries, such positions often require a subject area graduate degree in addition to the master's degree in library and information science. For these librarians, expertise in the area may reflect the incumbent's subject background, which may not provide sufficient knowledge of the broad field.

Many dance programs (both undergraduate and graduate) in colleges and universities are oriented toward performance rather than toward a knowledge of the field. Within that performance orientation, one may be able to specialize in a particular kind of dance, such as modern or jazz dance instead of ballet or folk. While a dance student will probably have an introduction to the techniques of the major theatrical dance forms, possibly to ethnic dance and to choreography, the program may provide a very limited exposure to dance history, criticism, aesthetics, notation, and preservation. These latter areas are critical to the documentation of dance; therefore, the dance librarian must acquire a solid grounding in them. In addition, given the number of technological advances made in the fields of preservation, audiovisual equipment, online databases, and digital imaging, the dance librarian, whose collection may depend heavily on nonprint materials, must continue to learn about these areas on the job and through special programs.

Paraprofessionals, Students, and Volunteers

Because the dance librarian cannot possibly do all the work associated with the smooth running of a dance collection, assistance in the form of paraprofessionals and/or student employees is critical. Some library systems have strict guidelines on what paraprofessionals may and may not do, particularly in technical services, and these guidelines are reflected in job descriptions that are used for hiring and for employee evaluation. Others may not be so strict, as long as the basic responsibilities of the job description are met. In many cases, libraries are so understaffed that paraprofessionals and even upper-level undergraduate and graduate students may be trained for duties often fulfilled by a dance librarian.

Volunteers can be extremely helpful to a dance collection with limited staff resources, and they may provide assistance and support in a variety of ways—both routine and ongoing—as well as for special projects. Because dance can be a very appealing subject to the public, it may often be easier to find volunteers to work in the dance collection than in other subject areas. Volunteers may come to the dance collection in a variety of ways. A "friends of the library" group may well be a source of volunteers for the dance collection. Some cities have a centralized volunteer agency that matches the interests of potential volunteers with groups and projects needing particular skills or assistance. Retired librarians are another valuable source for volunteers. While they may or may not have worked with dance materials previously, their knowledge of the library world can be very useful. Finally, dancers, dance teachers, and dance enthusiasts can make wonderful volunteers because of their knowledge and interest in the field.

The most important thing is to find volunteers who are dedicated and reliable, whether to a special project that occurs in a given amount of time or to an ongoing commitment the volunteer makes to the library. It is also important that the dance librarian keep in mind the needs of these people who give their time to come in and work. While it is not always possible to assign very exciting projects, the dance librarian should be able to make a volunteer assignment interesting. The better the dance librarian is able to make a volunteer feel a part of the important work going on in the dance collection, the more committed that person is likely to be. It is preferable to have fewer committed volunteers than numerous ones the dance librarian cannot count on.

If one dance librarian is directly responsible for supervising the work of both paraprofessionals and volunteers, the numbers of both should be within reason. That number will depend on the nature of the collection, the range of duties, and the hours of operation. If the library is only open during the daytime on weekdays, volunteer applicants may be limited to those, such as retirees, who are available during the scheduled hours.

Continuing Education, Recruitment, and Mentoring

Two organizations that provide a forum for dance librarians are the Theatre Library Association (TLA) and the Dance Librarians Discussion Group (DLDG) of the Arts Section of the Association of College and Research Libraries (ACRL), which also voted to form a Dance Librarians Committee at the Arts Section's 1993 annual membership meeting. The TLA has always supported dance as one of the several performing arts included in the organization's purview. With its charter in New York and its focus historically having been in the Northeast (and in particular at the New York Public Library at Lincoln Center, home of the Dance Collection), it is logical that dance has been an integral part of the association. Dance librarians have been members of the TLA, and articles on dance topics have appeared in the organization's newsletter *Broadside* and its annual *Performing Arts Resources*.

The DLDG was organized under the ACRL Arts Section in an effort to identify librarians working with dance materials, to provide a much-needed forum for them, and to begin to address the needs of the profession. Other organizations that include dance librarians as members and that provide insight into the current scholarly climate in dance are the Congress on Research in Dance, the Society of Dance History Scholars, and the American Society for Theatre Research.

Because of the lack of structured programs in dance librarianship, mentoring can be a very important part of the training process. In some established performing arts collections, an informal mentoring process has grown up over the years so that assistants may succeed their chiefs on retirement. Having worked with the chief and with the collections for years puts that assistant in a uniquely knowledgeable position. Others have returned to dance collections after work outside the area to assume the responsibilities of head librarian. In libraries with dance materials but without specialists in the area, the mentoring may be more general—for example, in the humanities or the arts. Nevertheless, many of the skills learned from a more experienced colleague are transferable from discipline to discipline.

Paraprofessionals in dance collections seem to choose on occasion to complete master's programs in library and information studies. They are often very directed in their job pursuits because they have worked in—and enjoyed—certain areas of the dance collection and wish to continue with a different level of work. These employees may benefit from mentoring by dance librarians in the field who inspire them, whether consciously or not, to seek the master's degree. Unfortunately, there are so few jobs in the field of dance librarianship that the paraprofessional may not be able to stay where he or she would like, when remaining would mean under-utilization and underpayment for the additional education.

COLLECTION DEVELOPMENT

Policies

In order to focus a collection, a collection development policy or collection management policy is a vital tool for dance collections in either academic or public libraries. It defines the collection and provides a framework for the dance librarian to consider materials that become available, as well as materials that are requested by patrons. For everyone involved in a dance collection at any level—administrator, librarian, staff, patrons, or potential donors—the collection development policy is a valuable tool.

Dance, as other disciplines, may be viewed in a variety of ways, and it is important for the dance librarian to establish how the subject is documented in that particular collection. The collection development policy should reflect the dance collection's mission within the context of the institutional mission and current collection practices in dance, including collecting levels in subdisciplines. It may include the collecting history of the library, as well as changes from earlier collecting policies. The collection development policy may identify the collection's clientele, the ways in which the collection supports use by its patrons and the types of materials, languages, or subject areas included as well as excluded. The policy may also include future collecting goals. It should identify real collection practices rather than ideal ones but may certainly describe as collection goals those that may not yet have been reached. Those goals may change over time, but they provide the dance librarian with a map for the future so that the dance collection develops with coherence.

It is important that the collection development policy be understood to be a document that is always in transition. Dance scholarship is a young field (in comparison with related disciplines in the visual arts, theater, and music). However, as the field of scholars grows, so will the literature available. In addition, advances in technology mean that dance—with its immediacy in terms of performance, its difficulty in documenting performance, and its close relationship to the other arts—will be available in a variety of physical formats. These formats will require special equipment and facilities for use, so the dance librarian must always be aware of what is possible technologically, the preservation implications of technological developments, the ways those developments may or may not serve the library clientele, and, of course, the practical aspect of the library budget.

The low level of publication in the field of dance certainly may affect the decisions a dance librarian may make on what and how much to collect. A study of books reviewed during the calendar year 1990 in *Choice* reveals that dance books made up only 0.21 percent of the total books reviewed (the lowest percentage of any of the subject categories), with dance books—averaging $29.89—at the low end of the average price per title (Soupiset 1991: 1073–1078). Similar evidence of low publication activity may be found in other standard sources, such as *American Reference Books Annual*, where the reviews of dance books are very meager in comparison to film, theater, and general works in performing arts. Even as late as 1979, a list of "Resources for the Dance Historian," prepared for the Dance History Conference, gave nineteen items as guides to reference sources, periodicals, books, and academic research but included only seven dance entries (Au 1979: 1–6). The remainder were divided among music, art, theater, performing arts, literature, and general sources. A final section included dance bibliographies published in books but no full bibliographic publications on dance.

Dance collection policies will be influenced by a number of factors that are both internal and external to the library. In academic settings, the nature of the dance program will affect acquisition for the collection. College and university dance programs occur in a variety of settings: as undergraduate or graduate degrees offered by a dance department, as a dance emphasis in an arts program, as a component of a physical education program, as a component of a music program, as a component of a theater program, or as a noncredit enrichment program. Degree-granting programs may vary widely in emphasis in subdisciplines (i.e., technique, choreography, history, notation, etc.). Collection levels in dance may also depend on the particular library and the way in which teaching faculty are consulted or solicited for input on library collections. A dance program with a very interested faculty member who requests materials actively, even though informally, may be better represented in library collections than one whose official library liaison faculty member is inactive.

Whether in an academic setting or not, the dance librarian should be responsive to the needs of the collection's clientele within the guidelines established in the collection development policy and the constraints placed by budget. Public libraries, for instance, may tend to acquire more "how-to" materials, particularly for currently popular dance forms. Research libraries may acquire dance materials in greater depth than required to support current dance programs. Research libraries often serve a broader clientele than the dance department, including disciplines such as the other arts, history, literature, language area studies, anthropology, religion, physical therapy, or sports medicine. These collections may also serve researchers from outside the local community, the region, or the country. However, even internationally known research libraries may collect at the local level. For example, The Newberry Library in Chicago established a collection to document the rich dance activities both past and present in that city (Sheehy 1990: 432–440).

Because the publication output in dance is small in comparison to many other subject areas, some dance librarians have the luxury of collecting the majority of dance materials appropriate to the collection as they become available. If publication in the field increases, as it seems likely to do, dance librarians who are currently able to buy everything may be faced with some difficult decisions in the future.

Due to the universal occurrence of dance (both historically as well as currently), the literature of dance is in many different languages. While visual documentation of dance may be easily transferable from one language group to another, the written documentation may be another story. In response to a dance collection's particular clientele and the common language(s) in the area, language may be used as a limiting factor in collecting materials; that exclusion will itself be a limiting factor in the broad development of a dance collection.

Since dance is done and written about all over the world, dance collections limited to a particular language will provide a very one-sided view of what is truly one of the most universal disciplines. For instance, much important material that documents the early development of western European theatrical and social dance was originally written in Italian and French (with significant publications also in German). While some of this material is available in translation, much of it exists in the original language, and some of it is available in facsimile editions. Much material on eastern dance is available only in the original language, so this also is an area that a collection may not adequately document if language is a factor in selecting materials. Currently, in areas of the United States with heavy ethnic populations, such as the Southwest, librarians may collect primarily in English and one other language, such as Spanish.

While public library collections are usually current collections, dance is one area in which historical materials are often retained. Frequently public library dance collections consist heavily of instructional and basic technique materials, as well as biographical and autobiographical works of major figures in the field. Public libraries, as well as academic libraries, may collect in particular areas because of some activity or organization in the community. For example, due to its proximity to The Ohio State University, which has a major dance notation program, the Metropolitan Columbus Public Library collects materials on dance notation, probably not a common collecting area for many public libraries.

Selection Tools

Dance materials may be—in fact, should be—located by using a variety of selection tools. Certainly, standard tools can be used for many publications. However, depending on the guidelines for collecting, the dance selector's pursuit of materials may need to extend beyond the standard sources. Many dance publications (particularly those on ethnic dance in both English and foreign languages, as well as foreign language materials on other aspects of dance) are often not available through the usual sources. The dance librarian should attempt to locate the small publishers and foreign language sources, as well as private publishers, of dance materials. For instance, the folk dance magazine *Viltis* frequently provides reviews or advertisements for privately printed folk dance materials that are not easily accessible through standard tools. Current writings on performance art may be found in "underground" magazines.

Librarians starting dance collections or beginning librarians who wish to evaluate the dance collections they have inherited may wish to start with the lists provided in *Guide to Reference Books* and *Books for College Libraries: A Core Collection of 50,000 Titles*. One must keep in mind, however, that these are very limited lists and should be used only as a starting point. For dance periodicals, *Ulrich's International Periodicals Directory* provides a useful list under "Dance" and also references to related publications in other areas; *Music and Dance Periodicals: An International Directory & Guidebook* (Robinson 1989) also assists in locating dance periodicals.

Because of the interrelated nature of dance with other arts, the dance selector may need to review theater, cinema, visual arts, and music selection tools. Yet because of the relatively small amount of publishing that is done in dance, this work may seem like searching for the proverbial needle in the haystack. In addition, given the fact that many librarians are selectors for two and frequently more disciplines, the plethora of these selection tools may be beyond the scope of the selection activity.

Publishers and Vendors

Several publishers have begun or continue to make significant contributions to the field of dance. The Princeton Book Company, publisher of Dance Horizons Books and distributor of other dance books, releases works on dance history, choreography and production, theory and criticism, dance education, physiology and anatomy, dance notation and movement, historic and traditional dance, and related works in physical education and gerontology. This company is also a large distributor of dance videotapes. Gordon and Breach Science Publishers/Harwood Academic Publishers offer dance monographs, as well as the dance book series Choreography and Dance Studies and The Language of Dance Series and dance journals. G. K. Hall has been a performing arts publisher for many years and produces the New York Public Library Dance Collection's annual *Bibliographic Guide to Dance*. (Materials listed in the Dance Collection's catalog, as well as those listed in *Bibliographic Guides to Dance* through 1990, are now covered in a CD-ROM, *Dance on Disc*.) Garland Publishing has inaugurated a Library of Dance series to publish scholarly works and resources in dance history, technique, and criticism.

An approval plan is one way in which the dance librarian can lighten the load of searching standard tools; however, the approval plan profile for the particular dance collection must be carefully constructed to provide maximum coverage for appropriate materials while minimizing returns of books that do not fit the collection. The dance librarian should understand clearly which publishers' materials will be available through the approval plan and which he or she will need to locate in another way. Some dance librarians prefer making direct contact with a publisher who regularly publishes dance materials in order to establish an ongoing relationship, which should bring with it regular notification of publications. However, depending on the structure of the acquisitions department, the dance librarian may not choose the particular distributor but may simply provide publication information.

Nevertheless, the more in touch the dance librarian is with a variety of publishers, distributors, and dance associations involved in dance publication, the better. The dance librarian should also review catalogs that provide selection information by format, such as film and videotape or microform. Several commercial micro publishers (for example, Emmett Publishing Limited, Inter Documentation Company, and Harvester Microform) have released important dance collections on microform. The Dance Film Association has been active in the publication of guides and catalogs to dance on film and videotape. The Dance Notation Bureau is a major source for dance in notated form, as well as information about it.

Donors and Donations

Many performing arts libraries are very dependent on donors for the development of collections. In particular, special collections (which are often not book collections) may have substantial relationships with donors and virtually no contact with publishers or approval plans. Because of the ephemeral nature of dance, much of the history and documentation of the field exists not in books but in letters, choreographic notes, notation, sketches, letters, business records, costumes, videotapes, news clippings, posters, photographs, and films. While some dance collections are sold as a collection, broken up into lots, or sold by individual pieces, many are acquired by libraries as donations. A good relationship with one's donors is, therefore, vital to the continued growth of the dance collection.

Donors may choose a particular dance library or dance collection for any number of reasons, but frequently the choice is made because the donor is an alumnus of the college or university or the donor's career is centered in a particular city that has an appropriate dance collection. With the advent of major developments in online access, facsimile transmission, and increased ease of travel, donors have begun to look increasingly to the dance collection that best meets their needs rather than the one that is the most convenient.

Normally, a gift agreement, which may specify any requirements or restrictions the donor has for the donation, as well as the manner in which the library will undertake to handle the collection, is reached with the donor. It is very important that an institution meet the commitment it makes because the best advertisement for potential donors is a satisfied current donor. In negotiating a gift agreement, the issues of property and creative rights may arise. Institutions have varying policies, and the dance librarian must be sure to follow the institution's policy. Some libraries receive only property rights when the material is formally given, while rights to the content of the material are retained by the rights holder who may not necessarily be the donor. Some institutions also negotiate rights other than property rights with the donor or rights-holder. In the case of dance, with the proliferation of documentation of choreography on video-tape, the question of creative rights becomes a very real issue and may need to be addressed in the negotiation for a collection.

TECHNICAL SERVICES

Cataloging

Most dance collections use either the Library of Congress Classification or Dewey Decimal Classification for book materials. As dance librarians and library patrons will readily attest, neither system is really adequate for their needs. Nevertheless, the two are the most frequently used standards and have the advantage of being widely known. Some libraries, such as the Juilliard School Library, have devised their own systems. As many dance librarians would agree, the Juilliard staff found that the Library of Congress Classification for dance was inadequate "to accommodate the materials now documenting an art which has blossomed into one of the typical theatrical expressions of the twentieth century" (Ludden 1968: 21). Juilliard's classification system removes dance from GV (Library of Congress location) to a new location in NN and NP, thereby situating it with the visual arts and theater. This system has proven for this library to be very satisfactory and a great improvement over the Library of Congress Classification.

Dewey Decimal Classification divides dance materials between 792.8 and 793.3, which is clearly a disadvantage. If dance must be divided, surely another division would have been preferable. As Dewey is designed, all nonballet theatrical dance is included under "Indoor Games and Amusements," along with folk and social dance, while in fact it may be more logically considered with ballet as theatrical dance. Many dance enthusiasts and participants would dispute the inclusion of ballet as a subdiscipline of theater rather than as an independent art form. Similarly, folk and ethnic dancers and scholars might disagree that a particular "social" form of dance is in fact a game or amusement.

In actuality, many patrons are not aware of the subtleties of the organization of dance materials and may simply find the right part of the library once and continue to go back there. Patrons frequently find what they want in public collections by browsing—they have found one book they like in a particular area and go back to the same place hoping for similar material. Since Dewey is commonly used in public libraries, this search method raises another problem. With the division of dance materials, patrons may easily miss what they hope to find because they do not physically search far enough along the shelf to find the subject they seek, for example, ballet. The larger the collection, the more pronounced the problem.

Browsing is not a sufficient method for any systematic search of library holdings since materials may not be on the shelves for a variety of reasons (in circulation, on reserve, missing, etc.). The patron must use the catalog to find out what dance materials are actually owned by the library and where those materials reside. With the advent of online catalogs, it is often possible for the patron to "browse" online by classification number.

But classification number is not entirely adequate as a search strategy either. Depending on both national standards and local practices, dance materials may be classified in a variety of ways. For instance, materials on such dance topics as injuries and treatment may be classified with medical materials; dance biographies, autobiographies, and memoirs under biography or literature; and many nonbook formats may simply not be classified at all. In these cases, a good subject heading list becomes a critical component in providing bibliographic access.

Unfortunately, Library of Congress (LC) subject headings for dance are inadequate in the extreme. The list lacks specificity and is too general for both large and small collections. For large collections, it is incredibly cumbersome since most dance headings begin "Dancing -" or "Ballet -" before proceeding to the description that more closely identifies the material. Ultimately, the patron may be the loser since he or she is at the mercy of both an insufficient subject heading list as well as the choices the cataloger makes in supplying subject headings from the approved list.

The Dance Collection of the Performing Arts Research Center of the New York Public Library at Lincoln Center has been the leader among dance collections in the United States in a great variety of ways, not the least of which is its development of an extensive authority file including names, subjects, and titles. This list is international in scope and would be much more useful for other dance collections of any depth than the LC subject headings. It is hoped that the Dance Collection authority list will become available to other libraries and will provide the framework for a standardized list.

Some dance librarians are more successful than others in having local practice adapted to suit the collection as well as the clientele. One factor in gaining accommodations may be the nature of the catalog department—whether it is highly centralized and standardized or whether the catalogers actually work in the dance library. In either case, it behooves the dance librarian to make the catalogers aware of problems that occur with the accepted practices. One should be aware, however, of the dangers of moving away from a national standard since that library's records will be less accessible to outside users.

The issue of classification of a particular item will frequently determine where that material is physically housed—in the same room, separate rooms, different wings, or different buildings. If housing is by strict call number order, then things may be "buried" in another part of the library. In decentralized collections, it may be possible to have a variety of call number sequences that are also found in other libraries in the system.

As mentioned above, many nonbook formats in dance collections may be cataloged or described using systems other than Library of Congress and Dewey. In fact, such a practice is necessary for materials for which those systems do not provide adequate access. Videotapes, films, and sound recordings (in various formats) are frequently organized in other ways, such as by accession number, so subject headings again may play a critical role in access if the materials are included in the common catalog. Some online catalogs provide for keyword searching, which may alleviate some of the problems of subject headings. Keyword searching may be provided for a limited number of fields in a catalog record or for all fields, may be limited to a particular vocabulary (i.e., LC subject headings), or may be an uncontrolled vocabulary. The difficulty with an uncontrolled vocabulary is that people describe things differently. If there is no standard language through which a patron may communicate his or her search, the material may be as lost as if the library had never acquired it.

If materials are not included in the common catalog, then the dance librarian must provide some kind of local access. This task has become much easier with the popularization of the microcomputer, which allows for searching of local databases. In addition to the formats mentioned above that may have other methods of access, special collections materials such as manuscripts collections, costume and scene designs, costumes, posters, photographs, and so on, will be handled differently from books.

At the national level, bibliographic access to many dance collections, particularly academic collections, may be available through the Online Computer Library Center (OCLC) or Research Libraries Information Network (RLIN). The type of access will depend on the record that the member library has submitted. Manuscript materials will frequently have a collection level record in the Archival and Manuscripts Control (AMC) format, which will provide a summary description of the collection. For detailed information and access, the patron would have to contact the library holding the material. Another source for dance collections is the Library of Congress's *National Union Catalog of Manuscript Collections* (NUCMUC). One of the projects undertaken recently by the Dance Heritage Coalition is the creation of a Union Catalog of Dance Documentation to "eliminate cataloging arrearages of dance materials, coordinate access to existing electronic records through a single national bibliographic database . . . and conduct a national assessment to determine archival needs" (Johnson 1992). This union catalog will be an important step in efforts to provide access to the materials that document dance.

Dance manuscript collections come to libraries in a variety of states, ranging from highly organized (according to the previous use of the collection) to boxed in no perceivable order. Collections may be the records of the activities of an organization or an individual or a mixture of the two. Collections may also consist of materials that have no functional relationship but have been assembled by a collector on a particular area of interest. The dance librarian, curator, or archivist must examine the materials and determine an order in which the materials will be arranged. The Society of American Archivists has many helpful publications that assist the dance librarian in working with manuscripts or special collections. For the dance librarian, the challenge may be in the great variety of physical formats and sizes that may exist within the collection—correspondence, photographs, posters, stage and costume designs, choreographic notes or notation, newspaper clippings, scrapbooks, music in manuscript and published form, sound recordings, video recordings and film in a variety of formats, costumes, and set pieces, to mention a few.

Processing, Binding, and Shelving

Not only will the above-mentioned formats require special attention in arrangement and description but also in where they are stored, how they are protected, and how they may be used by patrons. Many of the materials that are retained in dance collections are ephemeral in nature, not originally intended to be preserved permanently. In addition to preservation concerns based on physical condition, other issues that may affect storage, binding, and handling include uniqueness or rarity of material (is it widely available, somewhat available, or is this the only one of its kind?), the size of material (is it very large or very small?), and special equipment needs for use and security of materials (if it circulates, does this kind of material come back damaged or not at all?).

Conservation and Preservation

Environmental controls are essential to ensure the longevity of a library's holdings, be they nonbook or book materials. The dance collection, with its variety of physical formats, may be particularly vulnerable to humidity, light, extremes of temperature, and dust. In addition, while there are mixed opinions on exposure to magnetic fields, the conservative view is that such fields may endanger video- and audiotape materials. The general library environment should be considered, as well as the immediate environment, including shelving or cabinets for fragile items or materials that have special housing requirements.

Ideally, all dance collections should reside in an environmentally controlled facility where materials are protected from extremes of temperature, humidity, light, and dust. In addition, certain physical formats commonly found in the dance collection, such as audio-visual materials, have specific housing needs in terms of storage units, the manner in which materials are stored, and protection from magnetic fields. (Grounding of metal cabinets or shelving for magnetic tape materials should be considered.) Posters, light plots, set and costume designs, and any other large, flat pieces require map cases or appropriately sized archival boxes for flat storage. Helpful publications on preservation and conservation are available through a number of professional organizations, including the Society of American Archivists, the American Library Association, the Music Library Association, and the Theatre Library Association.

PUBLIC SERVICES

Reference and Information Services

It is clear from the problems noted in the section on cataloging of dance materials that public services librarians play an important role in helping patrons locate dance materials. It is necessary for public services librarians to understand the interrelated nature of dance materials with multiple disciplines and to know that dance materials may not be housed together but, in fact, may be in very different locations, depending on the particular dance topic or the physical format of the material.

Because of the lateness of dance in taking its place as a scholarly discipline, many of the standard tools that would be useful to dance librarians and patrons alike do not yet exist for the field. Several recent and forthcoming publications and projects will ease this problem to a certain extent. *The International Encyclopedia of Dance* (forthcoming), edited by Selma Jeanne Cohen and published by the University of California Press, will fill a huge void in dance reference literature. While a variety of music sources (including *The New Grove Dictionary of Music and Musicians* [Sadie 1980]) provide articles on dance, there has not been an adequate reference source of international scope for dance alone. Cohen's publication is a first and major step in that direction.

The lack of an ongoing index to dance literature in periodicals has frequently been cited as a major deficiency in the field. While *The Music Index* is used by some librarians (especially those with combined responsibility for music and dance), an analysis of a recent list of subject headings included in that index shows that only slightly more than 3 percent refer to dance; the actual number of dance titles indexed is small. The Dance Collection of the Performing Arts Research Center of the New York Public Library has remedied the situation, in part, with the publication of its *Index to Dance Periodicals*, which is international in scope and indexes some thirty periodicals.

Another project designed by dance scholars is the Dance Database Project based at the University of California at Los Angeles. This project is indexing not only periodicals but also books, portions of books, dissertations, theses, and other materials. This ambitious effort was begun in 1985 with the goal "to organize the efforts of an international group of dance researchers in the identification and indexing of dance materials to form a central, computerized data bank" used to develop "an annual bibliography of international scholarship, publication and performance documents of dance," which would also be available online (*Bibliography of Dance Studies* 1985: 4). *Dance Abstracts and Index* (1992) is one of the results of the project.

Access, Circulation, and Interlibrary Loan

One of the most valuable things that a dance librarian can do for patrons is to provide some kind of brief written introduction to the dance collection, describing its holdings, access, circulation, and usage policies, hours, and services. Whether a one-page flyer or a multipage booklet with photographs, this introduction will serve to inform both local and out-of-town patrons of the nature of the dance collection, its special strengths, and the conditions for its use. Particularly if access to the dance collection is not available in a catalog that researchers might encounter in their work, the introduction to the collection may be the only way in which potential users discover a valuable source. In addition, if the library system publishes a summary description of its holdings, a brief statement on the dance collection should be included. Another item that may be helpful to users is a printed search strategy for the dance collection. Particularly in special collections, access may not be as easy as with book collections, and providing a search strategy for patrons may save the dance librarian time in one-on-one instruction and save the patron a great deal of frustration.

Letters of introduction or appointments may be important for maximizing a dance researcher's time, particularly if the research is to be conducted out of town in a library with which the researcher is not familiar or for work in an archives or special collections department that may have restrictions on use of the collection. Circulation policies will vary from collection to collection, given the nature of the holdings, the service mission, and the clientele. Because of the many nonbook materials in dance collections, especially those that require specialized equipment for use or that may be damaged easily on wrong or bad equipment, use of the materials may be restricted to a supervised setting in the library. Similar decisions may be made for some book material that may be out of print or difficult or particularly expensive to replace, as well as for certain dance materials that are lost or stolen with some frequency. The dance collection must have a circulation policy, but that policy should be based upon local conditions and needs.

Interlibrary loan may play a very significant role in providing needed dance materials to patrons at schools that do not possess extensive dance resources. For book and journal materials, this method of access should be satisfactory, keeping in mind the inherent problems of interlibrary loan—the delay in obtaining materials, the short time that materials may be lent, and the possibility that the desired items cannot be obtained on loan. If it is discovered that the same materials are requested repeatedly, the dance collection should make every effort to locate and purchase those materials.

Unfortunately, in the field of dance, many materials are not in book or journal form. There is great difficulty in obtaining much dance material through interlibrary loan since it is in a variety of physical formats, such as videotape, film, sound recordings, and archival or special collections material. A large portion of this material may not circulate at the original holding library and may, therefore, either not be loaned externally or loaned only under very restrictive conditions. For the dance researcher who has access to a limited collection but needs a variety of materials, this may cause quite a hardship.

Because of scarce funds and the overwhelming increase in documentation in all areas, consortia sharing dance resources will continue to develop. In addition to major utilities, such as OCLC and RLIN, networks of libraries (regionally, statewide, and community-based) frequently share catalogs online. Consortia with other interests are also increasing. For example, the Consortium of Popular Culture Collections in the Midwest (Bowling Green State University, Michigan State University, and The Ohio State University) has been established by special collections departments whose holdings are related to the popular arts (including dance) and the mass media. The Consortium's purpose is to "develop joint projects to promote the common goals of member institutions and enhance local programs, priorities, and strengths" (*Prospectus* 1990: 1). The Consortium collaborates in collection development efforts; access through shared and cooperative finding aids, patron referral, and loan agreements; promotion of the collections through special programming; and cooperative preservation efforts.

A collaboration specifically of dance collections has been proposed in the recent NEA–Mellon Foundation report "to facilitate communication, joint activities, policies, programs and projects" (Keens, Kopp, and Levine 1991: 44). The dance librarian may find it advantageous to develop informal or formal agreements with other area libraries and even dance organizations in order to develop a collection and adequately serve patrons.

Copyright Issues

Copyright is an area of great concern for librarians and researchers in many subject areas. It is, or promises to become, a very complicated issue for dance because of the many forms in which dance is documented. While each library should have an institutional copyright policy developed in keeping with U.S. copyright law, the issues raised by intellectual and creative content are not easily resolved.

Not only is the use of dance materials in libraries affected by copyright but also the very creation of valuable resources on dance. Because of union contracts, it may be nearly impossible to adequately document theatrical dance in moving-image form. While several projects with very specific missions, such as the Theatre on Film and Tape Collection of the New

York Public Library, have been successfully undertaken and the resulting work placed in archives or special collections, access and use of the created materials is quite strictly limited. In addition, much dance material, such as videotapes of rehearsals or of the creative process, placed in special collections by choreographers or dance companies may come with restrictions placed on use. The dance librarian must scrupulously honor restrictions placed by donors while at the same time providing the best access possible for patrons.

Special Programs and Services

Depending on the size and staffing of the dance collection, a variety of user services and programs may be offered. Many of these services are common to other collections, such as photocopying, online searching, and facsimile transmission. If the library facility allows, a schedule board for dance events and speakers in the community is a helpful addition. Many libraries will schedule regular introductory tours to the collections as part of user education activities. These tours, with accompanying library literature, such as a descriptive brochure and search strategy, are to the advantage of the dance staff and users alike since they provide advance information about the use of the dance collection.

Public libraries, in particular, may have facilities for programs on dance and may sponsor such events for a number of age groups. These programs may include audio-visual presentations, speakers, and performances. Some libraries, especially dance archives or special collections that serve an out-of-town clientele, may offer research services for patron questions that are beyond the scope of a reference query. This type of service will again depend on library staffing, as well as on the library's policy on fees for service. One of the most visible programs that a library can implement and one that lends itself quite well to the materials of a dance collection is an exhibits program. Whether simply displays of dance book covers or more extensive exhibits of archival materials, the visual aspect of dance, even in still photographs, is very appealing to the eye. This kind of program serves to inform the public of the library's holdings and also does public relations work for the dance collection.

NEW TECHNOLOGIES

Software

Interesting software applications are making their way into the dance field in the areas of administration, notation, and creation. A number of performing arts administration software packages have been developed for use by arts companies and schools. While these packages may stream-line a dance company's operations, the use of such packages will have implications for the library holding the company's archives and will raise the issue of preservation and access for information that may no longer be paper-based.

Dance notation may be one area that will develop dramatically due to new computer applications. In recent years, dancers have turned to video-tape as a means of preserving their material, even though the medium is not stable. While great strides have been made in the development of notational systems, a major drawback has been the huge investment of time in writing and in reconstructing dances from detailed notations. While the computer will not obviate this problem, it will certainly alleviate it. Work is currently being conducted in the computerization of labanotation (the best known of today's dance notation systems) in the dance department at The Ohio State University, where a branch of the Dance Notation Bureau exists.

Academic libraries, in particular, have embraced CD-ROM (compact disc–read only memory) databases as enhanced access to information that is inexpensive to the user. In developing a CD-ROM network, care must be taken in the selection of hardware, software, and CD-ROM products to ensure that they are compatible. Both the dance librarian and the user need to be aware of the limitations of compact disc technology. While informa-tion may be issued on CD-ROM more quickly than in paper form, it will never be absolutely current because the disc will contain a finite number of records produced as of a certain date. By the same token, CD-ROM and online databases may not provide as much retrospective information as is available in print sources. In fact, Susan Cady (1990) views the proliferation of electronic technology as analogous to that of microfilm technology, which was predicted to revolutionize both scholarly output and library collections. While microfilm has taken its place as a significant preservation medium, it has not displaced print material, and Cady feels that electronic media are equally unlikely to do so (1990: 374–386). Therefore, the dance librarian must take care to assist patrons to use sources in a variety of media.

Online databases now seem to be an integral part of the academic library setting, although they still tend to be used conservatively by scholars in the arts and humanities. The sources available online to these scholars have not been as extensive as those for other areas, particularly the sciences. Nevertheless, some major general databases are worthwhile investigating for the dance researcher. The Arts and Humanities Search and ERIC (Educational Resources Information Center) are examples of helpful sources. The catalog of the Dance Collection of the New York Public Library is available on Internet. The dance librarian who provides online service should also give counseling to the patron on which databases will supply the best information for the particular query. With the advent of CD-ROM, some online search units seem to be experiencing a decrease in use by patrons. But both dance librarian and patron need to be aware that the two technologies will not always produce identical search results.

A number of general sources are available on CD-ROM that provide some information on dance, and *The Music Index* is also available as a more specific arts source that includes aspects of dance and performance art. Dance itself has moved into the CD-ROM market in a major way with the publication of the catalog of the New York Public Library Dance Collection by G. K. Hall. This CD-ROM provides the entire catalog and includes approximately 170,000 records. A source that was available for a time online but is now published in diskette form is *The Encyclopedia of Theatre Dance in Canada*. It was found that online access did not enjoy heavy use, so a change was made to a nine-diskette package.

Media and Hardware

The ever-expanding technological field that promises so many exciting advances for the moving, visual image and for data retrieval will also challenge the dance librarian. Dance has been slow to take its place as a scholarly discipline, in large part because of the difficulty in describing verbally what must be seen to be understood. Dance scholarship is now following the examples of the other arts with historical, critical, analytical, and aesthetic studies being published in a traditional printed form. Nevertheless, dance as an art with a major visual component is in an ideal position to take advantage of advances in imaging. Technologies that allow the art form to be viewed as by an audience member, analyzed by scholars, or reconstructed by other dance artists will bring dance documentation to a comparable level with the other arts. Dance practitioners have enthusiastically adopted videotape technology for recording movement ideas for later use, rehearsals, and performances. As other moving image technologies become available at an equally affordable price as videotape, dancers will choose the method that provides the highest quality image with the most convenient use. The same will hold true for audiovisual publishers who will embrace new technologies and, thereby, cause changes for both library and home use.

Dance librarians and patrons alike should be aware that new technologies will not solve all problems of documentation and access and, in fact, will create new problems. The incredible proliferation of audio and video formats and the rapid change resultant in the necessary equipment is an example of what can easily happen with new technological developments—the format one has in hand may be unplayable because it has been superseded in the marketplace, and equipment and parts are no longer available. Robert Wagner (1990) raises issues that should be considered by dance practitioners and dance librarians: "those concerned with the serious study and research of cinema, television, and video must take both a scholarly and practical look at the future of a field dependent upon photoelectronic artifacts which, while increasing in volume and cost, are decreasing in quality, becoming more complex in the technological and legal aspects of accessibility" (1–3). Nevertheless, the opportunities provided for the field of dance by these new technologies are legion, and their use has the potential to provide multiple new ways of documentation and access.

A new technology that promises to have great impact on the field of dance is the developing digital videotape format, similar to the digital audiotape now in use. This technology should allow for duplication of the captured image without the loss of quality inherent in the copying of the currently used videotape analog format (Calmes 1990: 5–6). While no adequate testing has yet been done to document its effectiveness, digital videotape could provide a partial solution to the problem of long-term preservation of the videotaped image—partial in the sense that tapes would still need to be recopied periodically, but a solution in that the image would not degrade on duplication.

Advances are being made daily in the area of visual technologies, so it is clear that the dance librarian must be responsive to developments in the technological as well as scholarly and creative fields in order to provide the best access possible. Interactive video is an exciting opportunity for dance practitioners as both a teaching and a creative tool, and to librarians as an informational tool. Interactive video is already being used by individuals for choreographic work, and theater interactive videos have been developed for instructional purposes. As developments such as high density technology occur in the world of television, the effect will eventually be felt by the dance librarian. The implications for format of collection materials and necessary equipment for use may be great.

FACILITIES

Space

The unfortunate reality of library life is that very few dance librarians will be in a position to participate in the design of a new library or to work with an entirely new space. Given that situation, one must make do with an existing facility, which is usually not ideal and often not even satisfactory. The layout of a dance collection will depend on the nature of the collection (is it a circulating book collection or archival materials?) and what equipment is required for the use of the collection, the clientele served and their needs (do patrons spend long hours in research, or do they pick out a book and leave?), the staff activities (is technical processing done off-site by centralized technical services or in-house, which requires large amounts of room, table, and shelf space for processing manuscripts and archives collections?), and other space needs (is a conference room or even theater required for classes or meetings that regularly take place in the library?).

Dance collections, as music collections, may have special facilities and equipment requirements that are not shared by other subject areas. Because of the highly visual nature of dance, libraries that maintain dance videotape and film collections must provide viewing facilities or must be willing to circulate those materials. Many public libraries made an early commitment to the purchase and circulation of dance videotape materials, so in-house equipment provision is not as necessary. Nevertheless, many public libraries do provide equipment for viewing and listening. On the other hand, libraries that do not allow dance videotapes to circulate must provide adequate in-house equipment for their viewing. This equipment should be located so that its use does not disturb other patrons.

Even though the standard equipment a dance collection could be expected to provide would not enable a large group to view videotapes, it is desirable for the viewing room or area to accommodate several people at a time since dance students frequently come together to see a particular videotape. The dance librarian should monitor periodically the use of the dance videotape collection to ensure that a sufficient number of viewing stations are available in the library.

All dance collections should make a commitment to providing access for handicapped patrons. The measures taken will differ for each library, according to the existing physical facilities. In addition to ensuring access to the library itself, dance librarians must be sure that all equipment, catalogs (in any form), and library materials are also available to the patron. In the case of dance collections that have long since outgrown their walls and that have been forced to move shelving closer and closer in order to accommodate the collection, the handicapped patron may be at a significant disadvantage. With the variety of kinds of equipment that may be used in the dance collection, easy access to controls should be considered in mounting and housing such equipment.

Hours and Security

While the hours for the general library may seem adequate, many dance collections may have more limited hours. In addition, in academic settings, libraries may be closed between sessions or open for limited periods. There are libraries that are not open to the public and for which a researcher may need a special introduction in order to use the dance collection; there are others that require an appointment scheduled in advance. In any case, it is to the researcher's advantage to communicate with the dance librarian before an anticipated visit and to provide information regarding his or her area of interest and research needs. Such a communication will ensure that the dance librarian is aware of the proposed visit, and this may well speed the research process.

Security of library materials is an issue for all librarians in any setting but may be of particular concern for dance librarians, whose collections may include extremely fragile, valuable, or desirable materials. Some materials, such as videotapes and popular dance books, may be desired by an individual who cannot or will not purchase the items; however, much dance material may have significant resale value and will, therefore, be a target for the thief who intends to make a profit. Many decisions regarding operation of the library will affect the security of dance materials.

A closed stack library, in which use of the dance collection is constantly monitored, will provide better security than an open stack, circulating collection. However, librarians know from experience that even closed stack collections are not safe from the determined thief. One aspect of the security issue that all librarians hate to face is the fact that a thief may be a library insider rather than an outsider. All decisions on how material comes to the library, how it is handled in processing, how it is used either in the library or in circulation, and how that use is monitored or controlled impact the security of library collections. Careful consideration should be given to each step of the process.

The dance librarian may know and accept that a certain amount of material will disappear each year. If so, consideration will need to be given to the replacement of such items and the cost that replacement entails balanced against the cost of additional security measures and the service mission of the library. Because the issue of security has become so critical, much study is being done and literature is being published on the subject by individuals as well as groups (such as the Society of American Archivists and the Rare Books and Manuscripts Section of the Association of College and Research Libraries).

BUDGET AND FINANCE

Ongoing Expenses

As is true for most library collections, personnel costs in dance collections form a significant part of ongoing expenses in the budget. While the relatively inexpensive availability of microcomputers has eased some aspects of work with dance collections, the field continues to be a labor-intensive one that requires staff to handle special dance collections, to accomplish preservation work, to work with donor development, as well as to perform standard technical and public services.

Depending on the variety of materials held by the dance collection, equipment required may range from nothing more than tables and chairs to a very high technology installation. Playback equipment may be needed for a great number of formats, including record discs in a variety of speeds; audiotapes in different speeds and perhaps sizes; videotapes in various sizes, on reels, or in cassettes; slides; films of various millimeters; microforms both reel and fiche; as well as the appropriate computer equipment for whatever software, online, imaging, and CD-ROM resources the dance collection may hold.

Given the variety of physical formats that may be held by dance collections, the implications for funding may be great. As was mentioned above, book publishing in dance has not been a huge industry; therefore, many dance collections have been well able to acquire the materials that are appropriate to their collection goals without the agonizing decisions that must be made in other subject specialties. However, dance librarians need to be aware that because of the vital visual nature of dance, not only will dance artists seize upon new advances in visual image retention, but any new technology in that area will be scrutinized and probably utilized for replication of the image. This use of new technologies will have significant impact on the materials that are published on dance and on the budgets both for dance materials and for the necessary equipment and facilities for viewing those materials.

Many libraries do not have integrated "dance collections" but may, in fact, have extensive dance materials spread throughout the library, which are purchased by different librarians from a variety of funds. For example, dance books may be found in arts or humanities departments, dance videotapes in an audio-visual section, dance journals in the periodicals department, and dance biographies in the biography section. If the bibliographer in each area has a specific fund for dance materials, then the collection as a whole may be well balanced. If funds are not specified, then the dance holdings may be very uneven, reflecting either the level of knowledge and interest of a bibliographer in a particular area or a collection development policy that is appropriate for the department but does not relate to the policies for other parts of the library.

Despite security measures, some libraries experience a high loss rate of materials. Because some dance books (especially facsimile editions of historical dance treatises) and visual materials may be quite costly on an individual piece basis, replacement funds may take a certain amount of the dance budget. This will vary from library to library, according to loss rate and to the replacement policy for lost materials.

Extraordinary Expenses

With the rapid development of new technologies for the visual and moving image, there will soon be serious budget implications for the dance librarian. With new technologies such as CD-ROM, interactive video, and digital video, the budgetary impact may be great. Workstations and drives, software and databases, computers with high resolution screens and videotape machines for different formats are some of the necessary purchases that will be expensive. Clearly the implications for dance librarians are immense, in terms of budget for acquisition, storage, use, and long-term retention of materials. Videotape is a prime example.

In addition to the initial cost involved in purchasing a dance videotape, there are numerous associated ongoing costs. To be adequately maintained, videotape requires an environment with temperature, humidity, and light controls; protection from magnetic fields; storage areas that allow for upright storage; proper winding; and periodic examinations of the videotape. Not only will frequent use degrade the image, but time itself is an enemy to the videotape, which has a limited life span. Equipment may be a very expensive requirement, particularly since a standardized video format was not established at the beginning of its use. While most libraries will have VHS, Beta, or both, special dance collections may well be faced with an even greater variety, including various sizes of reel-to-reel video-tape, which will require either conversion to a cassette format (with the automatic degradation of the image associated with later generations) or the maintenance of a multiplicity of machines, which are no longer available for purchase and which cannot be repaired due to lack of parts. In the end, the dance librarian, while attempting to simultaneously maintain videotapes and make them available for use, fights a losing battle against time.

So far videotape is a format that self-destructs, even when stored under ideal conditions and not being used; therefore, it cannot be a preservation medium for long-term documentation of dance. For the dance librarian whose charge includes such preservation, the costs may be prohibitive. One might copy videotapes on a periodic basis before the image decays on the original, but there will still be a degrading of the image for each copy generation. One might have the videotape transferred to film, which is a more stable, longer-lasting medium. However, both are ultimately expensive preservation methods.

Fundraising

"Marketing" a dance collection should begin at home. The dance librarian should make sure that the entire library system knows of the collection, its research value, and the way in which it fits with other library materials. The dance librarian should take advantage of internal publications, such as newsletters, to educate his or her colleagues about the collection and, in academic libraries, should promote the collection to the campus-wide community as well. While these groups may not provide extra funding for the collection, they may prove vital in supporting a grant proposal, both during the application process and during the completion of a funded project.

In order to meet the preservation and access needs of certain dance materials (for instance, large manuscripts collections in need of processing or collections requiring special preservation work), it may be necessary to seek funding from outside the home institution. Most libraries provide a certain basic level of commitment to materials, such as binding for books and a standard level of cataloging; however, for many dance collections, these levels are inadequate. While many dance librarians will agree that their libraries should support all materials according to their need and format, the reality is that in recent economic climates it is not possible.

Outside funding agencies have provided much-needed funds for preservation and access to dance materials; therefore, it behooves the dance librarian with special funding needs to search out those granting agencies and foundations whose interests are most closely in line with the collection in question. While federal agencies and major corporate foundations are frequently approached, one should not forget smaller private foundations, local and regional agencies, and even individuals who may have a related interest or connection to the dance collection. Depending on the size of the grant required, the dance librarian may put together a package of various outside funders to accomplish the entire project. A number of sources that give information about various funding organizations and programs are available to librarians. These will help narrow the search for the right funding agency. Alumni, another source of additional funds, should be informed about the dance collection, perhaps through a magazine, newsletter, or special mailing.

In fundraising from individuals, the person who actually makes the solicitation from an individual potential donor will depend on the structure of the parent institution and its development branch. In many cases, development is centralized, and all solicitation is done by a development officer who is assisted by the librarian and, perhaps, a member of the library's friends group. This structure may be a great advantage to the dance librarian, if the development department is well organized, since it may identify and provide information about potential donors and help finalize arrangements, including the completion of gift agreements.

Many dance librarians feel that for donors who give both collections and money, it is good to have the dance librarian handling the collection and someone else handling the financial aspect. There are disadvantages, however, since the dance librarian's priorities in fundraising may be different from the development department's or officer's, and certain institutional donors who would be logical to approach for particular projects may be off-limits. In other cases, if there is no development branch, the dance librarian may be free to approach any potential funder. A major drawback is that fundraising takes time and effort to do well, and the dance librarian most likely already has a full schedule just doing the daily job.

Friends groups can be very important, both in providing funds for the dance collection and in supplying an organization that can help in dance projects or events that ultimately may result in the solicitation of outside funds. Friends groups have traditionally been a source of funding for special purchases, in particular collection material, but also for equipment.

POLITICS

Internal

The chronic underfunding of the performing arts, in general, at the national, regional, and local levels in the United States is reflected in the funding for arts in schools at all levels and in libraries. This lack of funds may be the result of a lack of recognition or understanding of the value of the arts. The dance librarian should be prepared to fight the battle of justification over and over in trying to obtain administrative support and adequate funding for the dance collection.

Dance is intimately related to a number of other subject areas that may be found in the library, in particular to the other performing arts and to the visual arts. In fact, dance (in both its theatrical and social forms) is so intertwined with other arts, as well as the humanities and sciences, that frequently it cannot be separated from other disciplines. This is one of the strengths of dance as a discipline—that it so pervades human effort and interest. It can also be a drawback, in that dance may be perceived only in relationship to the primary discipline of the scholar. The challenge for the dance librarian is to give the dance collection coherence while working within the collection development policies for the library system.

External

The dance librarian is perhaps more fortunate than other library colleagues, in that dance is attractive and interesting to a great many people, and its documentation can also be extremely appealing visually. In seeking outside funding, especially within the community who can enjoy the dance collection firsthand, the dance librarian may have a distinct advantage. However, because of the weight given to the sciences over the arts and humanities in general, the disparity in funding between the two, and the perception of some that the arts are not necessary but a nice extra, "pretty" may not be enough. In order to firmly establish the dance collection with administrative support and adequate funding, the dance librarian may be faced with the task of proving the value of the dance collection, both locally and in the context of collections on a broader spectrum. The establishment of a good support base from the dance department of whatever academic unit offers dance or from the community, in the case of public libraries, may be vital to the health of the dance collection.

Censorship in the arts is not a new problem, nor will there be an easy solution, since objective methods for determining value cannot be established. Right and wrong exist only for the individual viewer, and that viewer's taste cannot constitute a standard for others. Dance and its practitioners have certainly been affected by censorship throughout the ages, and that situation continues today with recent focus on performance artists whose works incorporate movement. The dance librarian must attempt to document without prejudice the dance activities that fall within the scope of the particular collection policy and to make sure that documentation is available to patrons.

Dance and dance scholarship are at the threshold of an exciting time of potential. Advances in technology and the establishment of a solid base of scholars and scholarly works are coming together to provide opportunities that have not previously been available. The position of the dance librarian in this era of development can be an invaluable addition to this process by the expertise and helpful input he or she can provide. The dance librarian can assist not only in the research and the production of major tools in the field but in preservation studies of various physical formats of material. And, most important, the dance librarian's own discipline, dance librarianship, is just waiting to be developed.

REFERENCES

American Reference Books Annual. 1970– . Littleton, CO: Libraries Unlimited.

Au, Susan. 1979. "Resources for the Dance Historian: A Selected List of Bibliographies Published Since 1960." Prepared for the Dance History Conference, February 17–18, New York.

Bibliography of Dance Studies: A Research Conference, March 21–24, 1985, Library of Congress, Washington, D.C. 1985. Irvine, CA: Regents of the University of California.

Books for College Libraries: A Core Collection of 50,000 Titles, 3rd ed. 1988. Chicago: American Library Association.

Broadside. 1940– . New York: Theatre Library Association.

Cady, Susan A. 1990. "The Electronic Revolution in Libraries: Microfilm Deja Vu?" *College & Research Libraries* 51.4 (July): 374–386.

Calmes, Alan. 1990. "New Preservation Concern: Video Recordings." *Newsletter,* Commission on Preservation and Access 22 (April): 5–6.

Choice. 1963– . Middletown, CT: Association of College and Research Libraries.

Cohen, Selma Jeanne, ed. Forthcoming. *The International Encyclopedia of Dance.* Berkeley: University of California Press.

Dance Abstracts and Index. 1992. Los Angeles, CA: Dance Database Project.

The Encyclopedia of Theatre Dance in Canada. 1990– . CD-ROM. Toronto: Arts Inter-Media Canada/Dance Collection Danse.

Guide to Reference Books. 1929– . Chicago: American Library Association.

Johnson, Catherine. 1992. "Cataloging Council of the Dance Heritage Coalition." Unpublished electronic message.

Keens, William, Leslie Hansen Kopp, and Mindy N. Levine. 1991. *Images of American Dance: Documenting and Preserving a Cultural Heritage.* Report on the study sponsored by the National Endowment for the Arts and the Andrew W. Mellon Foundation. Washington, DC: National Endowment for the Humanities and Andrew W. Mellon Foundation.

Library of Congress. 1959/1961– . *National Union Catalog of Manuscript Collections.* Washington, DC: Library of Congress.

Ludden, Bennet. 1968. "The Dance Classification System of the Juilliard School Library." *Theatre Documentation* 1.1 (Fall): 21–29.

The Music Index: A Subject-Author Guide to Music Periodical Literature. 1949– . Detroit: Information Coordinators.

New York Public Library, Dance Collection. 1975– . *Bibliographic Guide to Dance.* Boston: G. K. Hall.

———. 1991– . *Dance on Disc: The Complete Catalog of the Dance Collection of The New York Public Library.* CD-ROM. Boston: G. K. Hall.

———. 1992– . *Index to Dance Periodicals.* Boston: G. K, Hall.

Performing Arts Resources. 1974– . New York: Theatre Library Association.

Prospectus. 1990. Bowling Green, OH; East Lansing, MI; and Columbus, OH: Consortium of Popular Culture Collections in the Midwest.

Robinson, Doris. 1989. *Music and Dance Periodicals: An International Directory & Guidebook.* Voorheesville, NY: Peri Press.

Sadie, Stanley, ed. 1980. *The New Grove Dictionary of Music and Musicians.* Washington, DC: Grove's Dictionaries of Music.

Sheehy, Carolyn A. 1990. "Chicago Dance Collection: A Case in *Pointe.*" *American Archivist* 53.3 (Summer): 432–440.

Soupiset, Kathryn A. 1991. "College Book Price Information, 1990." *Choice* 28.7 (March): 1073–1078.

Ulrich's International Periodicals Directory. 1932– . New York: Bowker.

Viltis. 1944– . Denver, CO: V. F. Beliajus.

Wagner, Robert. 1990. "Memo on Videotape Storage." Unpublished manuscript, Columbus, OH.

3

Film Studies Collections

Kristine R. Brancolini
and Beverly L. Teach

INTRODUCTION

Film studies can be defined as the examination of film as a cultural product—as fine art, as commercial entertainment, as social/cultural artifact. Generally speaking, one usually equates film studies with feature films. However, film studies collections are not limited to full-length feature films but can include as well documentaries, experimental or avant-garde films, films excerpted or adapted from feature films, examples of the very earliest motion pictures, and films that are representative of a range of filmic techniques. In academic libraries, collections to support film studies consist of print, film, and video materials.

Harold Geduld, Professor of Comparative Literature at Indiana University, notes that while film scholarship as an independent activity has flourished for most of this century, the introduction of film studies into colleges and universities is relatively recent, with programs first appearing in the 1960s and early 1970s (Geduld 1974: 2). In academic libraries, funding for print film studies collections has typically come from the related disciplines of literature and art. A subject bibliographer in one of these fields would assume collection development and selection responsibilities. The early audio-visual film studies collections were 16mm and generally developed under the auspices of an audio-visual center and not the university library. Most university libraries, particularly research libraries, did not begin developing audio-visual collections until after the emergence of video, and particularly ½″ VHS videocassettes.

Most films acquired in these initial film studies collections were not full-length feature films but rather documentaries, avant-garde films, or films with historical importance, to indicate only a few examples. Feature films on 16mm, if they were available to libraries at all, were very expensive ($500 to $2,500 or more) and available only on a lease plan. At the end of the lease (usually five years), the library had the option of renewing the lease at the current lease price or returning the title. Film studies faculty would rent feature films to show to their classes and, while the rental prices were also expensive ($50 to $150 or more), they were less expensive than leasing the title. Rental also allowed faculty more flexibility in the films taught from year to year. The availability of feature films on videocassette has had a major impact on the growth and development of film studies collections. As an example, *The Autobiography of Miss Jane Pittman*, which was originally available on a five-year lease in 16mm from Learning Corporation of America for $1,450, was available in 1991 with public performance rights from Lucerne Media, Morris Plains, New Jersey, for $1,250 in 16mm and $295 in VHS; it is also available without public performance rights from theatrical video distributors at a home video list price of $14.95.

The introduction of low-cost video in the home market has had a revolutionary impact on all segments of the audio-visual market, including the growth of video collections in public libraries. While many public libraries have had centralized 16mm collections, the availability of low-cost videocassettes and the demand for them by public library patrons has seen the growth and development of video collections in not only the system office but branch offices as well. Feature films account, on average, for approximately 50 percent of public library video collections (Dewing 1988: 62). By their nature, most of these collections take a more popular approach than do most college and university film studies collections.

Today, 16mm films are rarely acquired even in libraries that have large film collections. This is due to a number of factors, including stretching already tight acquisition budgets by taking advantage of lower list prices for video over film, user preference, and the availability of more and more titles only in video formats. The major focus of this chapter, therefore, is on the development and management of film studies video collections, rather than 16mm film collections. However, 16mm film maintenance is addressed, when appropriate, should librarians by choice or by default include films in their collections. Even with the evolving video technologies, there is still no video format that can match film for its impact, clarity, and resolution, including big screen video projection of laserdisc. The college and university film studies librarian should recognize that film studies faculty will still want to show their students films. To do this, they will continue to rent feature films on 16mm.

PERSONNEL

Staffing Levels

In colleges and universities without a separate library devoted to film studies or to the performing arts, staffing for any discipline may be minimal. (Even in a large research library, most subject bibliographers collect in more than one discipline.) Most academic libraries have established film studies collections within the last twenty years, and film studies librarians have been asked to assume responsibility for a film or video collection in addition to print resources.

Minimal staffing consists of one librarian and one clerical staffer in college and university libraries. As the Library of Congress classification for film studies literature is PN, the librarians who select literature may also select in the area of film studies. One librarian may select all film studies literature, or the librarians who select languages and literature may also select the accompanying film literature—French, Italian, Japanese, or Spanish, for instance. Depending upon how selection responsibilities are assigned among librarians, it may be desirable for English-language materials to be selected by one librarian and foreign-language materials to be selected by librarians who select literature in those languages.

There is not a special film studies librarian in most public libraries. Public libraries with established 16mm film collections usually have at least one staff member with both library and media training. These experienced media librarians have systematically incorporated the acquisition of both nontheatrical and theatrical videocassettes into their collections based on their collection development guidelines and the needs of their patrons.

Professionals

Desired qualifications for a film studies librarian include academic preparation in film studies and knowledge of building and maintaining audio-visual collections. Regardless of academic preparation and knowledge of audio-visual librarianship, it is imperative that the film studies librarian immerse herself or himself in the teaching of film studies at that particular institution. The teaching of film studies varies dramatically from one college or university to another. The course content of the program served by the library's collection should be the initial focus of the collection and the ongoing concern of the film studies librarian. This librarian must establish a relationship with the film studies faculty and work closely with them to develop a collection that serves their needs and the needs of their students. Of course, the depth of the collection will depend upon the overall mission of the library and its collection development policy. Whether the film studies collection serves the research needs of the faculty or the instructional needs of the faculty and students, the film studies librarian must communicate regularly with the faculty.

The development and maintenance of public library video collections should be undertaken with as much attention to the library's mission, goals, and objectives with regard to the needs of library patrons as the print collection. For this to happen, media librarians in public libraries must have traditional library training, as well as a strong background in the selection, utilization, production, and distribution of audio-visual materials. "Liking movies" is not adequate preparation for the position of media librarian.

Paraprofessionals, Students, and Volunteers

Paraprofessionals, students, and volunteers play varying roles in the management of film studies collections. In many public and academic libraries, paraprofessionals have complete responsibility for building the videocassette collection of feature films and managing the attendant services. Aside from general library experience, these paraprofessionals are often film buffs and may bring a wealth of film knowledge to the job. While not possible to write into a job description, this characteristic can add immeasurably to the success of a film studies collection, particularly in a public library. However, it is important to stress to such personnel that, as in building a print collection, personal tastes must not overwhelm building a film studies collection that meets the needs of users. Most academic libraries employ students, and it is desirable to hire film studies students or students who have studied film as part of another program.

Continuing Education, Recruitment, and Mentoring

Film studies librarians in academic libraries often find that they have no professional colleagues within their library with whom they can share their interests or expertise. They may not even have peers in other academic libraries in their state. Consequently, the film studies librarian may turn to film studies faculty for professional support and suggestions for continuing education opportunities. The film studies librarian may read publications such as *Journal of Film and Video*, published by the University Film and Video Association, which addresses issues and topics related to teaching film in colleges and universities. Within the American Library Association (ALA), film studies librarians may be members of the Video Round Table, the Arts Section of the Association of College and Research Libraries (ACRL) or the Audiovisual Committee of ACRL. However, in general, there is little support for film studies librarians within the ALA. Ironically, the ALA provides more support for film studies librarians as video librarians than as subject bibliographers. At this time, there is no film studies discussion group or similar organization within the ALA.

In addition to these formal organizations, there is another, more informal means of communicating with film studies librarians: computer listservs. For librarians with access to BITNET, film studies listservs can provide an immediate source of information and advice—almost instantaneous communication with hundreds of other film studies librarians, film buffs, film scholars, and film studies faculty. It is easy to subscribe to a listserv and easy to cancel the subscription. Three lists currently deal with film and film studies: CINEMA-L ("Discussions on All Forms of Cinema"), FILM-L ("Film Making and Review List"), and SCREEN-L ("Film and TV Discussion List"). The discussions range from obscure, very academic topics to film reviews and trivia. Due largely to the participation of librarians, collection development and reference questions appear from time to time. You need not be a subscriber to the listserv to post a query; just be sure to ask respondents to send replies directly to you rather than the listserv and include your electronic mail address.

To subscribe to any of these lists, a subscription message must be sent via electronic mail to the appropriate listserv manager. The subscription message should take the following form: *Subscribe [name of listserv] [sender's name]*; for example, *Subscribe FILM-L Kristine Brancolini*. To cancel your subscription, simply send the message *Unsubscribe [name of listserv]* to the appropriate listserv manager. To subscribe to CINEMA-L, send the subscription message to LISTSERV@AUVM.BITNET. To post a message to CINEMA-L, send it to CINEMA-L@AUVM.BITNET. To subscribe to FILM-L, send the subscription message to LISTSERV @ITESMVF1.BITNET. To post a message to FILM-L, send it to FILM-L @ITESMVF1.BITNET. To subscribe to SCREEN-L, send the subscription message to LISTSERV@UA1VM.BITNET. To post a message to SCREEN-L, send it to SCREEN-L@UA1VM.BITNET.

COLLECTION DEVELOPMENT

Policies

Whether establishing a new collection or expanding an existing one, the film studies librarian must begin with the collection development policy. The policy will delineate the boundaries of the collection and enable the film studies librarian to communicate effectively with other librarians and the film studies faculty. Many film studies librarians collect both print and audio-visual materials to support research and instruction in film studies. Because the collection guidelines differ so dramatically for print and audio-visual materials, it is necessary to have both a general collection development policy and one for audio-visual materials—usually video-cassette, videodisc, and/or film. The audio-visual collection development policy is actually a subpolicy of the overall collection development policy.

It is as imperative that a public library have a written collection development policy as it is for an academic library. While the video collection development policy in a public library will probably not be as comprehensive as that in an academic library, the policy should at least address the following issues: What is the overall goal of the collection? Will it support the popular entertainment requests of the local community, much as the local video stores? Will it attempt to collect the "classics," foreign feature films, or other theatrical works as well? Will it provide curricular support to the schools? Will it include nontheatrical materials, such as social documentaries, dance, music, drama, and other humanities programs; children's materials; how-to titles; and educational/instructional materials? In what proportions? While the following discussion is geared to film studies collection development in a college or university, the issues raised are also relevant to public library collection development policies. For examples of public library collection development policies, see James Scholtz's *Video Policies and Procedures for Libraries* (1991).

General Objectives and Subject Boundaries

The general film studies collection development policy should address the following issues:

What is the overall goal of the collection? Will it support faculty research? Will it provide curricular support? Describe the departments where film studies faculty teach. In some film studies programs, faculty are scattered throughout such departments as English, comparative literature, fine arts, telecommunications, and theater and drama. Film studies courses may also be taught in anthropology, history, and sociology. Does the collection support all courses, or will other subject bibliographers be selecting literature in those areas?

What areas of the film studies literature will be covered? Most collections include publications on the history and art of the film, history and art of directors, specific films, and actors and actresses. Will the collection cover all of these areas? Will the collection cover the techniques and craft of film production or the scientific aspects of filmmaking? Will the collection cover ethnographic and documentary filmmaking?

Will the collection cover English-language materials only, or will it also cover selected foreign languages? Which foreign languages will be covered? Will the collection cover the entire history of film, or will it cover only certain decades of film history? Which geographical locations will be covered? Will coverage be more complete for some continents and some countries than for others?

Which formats will be included and which will be excluded? Presumably books and periodicals will be included, but will 16mm films, video-cassettes, videodiscs, audiocassettes, microforms, published scripts, exhibition and museum publications, and audiocassettes be included in the collection? What about original scripts, film scores, press books, film memorabilia, posters, film stills, and 35mm and 70mm films?

Films, films on videocassettes, and other audio-visual materials on film studies may be selected by another librarian. The film studies collection development policy should note this as a related policy and discuss the scope of that collection. Any archival collections within the library system should be noted. Many colleges and universities have film studies collections outside the library system in an audio-visual center collection or in departmental collections. These additional film studies resources should also be acknowledged.

Specific Video and Film Policy

With the explosion in the home video market, feature films and short subjects are increasingly available on videocassette and on videodisc. Although ten years ago it was unusual for libraries to support the need of film studies faculty and students for films themselves, video has made this possible and affordable. However, many libraries collecting video-cassettes have yet to specify in their collection development policies the scope of their film studies collection and their selection criteria. In addition to the general areas discussed above, a collection development policy for video to support film studies should include the following elements:

How closely will the selection of video be related to faculty research and to the curriculum? Will the collection include "classic" films that may not be taught in film studies courses? How will "classic" be defined for the purposes of this collection? Will the video collection support recreational viewing? Will the collection include documentary video on film studies, such as biographies of directors and actors, the history of film, and examinations of specific topics in film studies? Will the film studies librarian attempt to purchase public performance rights for video?

Will the video collection include foreign films? Will foreign films be dubbed or subtitled? Will some foreign films be purchased in the original language without either dubbing or subtitling?

What video formats will the collection include—¾" videocassette, Beta, VHS, videodisc? Will the collection include American NTSC (National Television Standard Committee) standard only, or will foreign films be purchased in PAL (Phase Alternation Line rate) and SECAM (Sequential Color with Memory)? (If the film studies librarian decides to purchase videocassettes in non-NTSC standards, it is advisable to provide multistandard playback equipment in the library. On many campuses, this equipment will be unavailable otherwise.)

Selection criteria may be covered in a separate collection policy but are often included as part of the collection development policy. In addition to the general selection criteria for the purchase of video, the section dealing with video to support film studies may address regularly consulted review sources, acceptable levels of print quality, depth of coverage for directors, depth of coverage for genres, the balance among the various genres, and the balance between English-language and foreign-language productions. In the selection policy, the film studies librarian may also want to address Motion Picture Association of America (MPAA) ratings and content. Will the film studies librarian consider MPAA ratings during the selection process? Will movies rated NC-17 (no children under age 17) be included or excluded from the collection? While censorship is not an issue for most academic libraries, those public libraries and academic libraries serving colleges with a religious affiliation may be forced to confront this issue. What about foreign titles that may not be rated?

This section may also specify who is responsible for selection. Does the film studies librarian select alone or in consultation with other librarians and faculty? Does a committee make actual purchase decisions?

Depending upon the nature of the collection, the film studies librarian must decide how to handle decisions regarding replacement and weeding. Given the relative fragility of videotape and the vagaries of video distribution patterns, replacement is likely to offer more challenges than weeding. Repair and replacement of 16mm films may also prove challenging for similar reasons. Many of the companies that originally distributed films found in the early film studies collections are no longer in business. Rights to distribute these titles may or may not have been acquired by other distributors, and what rights were acquired may not have included video distribution.

Most collections supporting film studies require little or no weeding. They are small relative to the print collection and highly selective. Most titles are selected for their lasting value. However, if the academic program supported by the collection changes, the film studies librarian will want to have procedures in place for reevaluating the collection, particularly if storage space is at a premium. Similarly, the film studies librarian will probably want to replace damaged and worn video titles but be unable to do so. The policy should state the procedures for searching out-of-print sources in addition to the regular acquisitions channels. As the acquisitions department is likely to be unfamiliar with sources for out-of-print video-cassettes, the film studies librarian will have to maintain a list of contacts. Local video rental stores often sell used, out-of-print videocassettes, and there are now several national sources (see the "Publishers and Vendors" section in this chapter).

A film studies collection may be able to duplicate an out-of-print film or videocassette. Section 108, Subsection (c) of the copyright law gives libraries and archives limited rights to reproduce copyrighted audio-visual works "solely for the purpose of replacement of a copy or phonorecord that is damaged, deteriorating, lost or stolen, if the library or archives has, after a reasonable effort, determined that an unused replacement cannot be obtained at a fair price. The scope or nature of a reasonable investigation to determine that an unused replacement cannot be obtained will vary according to the circumstances of a particular situation" (H.R. Rep. No. 94–1476 at 75–76). Therefore, libraries should develop procedures that, in the opinion of their legal counsel, constitute a reasonable investigation to determine that an unused replacement cannot be obtained.

Selection Tools

For reviews and selection of current books, the film studies librarian will rely primarily on *Choice* and *Film Quarterly*. No other film journals devote much attention to reviewing film literature. In its summer issue, *Film Quarterly* publishes an annual book survey, covering English-language books that have not been reviewed in *Film Quarterly*. According to editor Ernest Callenbach, "While virtually all film journals and magazines review some books, *Film Quarterly* is the only publication that has tried to reflect in its book coverage a fairly complete sense of what has been written in the field" (Callenbach 1990: 21). The survey is divided into the following sections: autobiographies and biographies, criticism, history, reference, scripts, textbooks, theory, and miscellaneous. Published by the University of California, Berkeley, *Film Quarterly*'s annual book survey covers only those titles likely to be of interest to film scholars, so it represents an important tool for academic film studies librarians.

Film studies librarians in research libraries will want to use non-evaluative sources, such as *American Book Publishing Record, British National Bibliography*, and the Library of Congress's *CDS Alert*, to remain abreast of forthcoming and recently published film literature. As in other disciplines, these sources require the film studies librarian to make judgments based upon authors, titles, publishers, and subject matter, without critical evaluation. Film studies librarians who use these selection tools will probably want to use sources like *Film Quarterly*'s regular reviews and annual book survey to make sure that no important title has been inadvertently omitted from the selection process.

Selection tools for current videocassette and videodisc releases include library, film, and popular publications. From 1989 to mid-1992, Randy Pitman, publisher of *Video Librarian*, wrote "Video Movies," a regular column for *Library Journal*; in this column he focused on "lesser-known independent and foreign features" in an attempt to broaden the library market for these films. In July 1992, Pitman began publishing *Video Movies*, a monthly review source that expanded the purpose of the "Video Movies" column. However, this publication lasted for little more than one year. It ceased publication in October 1993, with volume 2, number 4. Each issue contained 18 to 20 lengthy critical reviews with a starred rating, 1 through 4. This publication will be missed by film studies librarians in both academic and public libraries who need evaluative information for new video releases beyond the "blockbusters" featured in general-interest magazines such as *Video Magazine*. Public librarians may also want to consult Pitman and Elliott Swanson's *Video Movies: A Core Collection for Libraries* (1990) for advice on collection building and an annotated list of 500 movies available on videocassette that are recommended for public libraries.

For reviews of laserdiscs, the most comprehensive source is Douglas Pratt's *The Laser Disc Newsletter*. Pratt provides technically oriented reviews, attempting to cover every laser videodisc that is released. To aid retrospective collection building, Pratt published *The Laser Video Disc Companion* (1992). This book includes a complete listing of over 5,000 discs released in the United States between 1981 and 1990, critical and technical reviews of more than 4,000 selected titles, and a suggested core collection of "One Hundred Great Discs." Pratt also includes an informative introductory essay and a bibliography. *Video Magazine* also reviews current laserdisc releases. Librarians will want to watch for a new collection of laserdisc reviews, *The Laserdisc Film Guide: Complete Ratings for the Best and Worst Movies Available on Disc*, by Jeff Rovin (1993).

Film studies librarians planning major retrospective purchases or collection evaluation have several tools available to them. Frank Manchel's *Film Study: An Analytical Bibliography* (1990) is a four-volume work unequaled in scope. Begun as an update to Manchel's 1973 work, *Film Study: A Reference Guide*, it includes extensive discussions of 500 books, annotations of 2,000 books, nearly 4,000 references to books, nearly 5,000 footnotes, and countless articles in its survey of film literature. Arranged by topical chapters, Manchel's work is indexed by author, article title, book title, film title, film personality, and subject.

Mass Media Bibliography: An Annotated Guide to Books and Journals for Research and Reference (1990) by Eleanor Blum and Frances Goins Wilhoit is the third, revised edition of *Basic Books in the Mass Media*. Updated to 1987, this work includes a chapter on film literature with annotated entries for 400 books. Written by librarians at the University of Illinois and Indiana University, *Mass Media Bibliography* has three primary purposes: to serve as a reference tool; to suggest materials for research or reading; and to act as a checking or buying list. Journals are covered separately, but film journals are not included in the listing. The authors recommend using Anthony Slide's bibliography of film journals, *International Film, Radio, and Television Journals* (1985). Arranged alphabetically by title, Slide profiles 200 major journals and an assortment of minor ones that have research value, whether scholarly or popular. Although radio and television are covered, film periodicals dominate the entries, as they dominate the publishing field.

In *Film, Television, and Video Periodicals: A Comprehensive Annotated List* (1991), another recently published reference work on film periodicals, Katharine Loughney covers the most widely used and accessible film, television, and video periodicals currently published in the United States. Arranged alphabetically by title, the book is indexed by geographical location, subject (film, television, or video), and intended audience.

On the Screen: A Film, Television, and Video Research Guide (1986) by Kim N. Fisher, a librarian at Pennsylvania State University, is a guide to important English-language reference works in the fields of motion pictures and television. Arranged topically, then alphabetically by title, *On the Screen* includes chapters on bibliographic guides, dictionaries and encyclopedias, indexes and databases and other types of reference works, a list of core periodicals, research centers and archives, and societies and associations. It is also indexed by author, title, and subject.

Publishers and Vendors

The acquisition of video or film requires the film studies librarian to become knowledgeable about the acquisitions process. Acquisitions is the process by which materials are obtained by the library, including identifying and selecting vendors, confirming title availability and price, organizing discounts, order verification, order transmission and fulfillment and tracking back-orders, and budgetary funds. In most libraries all of these tasks are performed by an acquisitions department or an acquisitions staff. For the acquisition of video, however, media staff usually find themselves performing all of these tasks (up to placement of orders).

Film studies librarians who select video or film must familiarize themselves with the system of video distribution, which includes three types of vendors: producers, distributors (wholesale and retail), and jobbers.

The producer is the corporate entity that actually finances and produces the film or video. The producer of an educational film or video usually retains the copyright and public performance rights.

Distributors contract with producers to sell their productions. They usually operate on a regional or national basis. Film studies librarians are advised to purchase from wholesale distributors whenever possible because they offer lower prices. However, most wholesale distributors of videocassettes work primarily with video rental stores and do not promote available titles beyond the "blockbusters." The film studies librarian will find them most helpful for providing new releases at reduced prices and locating back titles that are needed quickly. Wholesale distributors typically offer preorder discounts and a dealer discount. A current example will illustrate the pricing structure. *The Doors*, directed by Oliver Stone, has a preorder price of $67.45, a dealer price of $71.00, and a list price of $92.95. A wholesale distributor such as Major Video Concepts (MVC), for example, has a network of distribution sites. If a title is out of stock at their corporate headquarters in Indianapolis, they may be able to send it via overnight delivery from their distribution center in Richmond, Virginia. MVC's catalogs are filled with slick and sensational advertising, providing no evaluative information. They cannot be used as selection tools. A retail distributor, on the other hand, may provide more informative promotional materials.

Facets Video, located in Chicago, is a retail distributor. It does not offer reduced prices but represents a more academically oriented, specialized source for video. Facets is a nonprofit arts organization founded in 1975. In addition to video rental and sales, Facets offers daily screenings of foreign, independent American and classic films at Facets Multimedia Center (1517 West Fullerton Avenue, Chicago, IL 60614; 800-331-6197). Facets publishes an annual catalog, a monthly supplement called *Facets Features*, and topical catalogs—multicultural films, theater, French film, Slavic film, and more. *Facets Features* includes articles as well as listings of new releases, bargain videos, and laserdiscs. Each entry is descriptively annotated, providing selection information. Evergreen Video is a mail-order video company "dedicated to making its members aware of all quality films on video." Their annual catalog, *Evergreen Index*, and monthly newsletter, *The Evergreen Video Review*, emphasize the quality films that are often overlooked by video rental stores. All titles in their catalog and newsletter may be rented or purchased. Like *Facets Features*, *The Evergreen Video Review* highlights outstanding new releases. One issue (July/August/ September 1991) lists new releases, price reductions, "The Evergreen Gay & Lesbian Collection," "A Selected Director's List from the Evergreen Collection," and a list of used tapes.

If the film studies collection also contains documentary and ethnographic titles, programs on production techniques, programs on how a particular feature film was produced, and so on, the film studies librarian will need to familiarize himself or herself with the range of educational, nontheatrical distributors available. For example, the National Audio-Visual Center in Washington, DC, distributes documentaries produced by or for the U.S. government by Frank Capra, John Ford, John Houston, Pare Lorentz, Willard Van Dyke, and others. First Run/Icarus in New York City distributes *Making "Do the Right Thing"* (16mm $895; VHS $390). Pyramid Film and Video in Santa Monica, California, distributes a number of films done by experimental, avant-garde filmmakers, including Faith Hubley and Charles and Ray Eames.

The major video jobbers are Baker & Taylor and Ingram Video. They deal primarily with libraries and offer substantial discounts for volume sales. Film studies librarians purchasing a substantial number of recent-release feature films may want to explore the discounts available from these companies.

Many public and some academic libraries purchase used videocassettes and laserdiscs of feature films to replace out-of-print titles. These used films come from video rental stores that find they no longer need the extra copies of a once-popular title. Four sources of used videocassettes are AAA/Priority Video, Distribution Video & Audio (DV&A), Midwest Video Exchange, and Movies in Motion (Dick 1991: 49–50; Lora 1992:

72). Midwest Video Exchange inspects each videocassette for defects before selling it, but libraries that purchase used videocassettes may want to inspect them again before adding them to the collection. It is also important to select a vendor with a reasonable return policy for defective videotapes.

Donors and Donations

Donations are not a major factor in the development of a film studies collection in either academic or public libraries. Infrequently, a retiring faculty member or a department may wish to donate a locally developed book or videorecording collection. In the case of any donation of video-recordings, but especially those related to film studies, the librarian must determine the legality of the donated materials with regard to copyright. For example, a collection of videocassettes taped off the air or off cable cannot be added to the library's collection legally. Tapes that arrive in plain black boxes with hand labeling are always suspect.

More frequently, the film studies librarian might be approached to house a departmental or other specially developed video collection. In contrast to a donation, this arrangement may designate the film studies librarian as collection manager, responsible for providing storage, maintenance, and access, while the department maintains control of selection and funding. Such an arrangement should be approached cautiously, emphasizing to the donor department or unit that the materials must be available to library users on an equal-access basis.

TECHNICAL SERVICES

Cataloging

Print film studies collections should receive full descriptive cataloging and classification, the same as materials in other subject disciplines. This is not a controversial matter in most libraries. However, the video collection to support film studies may not receive the same treatment. In general, the cataloging of audio-visual materials has lagged far behind the collection of audio-visual materials. In reviewing the history of nonprint cataloging, Jean Weihs (1987) notes that in 1897 the Library of Congress had pictures and photographs in its collections, but Library of Congress rules for cataloging motion pictures, filmstrips, sound recordings, and two- dimensional representations were not published until 1952–1965.

Libraries continue to provide minimal bibliographic access to their audio-visual collections, particularly in public libraries. Because public library video collections tend to be small, most create title lists of their holdings. In a 1987 survey of 3,000 public libraries with videocassette collections, Martha Dewing found that over 90 percent of the 823 responding libraries had fewer than 1,000 videocassettes in their collections (1988: 52). The majority (57.8 percent) had 200 or less, and 80.9 percent had 500 or fewer videocassettes in their libraries. The majority of these libraries (73.2 percent) describe their collections in lists alone. A majority (56 percent) of libraries in large communities also list available videocassettes in their catalogs. Only 25.5 percent of libraries in small communities list available videocassettes in their catalogs. Approximately 38 percent of libraries in all sizes of communities use the original videocassette box to inform patrons about available videocassettes. Public library patrons like to browse the videocassette collection or may be seeking a particular title.

In academic libraries, on the other hand, title lists are not adequate. Most academic libraries shelve their videocassettes in closed stacks, making browsing impossible. More important, film studies students and faculty frequently want to search by access points other than title—director, country of origin, date released, screenwriter, language, and others. For this reason, full descriptive cataloging and thorough indexing are particularly important. The same film may have gone through numerous video releases. Full descriptive cataloging enables users to determine whether or not they have located the desired title. Films are collaborative endeavors, so the contributions of all participants should be recognized in the catalog.

Processing, Binding, and Shelving

Although the majority of videocassettes arrive without defects, each newly received item should be checked to be sure that it is the correct title and that it is free of defects. The case should be visually inspected for cracks, and the videotape itself should be viewed in its entirety. Many older feature films have been transferred from worn copies to videotape. It is important to establish standards for the quality of the video copy. Sometimes the film itself is so important to the collection that film studies faculty are willing to use a tape made from a scratchy print. Many older films and foreign films fall into this category. On the other hand, defects in the tape transfer itself should be unacceptable. The picture should not roll or be marred by dropout, which appears as horizontal white streaks or flecks across the picture.

If a film studies collection owns video inspection equipment, newly received videocassettes should be run through the inspection machine once to remove any excess oxide or cardboard particles left behind by the package. Videocassettes should always be transferred to a plastic case; particles from the original cardboard sleeve in which most feature films arrive can reduce the life of the videocassette and clog the heads on video playback equipment.

New 16mm film prints should also be inspected upon receipt to make sure prints are free of sprocket damage and splices. An inspection card should be filled out for each print, giving beginning baseline data, including whether the print is sound or silent; color or black and white; number of feet; number of splices and where splices occur; and general physical condition (excessive number of scratches, brittle, and so on). At least five feet of film leader should be spliced to the head and tail of the film to help prevent film damage from scratches and tears that can occur during threading and projection. Films should be evenly wound onto metal or plastic reels large enough to allow a ½" margin from the outside layer of film to the end of the reel. Improperly wound films can cause edge damage and abrasions.

Conservation and Preservation

The most important factor in the conservation and preservation of films and videocassettes is environmental control. Important environmental components include temperature, humidity, dust control, sunlight, excessive fluorescent lighting, and exposure to a magnetic field. The temperature and humidity should be maintained at constant levels of about 68 to 70 degrees Fahrenheit and 40 to 50 percent relative humidity.

Videocassettes should be stored in plastic, dust-free cases. Films should be evenly wound onto metal or plastic reels large enough to allow a ½" margin from the outside layer of film to the end of the reel. The reel should be placed in a film can or case and stored on edge. Storage shelves should be vacuumed frequently to remove dust. Do not store videocassettes or films on shelves in harsh sunlight or under uncovered fluorescent lights. Videocassettes should never be laid on top of videocassette players or televisions. If a library uses a magnetic security system, videocassettes should never be desensitized or placed near the sensitizing/desensitizing equipment. The actual gates through which patrons must pass will not damage videocassettes.

Videocassettes and videocassette players have a symbiotic relationship. Worn and dirty machines may damage or destroy videocassettes. Dirty and worn tapes can clog the heads of the videocassette player, shortening its life and perhaps damaging the next tape played in the machine. Therefore, it is imperative that both tapes and players be kept clean and in good repair. As a tape is played, magnetic particles flake away from the videotape surface. In order to minimize damage to the playback equipment, these particles should be removed from the videotape each time it has been played. Older tapes have usually sustained minor damage during playback. Unless this damage is detected, it may seriously damage playback equipment the next time the video is played.

No library offers a dust-free environment. When tapes are played with dust on the surface, those dust particles may gouge into the surface of the tape. The best way to remove magnetic particles and dust from the surface of videotape and inspect for damage is to use inspection and/or cleaning equipment. There are currently three types of machines available, all manufactured by Research Technology International (RTI) of Lincolnwood, Illinois. Although it is relatively expensive, TapeChek's™ value in preserving a library's videocassette collection and prolonging the life of its video playback equipment is incalculable. One series, TapeChek™ 400, inspects for physical damage, cleans the videotape, and rewinds it properly. This equipment cannot determine that a section of tape has been erased or copied over, nor can it detect magnetic defects, such as dropout. Until the introduction of TapeChek™ DVL, the second model, the only way to verify these kinds of problems was to view the videotape. TapeChek™ DVL inspects the video, audio, and control tracks for magnetic damage and can be set to varying degrees of sensitivity. A third TapeChek™ model, the XCL, was designed to be used as a backup to the 400 series and functions as a high-speed cleaner, conditioner, and rewinder, without the inspection capability. Some libraries inspect only periodically but clean and condition after each circulation. RTI also offers coin-operated TapeChek™ VHS videotape cleaner/inspectors.

Proper maintenance of video playback equipment is essential to the preservation of a videocassette collection. The videocassette player should be kept clean and away from dust. It should be covered with a dust cover when not in use. Library staff should follow a regularly scheduled maintenance routine. However, technicians do not recommend the regular use of head-cleaning tapes; they can shorten the life of the playing heads.

The longevity of 16mm film prints is dependent on proper handling and use and on regular inspection and repair. Most film damage is caused by improper threading and operation of the projector, dirt in the projector gate, improper handling (film should be handled only by the edges), worn or poorly maintained equipment, and lack of inspection and repair of the film. Film studies librarians with a 16mm film collection will find Craig A. Jones's *16mm Motion Picture Film Maintenance Manual* (1983) a valuable resource. In it, Jones provides detailed information on film structure and proper film storage, handling, inspection, cleaning and lubrication, and damage and repair.

Optimally, films should be inspected after each use so that any damage that occurred during projection can be detected immediately. Damage left unrepaired can quickly deteriorate the film, making the print totally unusable. Three common methods of repairing film include splicing broken films back together (or small damaged sections out), using sprocket repair tape, and ordering replacement footage. With the decline in overall film sales, many film laboratories are getting out of the film business, while others are reluctant to continue printing replacement footage sections, particularly if the needed footage is located in the middle of the film. For films no longer in distribution, replacement footage is an impossible repair solution.

Jones identifies three inspection methods—hand, machine, and visual (1983: 11–16). The hand inspection process, which involves a film inspector wearing cotton or nylon inspection gloves and using an electric or manual rewind machine, is an inexpensive method of locating film damage and can be used effectively by libraries with small film collections. Libraries with larger collections may wish to invest in electronic film inspection machines, which can locate sprocket damage, edge damage, breaks, splices, and sprocket repair tape through a damage detection system designed to stop automatically when damage is located. Visual inspection (i.e., viewing) of film is necessary to determine continuity (due to loss of footage) and sound problems. Visual inspection is particularly important when collections are adding prints of older, hard-to-find titles, such as feature films. Many of these prints have been well used and may contain a range of damage. The film studies librarian, as well as individual faculty members, should view the print to determine if its importance to the collection outweighs its faults. Visual inspection is also important to determine if an archival video copy can be made to preserve a well-used 16mm print that is now irreplaceable.

Videotape is not a preservation medium. According to Alan Calmes, preservation officer of the National Archives and Records Administration, the estimated life expectancy (shelf life) of a professionally produced master tape in 1″ C format stored under optimal environmental conditions, with careful handling and infrequent playback on a well-maintained machine, is 15 to 30 years. The estimated tape life expectancy of a master tape in VHS format stored under poor environmental conditions is 1 to 5 years. These figures are based upon accelerated aging studies of the chemical and physical breakdown of the tape itself and not of the performance quality of the tape (Calmes 1992). The tape life expectancy of library video collections probably comes closer to the one to five years prediction. Tape life is measured in number of plays as well as in years. With clean, well-maintained playback equipment, 500 or more plays are possible, but under normal library use conditions anywhere from 100 to 250 plays are average (Meigs 1984; Beacham 1991).

Many film studies librarians have turned to videodiscs hoping to alleviate the preservation difficulties associated with videotape. Videodiscs store information using a nonhelium laser beam to modulate the signal that cuts billions of micro pits in a smooth disc surface. Playback systems use a low-powered laser to "read" stored information, which may be digital, motion, audio, or still images and combinations of all four. The videodisc—manufactured in the same way as the audio compact disc—has three layers: a transparent core made of polyvinyl chloride; a reflective aluminum layer; then a protective acrylic layer (1.1mm). The videodisc derives its remarkable durability from two factors: its protective layer and the playback system.

Although users are cautioned to handle the videodisc carefully, experts disagree about the effects of dirt or fingerprints. Phillips DuPont Optical Company (PDO), the largest manufacturer of compact discs, advises users to avoid depositing oily fingerprints on discs and recommends handling them on the outer edges only (Day 1989: 24). Videodiscs are difficult, but not impossible, to scratch. Since the playback system employs no contact with machine parts, the disc does not wear as it plays. However, in 1988 and 1989, the popular press in Great Britain and the United States began reporting rumors that compact discs would deteriorate within eight to ten years. In a story in the *Guardian*, officials of Nimbus Records were quoted as saying that the inks used for labeling had " 'begun to eat into the protective lacquer' coating, oxidizing the reflective aluminum layer and making the CD's [*sic*] unplayable" (Day 1989: 23). Subsidiaries of Phillips and Sony, co-developers of the compact disc, issued denials to the press. They cited accelerated aging tests conducted by Sony that found no change of the product even after more than ten years. Sony contends that, with careful handling and storage, properly manufactured CDs will last "indefinitely." Douglas Pratt, editor of *The Laser Disc Newsletter*, notes that manufacturing defects have caused the premature deterioration of videodiscs, but this is not inherent in the format; "no one really knows what the life span of a properly manufactured laser videodisc is" (Pratt 1992: 7).

PUBLIC SERVICES

Reference and Information Services

Reference services for film studies require a broad array of reference books. The development of a film studies reference collection will vary depending upon the type of library. Public library film studies reference collections will emphasize books about films and film personalities. However, the academic library film studies reference collection will include dictionaries and encyclopedias, indexes and abstracts, guides to film credits, indexes to and compilations of film reviews, catalogs of film collections, directories and yearbooks, filmographies, bibliographies, and handbooks. The *Booklist* "Reference Books Bulletin" may be the best review source for new reference works in film studies, as well as revisions of older works. The sources cited previously as useful for retrospective selection and collection evaluation can also aid the development and evaluation of a film studies reference collection. In most academic libraries, there is a separate fund for the purchase of film studies reference sources. A member of the reference staff may be selecting these materials. However, the film studies librarian must be prepared to recommend titles for purchase and must be certain to apprise the reference staff of important changes in the film studies curriculum.

Access, Circulation, and Interlibrary Loan

Although an uncommon practice, the interlibrary loan of feature films on videocassette and perhaps videodisc will become increasingly important. Students and scholars need access to feature films held in other libraries for the same reasons they need access to books and journal articles. First, no one library has all the feature films. Even on the campuses of research institutions, libraries and audio-visual centers own a small fraction of the feature films available on videocassette. Given the politics of library collections, students and scholars are unlikely to ever find comprehensive feature film studies collections on their campuses. Second, most academic library collections have been built over decades, some over centuries; the relatively new disciplines and new formats are now underrepresented in these collections and are likely to remain so. Finally, feature films on video go out of print very quickly, making it difficult to purchase many feature films more than two years from the release date. It often takes this long for films to be incorporated into course syllabi. Many specialized and graduate film courses are only taught every few years. By the time the faculty request that the library purchase a film, it is often out of print. Interlibrary borrowing is often the only recourse for viewing a film.

Many film studies collections restrict the circulation of their video collections and so restrict the interlibrary loan of their video collections. Film studies librarians offer three major reasons for severely restricting or prohibiting the interlibrary loan of videocassettes. The first factor is the relatively high cost of videocassettes. Although feature films on videocassette typically range in price from $20 to $90, documentaries range in price from $50 to more than $700. The second factor relates to service to resident students and faculty. Many video titles circulate frequently. Some film studies collections operate a reservation system for faculty who want to show a particular film during a particular class period. How would the film studies librarian prevent these popular or reserved videos from being sent out on interlibrary loan? The third factor is the difficulty of replacing videocassettes. Many film studies librarians fear that an irreplaceable videocassette will be lost in transit or never returned by the interlibrary borrower. In these cases, payment for the item would be inadequate. Many film studies librarians have concluded that it is easier to restrict or prohibit the interlibrary loan of all videocassettes than to deal with the uncertainty and potential damage to public service on their own campus.

Speed and timing of delivery are other obstacles to the interlibrary loan of videocassettes. Most faculty want to borrow videocassettes to show in class on a specific date. There is little or no leeway to shift dates. Interlibrary loan is not designed to deal with an item needed on a particular date; most interlibrary borrowers want the material as soon as possible, not on a date three months in the future. However, instructors are reluctant to wait until two weeks before the video is needed to request it on interlibrary loan. Chances are that it will not arrive on time—if it arrives at all. This should not deter libraries from lending videocassettes, as there are many borrowers who want to use them for individual study and research. These borrowers do not need the videocassette on a particular date.

There are many film and video collections in colleges and universities that actively circulate videocassettes—some only within the university system, others on a regional or national basis as well. To maintain circulation controls and to be able to determine immediately if a title is available for a specific date, these collections have a scheduling system that can maintain a calendar of future bookings. Perhaps with time and the growth of video collections, collections that currently restrict their circulation will reexamine their policies with regard to the interlibrary loan of these materials. Without resource sharing, patrons will continue to be denied access to valuable information sources that are owned by other collections.

Public libraries readily circulate their videocassettes, sometimes charging a small fee for each circulation. Depending on the collection's size and volume, an advance scheduling system may or may not be required.

Copyright Issues

One copyright issue related to film studies collections concerns the public performance of videocassettes. Most educational, nontheatrical films and videocassettes either come with public performance rights, or they are commonly available for purchase at an additional charge. On the other hand, most feature films on video are licensed for home use only and may not be used in a public performance. Although some classic feature films may be purchased with public performance rights, current releases are not. Typical warning labels read "WARNING: The owner of the copyright of this motion picture has authorized its use in this cassette for the purpose of private home viewing without charge of any kind other than a purchase price or rental fee paid by the consumer for the videocassette. Any other use of this cassette, including any copyright, reproduction, or performance of any of the materials in it, is an infringement of copyright and may result in civil liability or criminal prosecution as provided by law." Film studies librarians have worried about adding these video-cassettes to their collections, particularly when many collections offer in-house viewing—either in addition to or in lieu of circulating video-cassettes for home use. Are these collections in violation of copyright law? Does the "fair-use doctrine" apply? If collections may not allow users to watch in-house a videocassette licensed for home use only, should the collection purchase these videocassettes? What about purchasing blanket licenses?

Section 106 of the copyright law (17 *U.S.C.* Section 101 *et seq.*, 1976) states the five exclusive rights of the copyright holder. The fourth right gives the owner of copyright the exclusive right to perform the copyrighted work publicly. "Perform" is defined as "to recite, render, play, dance or act it, directly or by means of any device or process or in the case of audiovisual works, to show its images in any sequence or to make the sound accompanying it audible" (17 *U.S.C.* Section 101 *et seq.*, 1976). Section 101 further clarifies that to perform a work "publicly" means "(1) to perform or display it at a place open to the public or at any place where a substantial number of persons outside of a normal circle of a family and its social acquaintances are gathered." All parties to the controversy agree that a library is a public place and that even one or two people viewing a videocassette in a library carrel or private room consti-tutes a public performance. However, experts disagree upon the im-plications for libraries.

Jerome K. Miller and Debra J. Stanek represent opposing viewpoints. In *Using Copyrighted Videocassettes in Classrooms, Libraries, and Training Centers*, Jerome K. Miller states, "Librarians must recognize that video performances for patrons in public libraries, except classroom performances authorized under Sect. 110(1), are copyright infringements. It is time for librarians to take appropriate steps to conform to the law" (1987: 26). Miller recommends that public libraries with video equipment for patron use consider purchasing from distributors licenses for in-house performances or purchasing blanket performance licenses. The Motion Picture Licensing Corporation of America (MPLC) secures nontheatrical public performance licenses from studios, then resells the rights to libraries, hospitals, nursing homes, churches, clubs, hotels, prisons, corporations, day care facilities, limousine services, and other organizations (Miller 1987: 74). According to Sal Laudicina (1991), MPLC vice-president, sales, the fee for an annual umbrella license varies among types of organizations. For public libraries, the fee is based upon a number of factors, including size of population served, the percentage of card holders, library seating capacity, and type of programming offered patrons. For academic libraries, the fee is based upon the number of carrels in the media center, at this time ranging from $1 per carrel per week to $2.50 per carrel per week. The MPLC licenses only library media center showings, not large group showings sponsored by student groups. The MPLC umbrella license offers libraries a relatively inexpensive way to license for public performance thousands of videocassettes and videodiscs sold with home viewing licenses.

Debra J. Stanek worked with American Library Association attorney Mary Hutchings Reed in preparing "Videotapes, Computer Programs, and the Library." She concedes that "a library's performance of a videotape to a large group of persons would, in fact, constitute a public performance as it is defined by the act" (1986: 47). However, Stanek believes that allowing individuals or small groups of persons to watch videotapes in private viewing rooms "may be fair use of the materials and therefore not infringing" (1986: 47). Stanek goes on to review fair use and to present her arguments in favor of permitting in-house viewing of videocassettes in libraries without purchasing public performance rights or an umbrella license. Stanek concludes, "It is reasonable to assume that performance of a copyrighted videotape with no user fee in a private room in a nonprofit library or school, where it is viewed by a single person, is a fair use of the videotape" (1986: 49).

Three recent publications support the copyright interpretation that would permit individuals or small groups to view videocassettes licensed for home use in the library. In a booklet published by the National Association of College and University Attorneys, attorneys Thomas M. S. Hemnes and Alexander H. Pyle write, "Although the boundaries of 'public performance' have not yet been tested, a screening in a private library carrel would probably not count as a public performance and would be allowed regardless of the purpose for the viewing. Probably, individuals and very small groups may be permitted to view a videotape in a study carrel or viewing room" (1991: 12). In an article published in the Spring 1992 issue of the *Law Library Journal*, James S. Heller, of the Marshall-Wythe School of Law at the College of William and Mary, concludes that students should be permitted to watch in the library videorecordings previously shown in class because the library is operating as an extension of the classroom. He further believes that allowing a student to view in a library a videorecording that has not been shown in class should be permissible under Section 107 (see below), the general fair-use provision (1992: 328). Librarians interested in this topic will also want to see J. Wesley Cochran's article in the Summer 1993 issue *Hastings Communications and Entertainment Law Journal (COMM/ENT)*.

For current copyright information, film studies librarians may want to subscribe to another listserv, sponsored by the Consortium for Networked Information (CNI). Subscribers include librarians, attorneys, and law school faculty. To subscribe to this listserv, send the subscription message described earlier to LISTSERV@CNI.ORG.INTERNET. To post messages to the listserv, send them to CNI-COPYRIGHT@CNI.ORG.INTERNET. Note that you must have access to the Internet to access this listserv.

Film studies librarians must decide for themselves the limits of the copyright law regarding the public performance of videocassettes licensed for home use only. While many public library boards have assumed a conservative stance, virtually all academic libraries offer in-house viewing of feature films on videocassette and videodisc. Many academic librarians view this as an extension of the face-to-face teaching exemption (17 *U.S.C.* Section 110[1], 1976). However, film studies librarians may want to explore the MPLC umbrella license (Motion Picture Licensing Corporation, 13315 Washington Boulevard, Third Floor, P.O. Box 66970, Los Angeles, CA 90066–0970; 800-462-8855) as an alternative to risking infringement of the copyright law.

In addition to the public performance issue, the film studies librarian should also be well versed in the issues relating to the duplication of films and videocassettes, in whole or part, and fair use. As stated previously, the copyright law grants the copyright owner five exclusive rights. The first of these exclusive rights is the right to reproduce the copyrighted work in copies; the second exclusive right is the right to prepare derivative works based upon the copyrighted work. The copyright owner generally assigns the first right to a distributor. In order to legally copy a film or videotape in whole or in part, including but not limited to the sound track and visuals, one must obtain a license from the distributor and/or copyright holder. Depending on the nature of the request, a license fee is sometimes (but not always) required.

This seems straightforward until the issue of fair use is considered. Section 107 of the copyright law reads as follows:

Notwithstanding the provisions of Section 106 (sole rights of copyright owners) the fair use of a copyrighted work, for purposes such as criticism, comment, news reporting, teaching, scholarship, or research is not an infringement of copyright. In determining whether the use made of a work in any particular case is a fair use, the factors to be considered shall include:

(1) the purpose and character of the use, including whether such use is of a commercial nature or is for nonprofit educational purposes;
(2) the nature of the copyrighted work;
(3) the amount and substantiality of the portion used in relation to the copyrighted work as a whole; and
(4) the effect of the use upon the potential market for or value of the copyrighted work.

The language is brief and vague, allowing the concept of fair use to develop and shift and the courts to interpret "fairness" within the context of the times. The biggest factor underlying fair use is, obviously, the economic one. Will the "fair use" exploit the commercial value of the original, resulting in economic loss to the copyright holder? (To argue that a copy made by an organization that does not have the funds to pay for it is not an infringement because the copyright owner did not lose a sale is not recognized as a valid legal point of view.)

Duplication and fair use are issues that face all librarians, and film studies librarians are no exception. Since film studies often requires the frame-by-frame analysis of all or part of a film, will the collection maintain "archival" copies of works that are still commercially available in order to preserve their original copy from possible undue wear and tear? Will the collection allow faculty to copy excerpts from works to facilitate their teaching? Will the collection allow faculty to create anthologies of these excerpts, either to use in their classes or to put on reserve for student use? Will the collection allow faculty to put videocassettes not owned by the library on reserve? What will the collection's policy be if it finds that a patron or faculty member has made a personal copy of a title in its collection? There are not always easy answers to these and the many other questions that can, and probably will, arise.

It is important for the film studies librarian to have a working knowledge of the copyright law and to have documented how the fair use guidelines will be interpreted with regard to the film studies collection. When in doubt, it is always best to seek permission. State institutions should be aware that the Copyright Remedy Clarification Act, commonly referred to as H.R. 3045 (Pub. L. 101–553, 1990), was signed into law on November 15, 1990. H.R. 3045 eliminates a technical defect in the copyright law that made the various states and their entities immune from damages in the case of copyright infringement. A written copyright policy approved by the library administration and its governing body is recommended.

Special Programs and Services

Public libraries frequently offer film showings and discussions. Public or academic libraries may bring in filmmakers to discuss their work. Thematic screening sessions can be scheduled throughout a month or a semester to showcase the works of a specific filmmaker or works in a specific genre that are available in the film studies collection. The film studies librarian may also wish to schedule traveling film exhibits or to submit programming proposals to the National Endowment for the Humanities or the National Endowment for the Arts. However, librarians are cautioned that any videorecordings used for these purposes must have public performance rights.

NEW TECHNOLOGIES

Software

A variety of databases and CD-ROM products provide reference and videographic information on a variety of films and videorecordings. Some of the newer computer-based film studies resources are *Cinemania, Videolog, Variety's Video Directory Plus*, and *The Motion Picture Guide*. For additional sources, consult reference tools such as *CD-ROMs in Print* (1987– , annual) or *Directory of Portable Databases* (1990– , semi-annual). *Cinemania*, however, is considered a multimedia tool designed for the consumer movie buff and videophile; it may never be listed in the library-oriented directories. For this reason, it is important for film studies librarians to regularly scan the popular literature. During the fall of 1992,

Cinemania was described or reviewed in *Fortune, Rolling Stone, Variety,* and *Video Magazine.*

Cinemania (officially, *Microsoft Cinemania*) is a multimedia film encyclopedia on CD-ROM, based upon *Leonard Maltin's Movie and Video Guide* (1992). This interactive movie guide lists over 19,000 films from 1914 to 1991, including studio stills and recorded dialogue from selected movies. Each film has a brief review and rating taken from Maltin. Approximately 750 classics and popular recent films have more detailed reviews and ratings from *The Motion Picture Guide.* In addition to movie information, *Cinemania* includes biographies, articles on movie topics, and a glossary of terms. For libraries with the necessary hardware and software (IBM-compatible PC, 386X or faster; CD-ROM drive; Microsoft Windows version 3.1 or 3.0 with Multimedia Extension; and a sound board), *Cinemania* is a bargain; the initial price is $80, with annual updates available for $30.

Videolog (Trade Service Corporation, 10996 Torreyanna Road, San Diego, CA 92121; 800-854-1527) is a computer file that can be loaded on the hard drive of an IBM-compatible PC. It provides a computer-based version of the loose-leaf service available in many video rental stores and libraries. *Videolog* includes 35,000 videorecordings, on videocassette and laserdisc, updated monthly. Although it lists educational titles, *Videolog* is most useful for feature films and other home-use titles, giving full videographic information and a price. While the distributor attempts to flag titles on moratorium, out-of-print titles remain in the listing. There is a startup cost of $250 and a monthly fee of $21 for updates.

Variety's Video Directory Plus (Bowker Electronic Publishing) on CD-ROM contains full videographic information, including price, and summaries for more than 70,000 videocassettes and laserdiscs in active distribution. It also includes full text reviews from *Variety* for more than 2,500 films. The database is updated quarterly, with an annual subscription price of $395. This source is a CD-ROM version of the print reference work *Bowker's Complete Video Directory.* Another similar directory, *The Video Source Book,* is available from Gale Research as a custom edition on diskette; its entertainment section can also be purchased separately on CD-ROM and is updated annually.

The Motion Picture Guide (Cinebooks, available from Baseline, 838 Broadway, Dept. CD, New York, NY 10003; 800-CHAPLIN) on CD-ROM represents yet another type of film studies reference tool. It is a computer-based version of the authoritative print reference source of the same name. *The Motion Picture Guide* offers librarians and film scholars a listing of 30,000 English-language and notable foreign-language films released theatrically and on videocassette, with complete filmographic and videographic data, complete credits, plus detailed synopses and starred ratings, from one through five. First published in 1985, the CD-ROM version of *The Motion Picture Guide* includes the information from volumes one through nine, which excludes the silent films, plus the annuals that have been issued since that time. The initial price is $997; annual updates, which replace the entire database, are $197.

Media and Hardware

Laser videodisc was developed at about the same time as ½" video-cassette systems—the late 1970s—but never became as popular with consumers. Originally, there were two incompatible systems, capacitance electronic discs (CED), which have not been produced since 1985, and optical or laser videodiscs. Videodisc players never achieved the popularity of videocassette players. The equipment was "read only" so consumers could not record off broadcast or cable television. Video rental stores were offering thousands of videocassettes, providing another source of programming. Soon the ½" videocassette player had captured the market. When RCA ceased production of Selectavision in 1985, experts were predicting the demise of videodisc. Video connoisseurs had always preferred the more sophisticated laser technology, and Pioneer continued to manufacture equipment. Since 1985, laser videodiscs have been gaining in popularity, probably stimulated by the popularity of the audio compact disc.

Consumers now have the option of purchasing a videodisc-CD combination player that can read any disc from three to thirteen inches in diameter. Record companies are experimenting with hybrid compact discs that feature a short music video followed by twenty minutes of music without video (Rogers 1989). In a 1990 article in *Library Journal*, Jeff Dick reported that the electronics industry projected more than one million videodisc players in homes by the end of the year. The software manufacturers hoped to have six million discs in production by the same date. As more players are sold, more programming will become available.

Videodiscs offer sound and picture reproduction superior to videotape: "For viewers with good-sized TV screens (27 inches and up) connected to their stereo systems, the advantages of laserdiscs over VHS tape are significant: a picture with 60 percent sharper resolution and clearer sound reproduction with a stunningly wide dynamic range. Outside of a Dolby-equipped movie theater, the experience is not to be surpassed" (Dick 1990: 37). More than simply videocassettes with improved sound and picture,

videodiscs can be used to retrieve images quickly, freeze them jitter-free
and carry as many as four audio tracks.

For film studies collections, the Voyager Company's Criterion Collection
exploits the capabilities of the videodisc format most effectively. Voyager
has used the multiple audio tracks to provide commentary and discussion
concerning a film. On the disc with *The Graduate* (1967, Criterion,
constant angular velocity [CAV] or standard play/full feature format, $99.95),
UCLA film professor Howard Suber provides a shot-by-shot discussion
of camera lenses and angles used to externalize the emotional states of the
characters. Suber also expounds upon his theory of comedic narrative
structure—"desire, deception and discovery"—and that protagonists are
usually passive for one hour, then "seize control of their destinies."
Supplementary materials include comparisons of scenes from the novel
with scenes in the film, rejected screen tests, and behind-the-scenes
photographs (Spotnitz 1991). While videodiscs in the Criterion series and
other connoisseur series range in price from about $100 to $125, most
prices range from $25 to $30. Douglas Pratt believes that volume sales
could bring prices down to $15. In an interview with Michael Rogers of
Newsweek, Pratt also predicts a thriving rental market, which would
stimulate additional releases and lower prices (Rogers 1989). Videodisc
players can also be interfaced with a computer for exciting entertainment
and educational possibilities. For these reasons, videodiscs are likely to be
the next audio-visual technology adopted by libraries, and feature films
are likely to be the most prevalent type of available programming.

Librarians who work in areas that are heavily influenced by the
consumer market—such as film studies—must read the popular press to
follow trends. Although public libraries are more likely to feel public
pressure to adopt the most popular audio-visual formats—½″ videocassettes, audiocassettes, and compact discs being the current favorites—
the development of academic library audio-visual collections is also
affected by the latest in consumer trends. The July 8, 1991, issue of
Newsweek reported the development of interactive video products for the
home market (Rogers 1991). If this market becomes viable, film studies
librarians will see an explosion of available materials—just as we have
seen with home videocassettes.

"Interactive multimedia" blends computers and television. To overcome the consumer's avoidance of computers, these new systems receive
input from a hand-held remote control unit, and they look similar to the
now-familiar audio compact disc player. Among the fifty programs
already in production, there are both educational and entertainment titles.
A Bach disc will give biographical information, but by pushing a button,

the viewer will be able to hear selections of music. *Hot Seat* presents ethical dilemmas in video vignettes. Viewers take time out to discuss the issue and then use the remote control unit to guide the action and see the results of their decisions.

Of course, there are incompatible alternatives for the "interactive multimedia" consumer. The multimedia systems currently being marketed to the general public include compact-disc interactive (CD-I), introduced in October 1991 by Phillips Electronics, the Dutch company that developed compact disc technology with Sony; multimedia personal computers (MPC), which combine a fully functioning personal computer with a built-in compact disc player that send digital audio to speakers or headphones; and compact disc television (CDTV), a CD player that attaches to a television like CD-I, but expandable, introduced in February 1991 by Commodore. Commodore's CDTV is limited to the company's own product line. CD-I products conform to an industrywide standard, accepted by Sony, Phillips, Magnavox, and others. As of this writing, CD-I systems cost approximately $1,000, MPC approximately $3,000, and CDTV approximately $800 for the basic machine (Schwartz 1991: 131). The $1,000 cost of a CD-I system is comparable to the prices of the first stereo compact disc players that came out in 1983 (Rogers 1991: 50).

FACILITIES

Space

Most video playback equipment for a film studies collection is housed in a library media center. Typically, the library media center offers small rooms for small-group study or seminars and carrels for individual viewing. When designing individual viewing space in the media center, it is important to consider six factors: space, number of carrels, sound, writing surface, light and glare, and policies.

Space: How much floor space will be allocated for carrels? Planning experts recommend thirty-five square feet per carrel (Vlcek and Wiman 1989: 403). How many viewers will be accommodated at each carrel? Some models have expandable sides, accommodating from one to six viewers. Each carrel should be surrounded by enough space to afford a degree of privacy, so viewers are not distracted by what students are viewing at other carrels.

Number of carrels: The number of carrels will depend upon the size of the academic institution, the size of the video collection, and the volume of in-house circulation. Vlcek and Wiman (1989) offer guidelines but caution against attempting to apply one standard to all colleges and universities. Ultimately, the film studies librarian must determine whether equipment is available in sufficient numbers to meet patron needs.

Sound: Carrel users need headphones. Each carrel should be equipped with the number of headphone jacks needed to accommodate the maximum number of viewers. Headphones should be selected for quality and durability. Some film studies librarians purchase high fidelity headphones, particularly those that collect videodiscs since videodiscs offer sound quality superior to that of videotapes.

Writing surface: The carrel top should be large enough to accommodate the writing materials of the maximum number of students. How bright will the film media center be? Does the unit need to equip each carrel with individual lamps?

Light and glare: Carrels with video equipment should be positioned away from windows, or the center should provide drapes or window shades.

Policies: Establish policies for use of the carrels and small group rooms. Can anyone use the equipment at any time or must it be scheduled? Will users be allowed to duplicate materials with the center's equipment? Will the unit operate a reservation system or will use be on a first-come, first-served basis? May patrons bring their own tapes into the center? Will they have access equal to users of other library materials? What if someone leaves a machine unattended and there are people waiting for a player? How will the center deal with waiting lines? Will staff monitor who is entitled to use the next available machine? Will the unit limit the length of time one person may use a machine? All of these questions have implications for staff time and stress and patron convenience. Most centers find that a simple set of rules works most effectively. However, each unit will want to consider each question and reach its own determination.

Hours and Security

Security and ease of access for patrons and staff are ultimately tied to space allocation, organization, staffing, and financial considerations. Most public libraries offer some form of browsing—usually the empty video-cassette case or cards with the information from the case. The cassettes themselves are shelved in plain plastic boxes behind a desk. While this system requires space for shelving the cassettes themselves in addition to space for shelving the cases, most film studies librarians find that patrons rely upon the information on the cases to select videos. Putting the videocassettes on public-access shelves is considered to be too risky and does not promote the collection as effectively.

In academic libraries, film studies video collections require careful security planning and may be the target of theft more frequently than the library's documentary and other video collections. Those libraries that began their film studies collections in the days of ¾" U-matic video-cassettes did not worry about theft. No one would steal videocassettes because they did not have easy access to playback equipment. Theft of 16mm films was always a concern, more because they were expensive than because they had high potential for outside use. Similarly, videodiscs may be less likely to be stolen than VHS videocassettes. However, the majority of academic library video collections are on VHS videocassettes. Most libraries rely upon closed stacks to limit access and reduce theft. Many academic libraries employ both closed-stack shelving and a security system. Unlike public libraries, most academic libraries do not feel compelled to offer patrons browsing.

James Scholtz (1989), speaking primarily of public library video collections, believes that with the decreasing price of videocassettes, such collections may want to consider less restrictive shelving patterns and just accept a level of theft. However, he considers an annual theft rate of higher than 5 or 6 percent to be unacceptable. Most academic libraries would not consider a theft rate of even 1 percent to be acceptable. Unlike public libraries, academic libraries endeavor to collect more esoteric titles. Often within a year or two, these titles are no longer available for purchase. Videocassettes stolen are often irreplaceable. Therefore, the costs of securing the collections are justifiable. Any theft is unacceptable.

BUDGET AND FINANCE

Ongoing Expenses

Libraries are print-oriented, and librarians often discriminate against audio-visual materials in budgeting and collection building. Despite anecdotal evidence to the contrary, studies have shown that all types of libraries—school, public, and academic—underfund the acquisition of audio-visual materials. Two recent studies of audio-visual collections in academic libraries (*Audiovisual Policies in ARL Libraries* 1990; *Audiovisual Policies in College Libraries* 1991) found that although 95 percent of the libraries in the surveys collect audio-visual materials, spending averages less than 1 percent of total acquisitions budgets. *Audiovisual Policies in College Libraries* (College Library Information Packet [CLIP] Note #14) reports the results of a survey of college and small university libraries with enrollments ranging between 1,000 and 5,000. With total acquisitions budgets for the CLIP Note sample of college libraries ranging between $36,680 and $1,220,000, expenditures for audio-visual materials ranged between $100 and $55,584. *Audiovisual Policies in ARL Libraries* (Systems and Procedures Exchange Center [SPEC] Kit #162) reports the results of a survey of the academic library members of the Association of Research Libraries. With total acquisitions budgets for the SPEC Kit sample of academic research libraries ranging between $1,330,069 and $6,500,000, expenditures for audio-visual materials ranged between $1,000 and $150,000. Most academic libraries spend very little of their acquisitions money on audio-visual materials.

The most significant factor in the amount of money spent on audio-visual materials appears to be the existence of a separate fund for the purchase of audio-visual materials. Both the CLIP Note and the SPEC Kit surveys found that libraries with a separate audio-visual budget spend more than double for audio-visual materials than those libraries without a separate budget. Sixty percent of the libraries in the CLIP Note sample have a separate audio-visual budget. The median expenditure for libraries without an audio-visual budget was $2,750; with an audio-visual budget it was $6,000. Fifty-seven percent of the libraries in the SPEC Kit survey have a separate audio-visual budget. The median expenditure for libraries without an audio-visual budget was $12,591; with an audio-visual budget it was $32,000. Further analysis of the SPEC Kit survey data revealed that despite size of the institution, size of the library collection, or size of the total acquisitions budget, the establishment of a separate audio-visual budget resulted in larger expenditures for audio-visual materials. When the purchase of these materials must compete with the purchase of print materials, print materials receive priority.

It is imperative that a separate fund be established for the purchase of film studies materials on videocassettes, videodiscs, and any emerging audio-visual formats. Particularly within academic libraries, the print bias is strong and likely to impede the development of these important collections. It is recommended that, within a general audio-visual fund, money be allocated internally for the purchase of feature films and other film studies materials on video.

Extraordinary Expenses

Most audio-visual collections can only be used with the proper playback equipment. This certainly applies to 16mm films, videocassettes, and videodiscs. Vlcek and Wiman note, "The largest and best media collection can serve no purpose unless appropriate equipment is available to allow patrons to 'read' those materials" (1989: 116). Most academic libraries offer in-house viewing, requiring the proper number of machines in the proper locations. Equipment needs for a film studies collection will vary, depending upon the formats collected, the size of the collection, and the viewing situations offered patrons. These factors will also affect the facilities in which the equipment is housed.

Equipment must relate to collection requirements and be compatible with the materials, so the mix of equipment should match the mix of formats. If 60 percent of a collection's in-house circulation is ½" VHS videocassette and 40 percent is videodisc, approximately 60 percent of the playback machines should be VHS and 40 percent should be videodisc. If the collection contains 16mm films, rear screen projection units or 16mm film preview units will also be required in proportion to the size and use of this component of the collection. The film studies librarian may not be directly responsible for selection and purchase of this equipment but will want to communicate with the librarian who is responsible to apprise that individual of shifts in circulation or in collection strengths. The film studies librarian will also want to monitor the number of patrons waiting for playback equipment; this may provide an early indication that more of one type of equipment is needed.

The equipment selected must meet user needs. Will the equipment be used by individuals in carrels? Will small-group playback in study rooms be provided? Will large-group playback in library classrooms be provided? How large will the groups be? Will equipment circulate to patrons?

Standardize equipment selections whenever possible. Standardization simplifies use of the equipment and reduces maintenance problems. Patrons prefer equipment with which they are familiar and dislike learning the details associated with many different makes and models. Maintenance technicians may have been trained on particular makes of equipment. They become familiar with the idiosyncrasies of particular makes and models, reducing the time needed to trouble-shoot equipment malfunctions. It is also easier to stock parts for only a few makes and models. However, models are discontinued regularly so film studies librarians may discover that, while it is easy to stay with one or two manufacturers, they must frequently change models.

Purchase high-quality and reliable equipment. Purchases should not be based on price alone. Select equipment that, according to your own judgment and that of your staff, will be dependable and will provide years of trouble-free service. Inferior video equipment can cause excessive wear-and-tear on film studies collections and even destroy them. The costs to the collection are far greater than the money saved by purchasing lower-quality equipment. Maintenance and repair costs may also exceed what the collection may have paid for better equipment.

Develop and follow a long-range equipment selection and purchasing plan. It is important to plan ahead in order to budget ahead. The plan should include a projected total number of machines and a realistic replacement schedule. A well-conceived equipment plan can help communicate to library administrators the need for reliable playback equipment in adequate numbers. Aging equipment often costs more to maintain and repair than it would cost to replace it. Aging equipment is also a risk to videocassettes and films. Vlcek and Wiman give the expected life expectancy of a videocassette player as eight years and a 16mm projector as ten years (1989: 118). These published figures should be measured against a collection's own statistics for individual machines. The film studies librarian should be prepared to use circulation statistics and user surveys to support requests for more and newer equipment. Document the length of time patrons must wait to use equipment if waiting lines exist.

Fundraising

Fundraising from external sources presents no special opportunities or difficulties for a film studies collection and is not a major consideration as a funding source for film studies collections. However, if fundraising is defined to include internal cooperative funding, the film studies librarian will want to explore the possibilities. Sources of funding can sometimes be found within the library from other subject-specific print materials funds. For example, foreign films without subtitles might be purchased from funds used to purchase foreign-language print materials. A comprehensive film collection on the Vietnam War might be partially funded by the history department's print materials fund. By establishing close working relationships with other subject bibliographers, the film studies librarian can extend what is likely to be a small fund.

The film studies librarian should also be aware of endowments or foundations that will accept funding proposals for collections. Many academic libraries have their own endowment programs, established with monetary donations and matching funds. For example, many libraries have endowments from the National Endowment for the Humanities, which may provide funding for film studies proposals. Special programs may also be available occasionally. For example, several years ago the MacArthur Foundation made a humanities video collection available to public libraries at very reduced rates and provided for libraries with limited acquisitions budgets to apply for partial funding through grants. The best way for libraries to stay informed about these national opportunities is to read publications such as *American Libraries*.

POLITICS

Internal

The development of film studies collections faces two biases within both academic and public libraries: the entertainment bias and the print bias. Although both biases can be countered with logical arguments, the nature of prejudice is its imperviousness to logical argument. Film studies librarians may find themselves besieged with arguments that their collections—both print and audio-visual—are too popular and that money spent on them could be better spent saving a few journals in the physical sciences or adding more books. Film studies librarians can take a number of steps to protect their funds and their collection, particularly during times of materials budget crises.

Develop strong collection development policies for both print and audio-visual film studies collections. Confront the biases of others and incorporate convincing rationales for the collections. In academic libraries, work closely with the teaching faculty and librarians in contingent disciplines to develop these policies, incorporating a discussion of the research and instructional significance of film studies collections. In public libraries, work closely with the library community served. Resist the temptation to build circulation statistics with only entertainment video. This practice undermines the efforts of other librarians to demonstrate the legitimacy of video collections.

Develop close working relationships with film studies faculty, students, and library patrons. Survey them formally and informally. Invite their suggestions for purchase. Ask their help in identifying new research trends. In the final analysis, the goal of the film studies collection is to serve the needs of its users—either faculty and students or the community. The users are in the best position to explain to skeptics the importance of these collections to either their work or their recreational, cultural, or informational needs. If the funding of film studies collections is threatened, mobilize these people. They will provide the most effective voices within the library for preserving the funding, if not increasing it.

Remain current with film studies scholarship. Scan the literature regularly and note new trends. Communicate with the college or university's faculty to determine if these trends are likely to have an impact on local faculty and student research. Despite the general resistance to audio-visual collections in libraries, film studies seems to be a logical discipline for building such collections. The film studies librarian should develop a personal philosophy in this regard and be able to articulate it to others. The film studies librarian will not be an effective advocate for these collections if she or he does not believe in their importance to the library and to the institution.

External

Academic libraries are rarely the target of censorship, but the film studies video collection is more likely to be censored than either the print collection or the documentary film or video collection. Film and video provoke strong reactions among would-be censors. People fear the power of film to influence behavior and to reinforce stereotypes. Many libraries practice self-censorship, preferring to avoid controversial materials than to be forced to defend them. This practice is particularly reprehensible in academic institutions, where students are supposed to be exposed to a wide array of opinions and perspectives. Academic libraries are less likely to be censored for sexually explicit materials than for politically sensitive materials—those dealing with sexism, racism, and politics. With regard to feature films, the collection may be criticized for purchasing a film that depicts women or minorities in an unfavorable light. Film studies librarians must confront their own biases with regard to objectionable materials. As individuals, all film studies librarians find some films offensive. What will be our response? One of the principles affirmed in the American Film and Video Association's *Freedom to View* statement, originally adopted in 1979 and revised in 1989, is "[t]o provide film, video, and other audio-visual materials which represent a diversity of views and expression. Selection of a work does not constitute or imply agreement with or approval of the content." Film studies librarians must allow our users to decide for themselves what they wish to view.

Faculty and students of film studies must have access to a collection that contains both print and audio-visual materials. And, while print materials are important, ready access to a wide range of film and video materials is essential. Film studies is, after all, the study of film—its history, adaptation, production, social expression, political statement, and moral and artistic visions. In film studies, the film is the text. As one film professor notes, "While poems, for example, can be re-read many times before a class discussion, students will likely have seen the film to be discussed only once" (Grant 1989: 15–16). Students can study screenplays of the films, but video offers an alternative solution. According to Grant,

"While video viewing should not be practiced as a substitute for the experience of the large screen, it is perfectly suited to the task of close analysis which may follow a regular 16mm screening" (1989: 16). To try to teach film studies through print alone would be ludicrous, if not impossible.

The theatrical and nontheatrical video collections in public libraries are important and must be developed with as much thought to the entertainment, cultural, and informational needs of their library patrons as possible. We live in an age where electronic information is commonplace, and a new generation of library patrons will not be content to rely on print alone when video or another emerging technology can better provide the information. It is imperative that public library video librarians have a well-defined plan for the growth, development, management, and maintenance of their collections.

REFERENCES

American Book Publishing Record. 1960– . New York: Bowker.

American Libraries. 1907– . Chicago: American Library Association.

Audiovisual Policies in ARL Libraries. 1990. Compiled by Kristine Brancolini, SPEC Kit no. 162. Washington, DC: Association of Research Libraries.

Audiovisual Policies in College Libraries. 1991. Compiled by Kristine Brancolini, CLIP Note no. 14. Chicago: American Library Association.

Beacham, Frank. 1991. "Videotape's Wonder Years." *Video Magazine* 15 (October): 50–51, 94, 96, 98.

Blum, Eleanor, and Frances Goins Wilhoit. 1990. *Mass Media Bibliography: An Annotated Guide to Books and Journals for Research and Reference*, 3rd ed. Urbana: University of Illinois Press.

Booklist. 1905– . Chicago: American Library Association.

Bowker's Complete Video Directory. 1990– . New York: Bowker.

British National Bibliography. 1950– . London: British Library.

Callenbach, Ernest. 1990. "The Annual *Film Quarterly* Book Survey" (Introduction). *Film Quarterly* 43.4 (Summer): 21–22.

Calmes, Alan. 1992. "Preservation of Video Recordings." In *The Video Annual 1992*, edited by Jean Thibodeaux Kreamer, pp. 23–27. Santa Barbara, CA: ABC-CLIO.

CD-ROMs in Print. 1987– . Westport, CT: Meckler.

CDS Alert. 1982– . Washington, DC: Library of Congress.

Choice. 1963– . Middletown, CT: Association of College and Research Libraries.

Cinemania. 1992– . CD-ROM. Redmond, WA: Microsoft.

Cochran, J. Wesley. 1993. "Why Can't I Watch This Video Here? Copyright Confusion and Performances of Videocassettes and Videodiscs in Libraries." *Hastings Communications and Entertainment Law Journal (COMM/ENT)* 15.4.

Day, Rebecca. 1989. "Where's the Rot? A Special Report on CD Longevity." *Stereo Review* 54 (April): 23–24.

Dewing, Martha, ed. 1988. *Home Video in Libraries: How Libraries Buy and Circulate Prerecorded Home Video.* White Plains, NY: Knowledge Industry.

Dick, Jeff T. 1990. "Laserdisc Redux." *Library Journal* 115 (November 15): 37–39.

———. 1991. "Secondhand Videos." *Library Journal* 116 (November 15): 49–50.

Directory of Portable Databases. 1990– . New York: Cuadra/Elsevier.

Facets Features. 1975– . Chicago: Facets Multimedia.

Film Quarterly. 1945– . Berkeley: University of California Press.

Fisher, Kim N. 1986. *On the Screen: A Film, Television, and Video Research Guide.* Littleton, CO: Libraries Unlimited.

"Freedom to View." 1991. In *Whole Library Handbook: Current Data, Professional Advice, and Curiosa about Libraries and Library Services.* Compiled by George M. Eberhart, p. 386. Chicago: American Library Association.

Geduld, Harry M. 1974. "Film Study in the University." In *From "A" to "Yellow Jack": A Film-Study Film Collection,* p. 2. Bloomington: Indiana University Audio- Visual Center.

Grant, Barry Keith. 1989. "Film Studies in the Undergraduate Curriculum: An Overview." In *Film Studies,* edited by Erik S. Lunde and Douglas A. Noverr, pp. 8–21. New York: Markus Wiener.

Heller, James S. 1992. "The Public Performance Right in Libraries: Is There Anything Fair About It?" *Law Library Journal* 84.2: 315–340.

Hemnes, Thomas M. S., and Alexander H. Pyle. 1991. *A Guide to Copyright Issues in Higher Education.* Washington, DC: National Association of College and University Attorneys.

H. R. Rep. No. 94–1476, 94th Cong. 2d Sess. (1976).

Jones, Craig A. 1983. *16mm Motion Picture Film Maintenance Manual.* Consortium of University Film Centers, Monograph Series no. 1. Dubuque, IA: Kendall/Hunt.

Journal of Film and Video. 1947– . Boston: University Film and Video Association.

The Laser Disc Newsletter. 1984– . East Rockaway, NY: Pratt.

Laudicina, Sal. 1991. Telephone interview with Kristine Brancolini, October 4.

Lora, Pat. 1992. "Money, Money, Money: Video Funding and Spending." *Wilson Library Bulletin* 66 (May): 71–72, 132.

Loughney, Katharine. 1991. *Film, Television, and Video Periodicals: A Comprehensive Annotated List.* Garland Reference Library of the Humanities, vol. 1032. New York: Garland.

Maltin, Leonard. 1992. *Leonard Maltin's Movie and Video Guide.* New York: Penguin.

Manchel, Frank. 1973. *Film Study: A Reference Guide.* Rutherford, NJ: Fairleigh Dickinson University Press.

————. 1990. *Film Study: An Analytical Bibliography*. Rutherford, NJ: Fairleigh Dickinson University Press.

Meigs, James B. 1984. "How Long Will Videotape Really Last?" *Video Review* 5 (July): 24–26.

Miller, Jerome K. 1987. *Using Copyrighted Videocassettes in Classrooms, Libraries, and Training Centers*, 2nd ed. Copyright Information Bulletin no. 3. Friday Harbor, WA: Copyright Information Services.

The Motion Picture Guide. 1992– . CD-ROM. 2nd ed. New York: Baseline.

Pitman, Randy, and Elliott Swanson. 1990. *Video Movies: A Core Collection for Libraries*. Santa Barbara, CA: ABC-CLIO.

Pratt, Douglas. 1992. *The Laser Video Disc Companion*, updated edition. New York: New York Zoetrope.

Pub. L. 101–553 (November 15, 1990), Copyright Remedy Clarification Act. 104 *Stat.* 2749.

Rogers, Michael. 1989. "A New Spin on Videodiscs." *Newsweek* 113 (June 5): 68–69.

————. 1991. "Is This the Next VCR?" *Newsweek* 118 (July 8): 50.

Rovin, Jeff. 1993. *The Laserdisc Film Guide: Complete Ratings for the Best and Worst Movies Available on Disc*. New York: St. Martin's Press.

Scholtz, James C. 1989. *Developing and Maintaining Video Collections in Libraries*. Santa Barbara, CA: ABC-CLIO.

————. 1991. *Video Policies and Procedures for Libraries*. Santa Barbara, CA: ABC-CLIO.

Schwartz, Evan I. 1991. "Multimedia Is Here and It's Amazing!" *Business Week* 3244 (December 16): 130–131.

17 *U.S.C.* Sections 101–914 (Copyright Revision Act of 1976).

Slide, Anthony, ed. 1985. *International Film, Radio, and Television Journals*. Westport, CT: Greenwood Press.

Spotnitz, Frank. 1991. "The Caring Disc." *American Film* 16.1 (January): 50–51.

Stanek, Debra J. 1986. "Videotapes, Computer Programs, and the Library." *Information Technology and Libraries* 5.1: 42–54.

Variety's Video Directory Plus. 1986– . CD-ROM. New York: Bowker.

Video Librarian. 1986– . Bremerton, WA: Randy Pitman.

Videolog. 1990– . CD-ROM. San Diego, CA: Trade Service.

Video Magazine. 1978– . New York: Reese Communications.

The Video Source Book. 1979– . Detroit: Gale.

Vlcek, Charles W., and Raymond Wiman. 1989. *Managing Media Centers: Theory and Practice*. Englewood, CO: Libraries Unlimited.

Weihs, Jean. 1987. "A Taste of Nonbook History: Historical Background and Review of the State of the Art of Bibliographical Control of Nonbook Materials." In *Policy and Practice in Bibliographic Control of Nonbook Media*, edited by Sheila Intner and Richard Smiraglia, pp. 3–14. Chicago: American Library Association.

4

Music Collections

Rosalinda I. Hack
and Richard Schwegel

INTRODUCTION

The attempt to include the discipline of music in a library results in something very special and unique. From cataloging and acquisition to the storage and retrieval of a bewildering array of formats, there is probably no other subject area that offers a manager as many problems to solve and creative opportunities to exploit. This chapter touches on many of the issues that managing a music collection presents, noting the differences and similarities of public and academic libraries, and examines the difficulties and challenges that arise with this most unique of the performing arts.

PERSONNEL

Staffing Levels

Do we ever have enough staff? Public libraries (like most governmental agencies) will in a resounding chorus answer "no!" Yet we open the door every morning, answer the telephone by the fourth ring and, on occasion, still find time for lunch. The crucial test of a manager's skill is not running a well-fed, well-oiled, and fine-tuned machine. It becomes, rather, the ability to make that overburdened machine rattle, creak, and struggle forward with the means at hand.

Undoubtedly, the most important resource a music collection has is its staff. Can quality make up for the lack of quantity? What is the necessary supply to meet the demands of service and basic operation? On a professional level we can begin with the absolute minimum of one. We will put aside the hundreds of libraries that do not have a sufficiently large music collection to merit full-time attention. Accepting that, the first question arises: What constitutes a large enough collection? This has three answers:

- Any collection that integrates books about music, musical scores, and recordings as a distinct entity.
- Any library whose volume of music-related inquiries and circulation require a reference service point for the music materials.
- Any library that maintains an undergraduate study level as the minimal collection development profile for the music materials.

Given the many variables involved, it would be difficult to measure uniformly at which point or at what ratio additional professional positions are required. Complicated equations can be made to compute the number of service points, open library hours, and so on. Consideration must be given to allotted vacation and sick days, the ability to close off certain parts or services of the collection, and the volume of inquiries. Other factors include overtime or compensatory time for working weekends and evenings, the size of the materials budget, the quality and quantity of support staff, and managerial commitments. Academic libraries can and do limit hours that librarians are available or at least on call. Public libraries generally must staff reference desks for all open hours. Academic music librarians are often classed as reference, collection development, or technical services, while public librarians are responsible for a wide range of tasks. Such a multitude of activities requires a great deal of attention to scheduling. One formula will not work for all libraries. A basic truth, however, is that adequately meeting the needs of the patron is the primary factor in determining the need for additional staff.

Professionals

Managers of music collections can easily and often effectively make the argument that music as a subject is special and different—wrapped in mysterious terminology, concepts, and formats that only the initiated could possibly comprehend. To some degree this is a conceit that becomes a useful tactic in bureaucratic maneuvering, but the mystique is projected from a basic truth. Just as a foreign-language collection requires staff with language skills, a music collection must have professionals with musical skills, either as performers or through education. These skills are the ability to read music notation, the ability to understand terminology, and the ability to interpret the wide array of physical reproductions of what is intrinsically a temporal and intangible medium. Retrieving a sonata by Beethoven requires a far greater number of decisions by the librarian than finding a novel by Mark Twain.

The basic qualifications for a music librarian, as outlined by the Music Library Association (MLA), require that a professional have at least a bachelor's degree with concentration in music, a substantial liberal arts background, a knowledge of foreign languages, and, of course, a master's degree in library science. Many academic libraries prefer, if not insist on, a master's degree in music as a prerequisite to employment. Public libraries must embrace the whole spectrum of music in all its forms, so at least one staff member should be familiar with or at least enthused about commercial popular music, including musical comedy. A survey of public library music collections would most likely show that as much as 50 percent or more of the inquiries relate to the popular side of the subject.

Paraprofessionals, Students, and Volunteers

To cope with seemingly ever-present staff shortages in music collections, managers must often rely on paraprofessionals and volunteers. "Library associate" is a common job title given to full-time staff who have an undergraduate degree. Even without formal library training, in many instances associates offer attractive benefits to the institution. As with professionals, a music collection should employ individuals with a knowledge of music. Given the instruction to refer to the librarian any inquiries that they are unable to handle, paraprofessionals can do a reasonable job with basic reference at off-peak hours. If they play an instrument, they can often make suggestions for needed titles in scores and recordings. If they are performers, they often have contacts in the field and can suggest musicians for events or even arrange concerts and programs (a luxury for which many librarians do not have the time).

The critical issue with volunteers is finding tasks that are rewarding enough to keep their interest but are not one of the responsibilities that make the music librarian's job interesting and enjoyable. At some unionized institutions, the fact or even impression that volunteers are being used to replace or get by without regular staff should be avoided.

Experience has shown many music librarians that volunteers will work in a music collection for only a short time. They tend to fade away when they realize that the tasks that the music librarian feels appropriate to assign to them are detail oriented and repetitive. Ideally, volunteers should not be treated as simply additional clerical staff. Work entrusted to them should be projects that the institution would like to undertake but does not have the staff to accomplish now or in the foreseeable future. Such jobs may be inventorying and organizing gift sheet music and record collections, indexing song anthologies, assisting in running programs, or maintaining a bulletin board of current events. Volunteers require a percentage of a manager's available time for training, supervision, and social interaction— one of the major reasons that they have come to your door.

To establish a quantitative ratio of paraprofessionals and volunteers to music librarians would be very difficult. At the minimum, each of these staff would require 5 to 10 percent of a supervisor's time. Should one institution have a large number of these employees and volunteers, it might be suggested that one music librarian be given their supervision as a primary responsibility. The diversity of talents and capabilities of these employees make the deciding factor one of how much supervision they will require.

Continuing Education, Recruitment, and Mentoring

Every opportunity for continuing education for music staff, both professional and support, should be seriously considered. Whether it is to pursue graduate studies in music or a half-day seminar in telephone courtesy, the institution will reap benefits both in staff competency and morale.

A music librarian working toward an advanced degree will improve his or her bibliographic skills while simultaneously finding reference works old and new that may not, but should, be among the collection's holdings. Ideally, term papers, projects, and theses carried out in course work could cover topics of relevance to the music collection. Writing on a topic of repeated patron interest could be subsequently developed as a pathfinder or bibliography. Analysis, inventory, and organization of a gift collection of historical significance could bring to life those boxes now in storage while providing a satisfying and original major project for the degree-seeking music librarian. In public libraries, personnel department–sponsored courses in management theory, new technology, organization, customer relations, and so on have practical value and can additionally be used by managers as one of the few reward options. Participation in national and local chapter meetings of the MLA provides an excellent opportunity to learn the latest developments in the profession, to discover how various institutions handle similar problems, and to find and meet publishers and jobbers of music materials.

Music collections, like libraries in general, are facing a growing shortage of qualified applicants for new and entry-level positions. Though not widespread in the music profession, mentoring is one technique being promoted as a means of encouraging students to choose music librarianship as a career. A successful mentoring program will introduce the student to most, if not all, of the many activities and workings of the music collection, from shelving books to collection development. Making a program successful and worthwhile to both student and staff requires considerable one-on-one time to introduce, instruct, and supervise the student in all of these activities.

In a music collection with a large staff, this responsibility can be shared among all of the employees, giving the student differing viewpoints and experiences while enabling the other staff to carry out their duties largely unhindered. Typically, mentoring programs occur during the summer months when music collection use declines. Music collections with one or two professional staff should take a serious look at their capacity to work what is essentially full-time with a student who will be with them for only a matter of weeks. Applicants should be screened for proven academic ability and potential interest in the field of music librarianship. A successful mentoring program can be a personally rewarding experience with the added benefit of improving the pool of talent the profession will have to draw upon in the future.

COLLECTION DEVELOPMENT

Policies

The importance of a written collection development policy is an issue drilled into librarians in graduate school. How often, though, do the exigencies of the real library world leave us without one? To have one is undoubtedly a good thing, but the form it takes can be left to the conscience of the individual librarian. Whether written as a generalized statement for the institution as a whole, as a detailed document of goals and objectives specifically for the music department, or one that is handed down as an oral tradition, the policy should become the practice as it is and will be, not only as it might or could be.

Peculiar to and necessary in the collection development policies of music collections, both public and academic, that have circulating collections is the need to include a statement regarding the policy of purchasing or not purchasing in particular formats. One patron may desire a Beethoven symphony on a cassette and another in a compact disc (CD) version. There will also be the one who complains that he cannot afford a CD player and must have an LP (long-playing) recording. What music collection has a budget sufficient enough to duplicate repertoire in all formats? Similarly, whether to purchase music scores in parts or full score and in what size (from trio to complete orchestra) are issues that need to be resolved and included in a collection development statement.

Selection Tools

In addition to using the standard selection tools for books about music that libraries in general use, one important source is the "new books" section found in each quarterly issue of *Notes: The Quarterly Journal of the Music Library Association*. This list includes books on all types of music, arranged by the language of the text. As might be expected, many music journals, both scholarly and popular, feature book reviews. The annual *Bibliographic Guide to Music* (New York Public Library 1975 –), though a year behind, is helpful in finding titles one may have missed in subject areas of interest to a particular library. Core music collection lists have been published by the American Library Association (ALA).

Unlike most other subject areas, music collections must use specialized selection tools for printed music and sound recordings. Although *Notes* provides a quarterly list of scores as it does for books, music collections more often rely on publisher and jobber catalogs. If one is developing a specific area of the collection, for instance string ensemble music, a number of catalogs from various publishers can be found that will cover only that material. Several major jobbers provide an ordering card and approval plan system to match a music collection's specialized needs.

It is highly recommended that music librarians use a jobber for acquiring sound recordings. These businesses provide their own compiled lists, as well as catalogs of individual companies. There are a number of comprehensive listings of available recordings, such as *Phonolog Reporter*, the *Schwann* series of catalogs, and foreign listings, such as Great Britain's *Gramophone* and Germany's *Bielefelder Katalog*. Automatic purchase plans in certain areas can save staff time and insure timely and comprehensive coverage of high demand recordings, such as *Billboard*'s top ten.

Publishers and Vendors

In old World War II films, one will often find a scene where the men of a supply unit miraculously come through with the desperately needed equipment. So, too, music librarians sometimes expect miracles of their jobbers and vendors to get that high demand or rare item as quickly as possible. More realistically, many simply expect a reasonable performance in supplying books, scores and records within an average time frame and with a customary and fair discount. In either scenario, good relations with a jobber are important to keep a steady supply of materials and to overcome the occasional but inevitable problem. For music librarians, having to deal with not only one but three or more different media suppliers just compounds the problem. Select a jobber or vendor that will communicate directly with staff, solve problems, and handle those rush orders.

Relatively new as a service offered by jobbers to music librarians is supplying cataloging and cards for records and videos. These formats are often the bane of cataloging departments and end up in various stages of backlog. Music librarians should consider requiring this feature of their vendors, in order to shorten the time it takes to get recorded sound and video materials onto the shelves and into the hands of their patrons. Especially for public libraries, where the demand for current chart hits is considerable, actually having the recording on the shelf when it is in greatest demand is obviously fulfilling the needs of that particular segment of users. Similarly, academic libraries can more readily meet deadlines for having materials in the library and ready in time for class assignments.

Donors and Donations

Donations offered to music collections can range from a handful of dusty 78 rpm phonodiscs from somebody's attic to an entire library of scores or to rare and unique documentary items. There is certainly a proportional ratio of time spent working toward a donation to the value and importance of the potential gift to the music collection. This does not exclude, however, a few basic policies to follow that apply to every such situation.

Prior to accepting any gift, a well-defined written or established gift policy should be in place. Important issues ought to be spelled out, such as ownership rights, collection development profiles, and the recognition of an institution's capacity to handle the housing and staff time needed to manage, process, and organize materials. A clear understanding of these matters is essential from the start, as it is very important to be up-front with a potential donor from the very beginning, even if it places the gift at risk.

It is quite common, and not at all unreasonable, that a donor will place a much higher value on his or her materials than would the music librarian, who will more likely be aware of their true value. In the extremes, these situations can range from the patron who has a 78 rpm of Enrico Caruso singing "Vesti la giubba" and, thinking it a rare find, does not understand why the music librarian would not want such a wonderful thing, to the lifelong fan who wishes to donate his comprehensive collection of Louis Armstrong recordings and memorabilia. That latter donation would in itself be fine, but he also wants a separate room to display it and a salary to be the curator.

Both types of donors deserve the same courtesy and clear explanation of why their gifts cannot be accepted, as well as a suggestion of another library that might be interested in them. In the latter case, an up-front explanation of what the music collection can and cannot do becomes a solid basis for negotiation. Often this will result in the donor eventually coming around and presenting it to the music collection without preconditions.

Acquiring a gift may be as simple as an over-the-counter transaction or as complex as arranging for shipping, finding custodial staff for moving, and reorganizing one's space to make room. It is helpful to have a preset system for storing and retrieving gift scores and recordings so that new materials can easily be added. As is often the case, closed library stacks can become the limbo where boxes of donated material are sent to remain while the knowledge of their contents disappears as library staff come and go. A simple composer/artist arrangement for recordings and composer arrangement for music scores often make useful and valuable gift materials retrievable. Indeed, remedial organization and storage of gift materials will save the music librarian considerable embarrassment should a donor return a year later to see what has become of his or her donation.

An inventory of any materials donated to the music collection should be made at the time of acquisition. Whether as thorough as an item-by-item description or simply a register indicating a "box of sheet music" with donor and date of receipt information, it is important that this be tallied. Questions may arise as to true ownership of missing materials, even leading to an Internal Revenue Service investigation.

As a rule, any donation to the music collection should become the library's property with full right of arrangement, organization and disposal. This is done to protect the institution from committing money, space and staff time only to have the gift withdrawn by the donor after a period of time. However, long-term commitments to keep music collections intact—to display, promote, and organize large donations—cannot be realistically made in government-funded public institutions. Such libraries need the complete freedom that sole ownership brings. Public libraries, by and large, do not receive music manuscript materials where the literary rights are an issue. There are those who argue that the copyright in such cases must be transferred to the institution along with the physical item. On the other hand, it is possible to recognize the rights of the original copyright holder as one would with any published materials the music collection routinely purchases.

The situation in academic libraries is a complex one. The close inter-relationship of faculty and alumni with the music collection can create intricate and ambiguous legal difficulties as to true ownership and rights.

TECHNICAL SERVICES

Cataloging

It is in the areas of bibliographic access, cataloging, and classification that the uniqueness and need for special treatment of music materials is most evident. In attempting to reconcile the bibliographic access require-ments of different types of users, no other subject matter has engendered more schemes, home-brew systems, and in-house adaptations of the Dewey Decimal Classification (DDC) and Library of Congress Classification (LCC). The issue is to find a system that will allow a patron to find material organized by composer (all of Bach's works together in one place), by medium (all the works for flute and harp in one place), and by form (all the sonatas in one place).

A second problem is one of the differing versions of a particular work. A single composition may exist in an edition for piano solo, piano duet, violin and piano, guitar solo, chamber orchestra, or for xylophone. The argument as to whether one should shelve these versions altogether under the composer or whether to arrange them so the piano duets and such are together is at the heart of the differences in the various classification schemes.

The DDC and LCC systems have approached these difficulties by arranging the items on the shelf by medium and using a card catalog to group works together by composer and form (subject). Although DDC is certainly the most widely used system in public libraries, it is the less satisfactory of the two. Part of the problem stems from the numerous alterations and changes in the many editions of the scheme. More signif-icant is the placing of books and scores in a single sequence. Many libraries alter this by separating the media and/or adding an "M" or other designa-tion to scores. Such steps are taken because the majority of users are seeking one or the other format for entirely different purposes. There is also the practical difficulty of accommodating such a wide array of formats—from miniature to full orchestral part scores—in a single sequence.

The Dewey system is also inadequate in its treatment of music of different cultures, a problem that will grow with the increasing interest in world music. The recently devised Phoenix Schedule for music addresses these disadvantages by allowing for format differentiation and establishing a new area for popular, folk, jazz, and world music. Music collection librarians contemplating converting to this revision must examine the possible major dislocation of their collections and the cost of relabeling.

The LCC works best with larger collections and has the advantage of separating material into three distinct groups: musical scores, music literature, and music instruction. A frequent criticism of this schedule is its inability to handle new subject areas.

In cataloging music, several problems stand out. The first is one of title. A single work can show as many different titles as there are published versions. This is especially true of pieces whose title is derived from the musical form it takes: sonata, symphony, prelude. An English edition may read "piano sonata," the German "*klaviersonaten.*" Another may indicate a key signature ("Sonata in C Minor"), another its opus number ("Sonata op. 27, no. 1"), and yet another the popularly known title ("Moonlight Sonata"). Proper identification is such a difficult problem that music catalogers must make extensive use of the "uniform title." This practice, codified in 1941, establishes an official and generally recognized title for a particular work, while preserving the existing edition title. The decision in the second edition of the *Anglo-American Cataloguing Rules* to use the language of the work as it was first published to determine the uniform title is causing consternation among many music librarians. The typical user will not, as an example, look for Tchaikovsky's *Swan Lake* under *Lebedinoe Ozero* in the catalog.

Another problem is the question of excerpts. In no other subject, except perhaps poetry, is there such significance placed on the individual parts of a whole. This can be taken to the extreme where an excerpt, such as an opera aria, is far more important than the opera itself. Examples abound in which the average patron or student requests a title completely unaware that it is from a larger work. Vivaldi's highly popular "Four Seasons" are actually part of *Il cimento dell'armonia e dell'invenzione* and are filed under that collective title.

Other factors of importance in accessing and cataloging music are content notes. While it is relatively easy to give added entries for 10 or so individual pieces in an anthology, there are many collections with 100 or more songs by different composers. The same applies to sound recordings which may range from one symphony to 25 Renaissance madrigals. The level and depth of cataloging required is an important area of discussion with the library's cataloging unit, since it may not correspond with the levels preferred by other library units or the institution as a whole.

Although cataloging recordings in MARC (Machine Readable Cataloging) format is quite common, in public and academic libraries with smaller audio collections assignment of call numbers from the schedules is infrequent. One system successfully used by many libraries is the ANSCR (Alpha-Numeric System for Classification of Recordings) system. This quick and easy-to-use method organizes recordings in subject categories, followed by the first four letters of the artist or composer, the album title initials, and a unique number. The system is quite effective for libraries with browsing collections. For example, *Ella Sings Cole Porter* on the Verve label, number 64049, would be assigned MA FITZ ESC F49. MA is the category code for pop music.

The problems that arise from the cataloging of music create difficulties in online catalogs and circulation systems. Multiple hits on a search request often result in abbreviated record displays. The trick is to provide sufficient space for the many instances in which the unique identifiers for a work are at the end of a uniform title, that is, opus number, arrangement, and so on. When reviewing a system's featured response time, does having to scroll through several hundred entries for "Beethoven" impact on its usefulness? A system should also identify whether an item is a score, the type of score, a recording, or a book. In addition, searches should be possible using a delimiter by medium so that a patron can search for only recordings or only scores.

Depending on one's view, music collections (both public and academic) are either plagued or blessed with any number of boxes of gift sheet music, recordings, programs, and assorted ephemera hidden in the stacks. Academic libraries may receive the papers of a composer or research of a faculty member, the records of an opera company or the documents of a well-known performer. Certainly for public libraries, and perhaps less so for academic institutions, the possibility of timely MARC format cataloging is not to be expected in the near or long-term future. To make these collections accessible to users requires the creation of printed checklists, inventories, or, more frequently these days, database indexes.

The computer's capacity to search text makes it an especially valuable tool for music collections. In-house indexing of anthologies, uncataloged sheet music, and gift collections will generally include a title field. Patrons are often unsure of song titles, and keyword searching greatly increases chances of finding the right song. The famous piano bar song known to most everyone as "Melancholy Baby" is actually titled "My Melancholy Baby." A keyword search under the rather unique word "melancholy" would identify the song immediately.

In-house cataloging or indexing of such material is advisable if one has the necessary equipment, time, and staff. Determining if the material merits the expenditure of that equipment, time, and staff is equally important. These databases can be simple inventories by title or as complex as MARC format simulations. The key is to balance the ease and efficiency of rapid data input with the need for the extensive access points that music requires.

There are a number of available software packages, each with advantages and disadvantages, such as dBase, Revelation, and Paradox, that are capable of handling large data files with reasonable retrieval speeds. A key feature of any software—and indeed one of the primary advantages of creating an online index over a paper one—is the ability to search by individual words within a given field. In music collections, one will time and again find patrons who are unsure of a correct title. Being able to search by any one of the words increases the chances of finding what that patron needs.

Processing, Binding, and Shelving

Due to the variety of formats and media found in a music collection, one would expect a need for special treatment, and indeed this is the case. The handling of books, of course, is the same as any other subject area with perhaps a greater number of mixed media sets and the accompanying decisions as to whether to shelve sets together as a book, or cassette, or separately.

Musical scores, on the other hand, present some of the most difficult binding problems. It is generally recommended that all types of scores receive some form of binding prior to being placed into circulation. The type of binding required relates to either the type of material or to the expected shelf life of the score. Many popular song anthologies are cheaply made with glue binding and pages that start to fall out fairly quickly. These scores are also subject to a higher loss rate through theft and failure to return. Expensive binding of these scores is often a waste of money, and it is probably wiser to use a less expensive clear plastic slip cover.

It is imperative for scores with sewn bindings that the stitching is sewn through the fold and not sideways into the gathering, as scores need to lay flat on a music stand. Nothing is more aggravating to a performer than to have pages turning over too soon or having to hold down one or both sides with other books, which only makes it more difficult to turn the page at the right moment. Sheet music and scores that have only a few pages should be sewn through the fold and placed between stiff cardboard covers, especially if they will be shelved in the general score sequence. An exception is often made with rarely cataloged popular sheet music, which is often filed by title or composer in a separate storage medium. If a library can afford acid-free file folders, the wear and tear of pulling and returning these often fragile items will be substantially reduced.

Musical scores with multiple parts present problems all their own. Generally, one part (usually the largest or piano part) is sewn in cardboard covers with the individual parts placed in a side pocket. Larger sets may be placed in cases with a pocket for all the parts. If one can afford it, these individual parts should be separately bound in lighter weight cardboard. Call numbers and ownership stamps should be placed on all parts. A book card indicating the number of parts will help the circulation staff know what elements complete an item. Clear instructions should accompany all materials to the bindery. It is certain that nearly every music librarian has seen examples of improper binding, such as a set of beautifully bound and sewn together individual string quartet parts, a situation which makes it impossible for four players to perform.

Score binding can be the most expensive part of a bindery budget. Buckram binding can sometimes exceed the value of the item being bound. A considered study should be made to determine which types of scores require long-term binding and the more ephemeral materials that merit less expensive methods.

Processing requirements of LP recordings and cassettes are considerably less than those of scores. Circulating LPs should be placed in clear plastic covers. LPs should never remain in the original shrink-wrap. The book card or an affixed label should indicate how many recordings are in the set and if there are any accompanying materials, such as a lyric sheet or libretto. The disc itself should have either an ownership label and written call number or be imprinted with an engraving pen. Cassette boxes are sufficient binding in themselves, although a supply of replacement boxes should be on hand.

Compact discs are a major topic of conversation whenever music librarians, especially those in public libraries with circulating collections, get together. The jewel box cases that CDs are currently sold in are fragile. The industry is currently marketing alternate types of packaging which will only cause further consternation of music librarians. As with any radical new medium, the jury remains out on a number of practices. Does a label placed on the disc itself affect playing? Will the adhesive chemically react with the plastic coating? How do you clean a CD? A constant perusal of music trade magazines, library technical reports, and consumer and professional audio equipment magazines is necessary to keep abreast of trends and current thinking on this ever-changing issue.

Just as scores and recordings require special binding and processing, so also do they require special shelving. An excellent source and detailed study is Robert Michael Fling's *Shelving Capacity in the Music Library* (1981). In general, shelves must be divider type, preferably with backing. Fourteen-inch shelf depth for recordings and twelve-inch shelf depth for scores are advisable. In public libraries, heavily used areas (such as popular music) are impossible to keep in call number order. If space is available, it is recommended that these recordings be placed in bins.

Storage of CDs and cassettes presents special problems due to their compact size. Conventional shelves are inadequate, and no uniform method has appeared. Slanted shelves, cabinets with drawers, special shelving inserts, and record store–type display furniture can be found from library to library. A primary determining factor is the size of the music collection and the type of user. A smaller browsing collection for circulation has different requirements than a classified reference collection of 10,000 items. In general, one must find a system that prevents the fragile CD jewel box from falling off the shelf and one that makes the identification and reading of the spine easy for the user.

Conservation and Preservation

Because of historic documentation or rarity of materials, some music collections in academic libraries are relegated to a special library or archives. In large public libraries this may also be the case. The variety of formats—print, nonprint, microform, sound and video recordings, musical instruments, CD-ROM (compact disc–read only memory), online databases—all present conservation challenges for the music librarian. Attention to paper formats is generally observed, but the music manager must see that the nonprint media receive equal attention, for those formats are less stable than paper.

Ideal storage conditions vary and are difficult to control, even with the best of plans. Environmental conditions (proper temperature, light, moisture, and pollution control) play an important part in prolonging the life of a music collection. Newer recording formats are proliferating, complicated by varying sizes, composition, and playback equipment.

Time has yet to judge their longevity, and the many theories on proper treatment that one will find in the literature have yet to be proven. Degradation of sound or video through frequent playback or improper maintenance may require intensive preservation, restoration, or replacement.

The formulation of procedures on proper use and handling of music materials should include a periodic inventory for up-to-date reports on the need for mending, rebinding, and cleaning. Prior to accepting a gift collection, it is important to evaluate its condition and preservation needs. The knowledge and skill of a trained conservator may be required to review the need for deacidification, cleaning, repair, encapsulation, microfilming, or rerecording. It is also advisable to have a disaster preparedness manual, along with documentation on the location of important items.

As the previous paragraphs and information elsewhere in this chapter imply, conservation principles begin with the acquisition of a collection. The goal for any music collection is to provide music materials for present and future users. While general storage and circulation procedures are well-known, security and environmental concerns must be studied and given equal consideration in the planning of facilities, storage, budget, and staff allocation.

PUBLIC SERVICES

Reference and Information Service

As stated previously, a music librarian must make many more decisions on a typical reference inquiry than librarians in other subject areas. In addition to format and media, other possible determining factors for music scores are edition, arrangement, study score, full score, separate parts, and language of text; for recordings they are performer, conductor, orchestra, arrangement, and language.

The reference interview itself can take longer than those in other subject areas. It is one thing to ask for a book by Agatha Christie. A patron or student requesting music by Igor Stravinsky needs to define whether it is a recording, score, or book about his music. If it is a recording, would it be with Stravinsky as conductor or composer? What format is acceptable? If it is a score, will it be for study or performance? Is there a particular arrangement needed?

The use of uniform titles insures proper identification of what the patron is requesting, whether from personal knowledge or consulting reference tools. For scores and recordings, locating individual titles in anthologies and larger works is time consuming and requires considerable skill in sensing the likely sources from the less likely.

Successfully answering a music question may take more than thirty minutes. Administrative decisions must be made regarding call-back policy and under what circumstances an inquiry is allowed to monopolize staff time. In public libraries, which provide basic reference service to more clients with no search skills, in contrast to academic libraries whose students presumably have some research training, this is a matter of some importance.

As an example, it is by no means infrequent in a public library for a patron to request ten or more individual songs either in printed score or in recording. Such a search can be very extensive. While a patron may begin a search, he or she will be unfamiliar with the many tools (both published and in-house) and search strategies than a music librarian can provide. How does a music librarian balance a patron's needs with the level of service that can reasonably be offered in such cases? Does a music librarian arbitrarily set a limit of three titles, five minutes, or make it a case-by-case decision? Does the music librarian's need for longer search times conflict with the reference policy of the library as a whole? As a manager, the music librarian must be able to use these facts to justify the need for trained staff, increased service levels and flexibility in interpreting a reference policy that may work for the library as a whole but is unrealistic for the music department.

Access, Circulation, and Interlibrary Loan

Public libraries by their very nature are open and accessible places. Restriction by special use forms, letters of introduction, and appointments are found far more often in an academic setting. Indeed, any restrictions in public libraries can be difficult to enforce as they traverse issues of discrimination and rights of taxpayers. Academic libraries, for justifiable reasons, may limit access to their holdings. Many such institutions require an information pass from another institution or set certain hours that the public at large may enter to make use of their resources.

Materials in performing arts collections will always include hard-to-circulate items such as sheet music, photographs, scores, and recordings. In many instances, these materials are not cataloged (except in only general terms), so that it is difficult for anyone outside the library to discern the extent, depth, and contents of such collections. It would be beneficial to both lending and borrowing libraries, as well as to the patron, if some inventory list, brochure, or published source (whether print or online) provided some means of description and access.

Access may be deterred, but not denied, by requiring the music patron to wait until a future date when material can be taken from storage or a dub copy of a recording can be made for in-house use. Fragile music manuscripts, rare books, and scores need special handling and should be stored in a secure environment. Appointments may need to be made to arrange for retrieval and monitoring of these materials. An area can be set aside that may limit the chances of theft and deliberate or accidental mutilation. For music collections with large 78 rpm collections, time may be necessary to dub a working copy on cassette and to allow for the extra effort necessary to filter out background noise.

Academic music collections, on the whole, circulate scores and, less so, recordings and reference books to their students and faculty. Public music collections are dedicated to circulating materials; only in the largest music collections are there substantial reference-use-only collections. Music librarians may feel it necessary to limit the length of borrowing time and the quantity of materials allowed to be checked out in cases of high demand/few copies areas or where certain materials are prone not to return. This is true whether it is the latest hit by Madonna or the listening assignment of a music school professor. In public institutions there are cases where patrons go from branch to branch or return several times a day to the same library in order to take music materials out of the library and sell them. A default in an online system that limits the number of items charged to a patron record greatly aids in preventing such instances of wholesale theft.

In circulating music materials there is always the problem of missing parts to scores and missing discs or textual inserts in recordings. Each item should include the information as to how many parts or discs are included to enable the general circulation staff to know what to look for when materials are returned. If there is sufficient staff, a music department should provide its own circulation desk for scores and recordings. Having a staff trained in knowing what to look for helps prevent the loss of materials (especially popular recordings) between the general circulation desk and the music department.

Most libraries of any type will participate in statewide and national library system services. Cooperative collection development programs among geographically linked libraries enable each institution to develop its special areas of interest while still meeting the needs of the users as a whole. An interlibrary loan request is the most common type of service provided between cooperating libraries.

Interlibrary loan issues that music librarians must concern themselves with include whether or not to allow the loaning of recordings and the photocopying of copyrighted materials. Recordings are fragile and irregular in size. Music collections that agree to loan such materials must have the proper mailing cases and be willing to cover the extra postage costs. Interlibrary loan requests to music collections usually involve finding a specific piece of sheet music. For public libraries, this is more often a popular song; for academic libraries, a vocal solo or piano work. If the sheet music is for reference use only, music staff will often fill the request by photocopying the requested item. This is especially true for anthologies, which if loaned makes all the other songs contained in the volume unavailable to other users. This is more than likely a violation of copyright. Although it occurs frequently and rarely results in lawsuits, an institution needs to consider its interests and set an established policy.

Copyright Issues

The introduction of the photocopy machine, the tape recorder and now digital audiotapes (DAT) and recordable compact discs have created complex issues regarding music collections and copyrighted materials. Particularly for popular song sheet music, a large component of many public libraries, the problem is very clear. Whereas a patron is unlikely to photocopy an entire novel, the average song consists of two to four pages and in practice will nearly always be copied in its entirety. The patron's view is, of course, that the price of sheet music is too high. In their minds, it is unreasonable to pay $2 to $3 for a folded piece of paper. As before, a similar situation exists for classical vocal pieces and piano compositions in academic libraries. For the library's part, a photocopy machine helps to keep down instances of theft and ripped out pages from anthologies. On the other hand, the publisher will argue that the cost of printing music is high and their profit margin low. Furthermore, the rampant practice of photocopying reduces demand, which in turn leads to less stock and less material being published.

Music librarians generally address, if not solve, this issue by posting warnings about copyright infringement at each copy machine. This places the responsibility upon the patron, at least in the view of the library if not of a copyright lawyer and music publisher. In some music collections, the same tactic is used for recorded materials, although providing a linked phonograph or compact disc player with a cassette or dual cassette player and allowing patrons to record materials is not very common.

A new issue for music librarians is the question of video formats and public performance. Legally untested guidelines have been written by interested organizations with differing interpretations. While academic use is clearly educational, does on-site viewing in a public library constitute a public performance? Some music collections attempt to resolve this question by limiting viewing to a single patron and/or preventing a user from watching a video in its entirety by only allowing thirty minutes to be seen. A manager must make the effort to research these issues. Consult with colleagues and your institution's legal advisers to find a policy with which the library can be comfortable. Such a policy should balance the rights of the producer, artist and manufacturer with the desire to provide materials and services to the user.

Special Programs and Services

Specialized user services in public libraries with music collections most often consist of listening centers, which allow patrons to use recorded sound materials in the library for study or entertainment. Whether such a service is hands-on or hands-off depends on the variables of staffing, size, and historical value of the collection. Each method has its advantages and drawbacks. The latter requires equipment and staff in order to protect library materials, and the former requires increased maintenance of equipment but less staff time. The crucial question is the level of control one wishes to maintain over one's collection. Most public music collections with listening centers opt for the hands-on system. Hands-off systems will more frequently be found in universities.

Practice rooms with pianos will be found in music collections and can be a very popular service. Although the music librarian's intent may be that these rooms are for trying out music before borrowing it, many patrons will use them as an alternative to disturbing their neighbors at home. The importance of adequate soundproofing of these rooms cannot be overstated.

One service that is recommended for all music collections is the maintenance of a bulletin board featuring current and upcoming musical concerts and events. Such a service promotes attendance at concerts, generates materials for local history collections, allows the music staff to be aware of what may be in demand, and brings the music collection into contact with the local community of performers.

Bibliographies and pathfinders covering frequently asked-for subjects help both patrons and staff. Wedding music, figure skating selections, and holiday music are typical examples of frequently asked-for subjects in public libraries. Academic music collections may produce guides to basic research, using periodical indexes in music or finding analyses of pieces.

NEW TECHNOLOGIES

Software

As in most subject collections, computers can be found at work in music collections as well. From instructional software to indexing, many of the uses are the same. What may be different for music collections is the type of computer keyboard, one that looks more like a piano than a typewriter.

The development of musical instrument digital interface (MIDI) as a tool for performers, composers, and arrangers enables the electronic keyboard instrument to communicate both with computers and each other. A very simplified analogy is that of a player piano. With this technology, basic music theory, keyboard instruction, and ear-training can be taught interactively. For example, the computer can play a brief melody and request the student to repeat it as an ear-training exercise. A more complex application is using the keyboard synthesizer to input musical compositions as computer data. Once digitized, these pieces can be edited (adding dynamics and text), rearranged, and printed out in notation in a way similar to word processing. Sophisticated systems can play back pieces with a complete palate of orchestral sounds—a wonderful alternative when the composer does not have a live ensemble at hand. Furthermore, some software enables the score to be printed as a whole or in separate parts for each instrument.

Such applications of computer technology are found more often in academic music collections, which have appropriate facilities and staff necessary to operate such services. Public music collections with computer centers may offer basic music instruction software for loan or on-site use.

Keyword searching is an important feature of one of the few CD-ROM products for music. *CAT CD 450 Music Cataloging Collection* from OCLC (Online Computer Library Center) is a file of all sound recording entries from the OCLC database. In addition to the title, composer, and performer fields, other searchable fields include publisher, notes, instrumentation, and year. A similar product from Pro/Media Services Corporation, *BiblioFile: A/V Access*, contains 100,000 records with quarterly updates. A most welcome new product is *Music Index on CD-ROM* with cumulated entries from 1981 to 1988. *The Music Index* is the primary periodical indexing source for the subject; its appearance as a CD-ROM will make searching easier and more efficient. *NewsBank* offers a CD-ROM index to its microfiche collection of performing arts articles taken from 80 newspapers across the country. Concert reviews, feature articles, and news items are accessible by keyword.

With the exception of a few music business–oriented publications, there has been little development in full text online for music. Full text articles from Dialog are, more often than not, record reviews or newspaper features. Part of this may be explained by the fact that the need for rapid retrieval of up-to-date information is very low in music research, and the demand for music journals online is insignificant in comparison to mass-market publications and business and science journals.

A number of new products are in the planning and production phase, and this new technology will have a growing impact on music collections. Along with these reference tools are a few CD-Is or interactive CDs for music. Several of them focus on a specific composition, providing a performance with accompanying score, background, and biographical information and analysis of the work. Both public and academic music collections should prepare to add this new and promising technology to their libraries in the coming years.

While not readily apparent for music, digital imaging technology may be of use to those libraries with large special collections or archives. Photographs of performers, concerts, manuscripts, and sheet music can be preserved and reproduced with the additional feature of an automated finding aid. The potential of CD-ROMs containing, for example, tens of thousands of pieces of music makes its development an area of which music librarians should keep apprised.

Media and Hardware

The ever-increasing rate of advances in technology will have a profound impact on music collections, which maintain extensive holdings of non-book materials. Just as music librarians were making the decision to embrace the new compact disc (or letting market factors make that decision), the industry introduced DAT. Music librarians should not be expected to be on the forefront of this revolution. In order to avoid what may be passing or superfluous technology, not until a new format has gained acceptance and patrons have begun to request materials should a music librarian invest in new media and playback equipment.

On the video end of audio-visual, there are well over 2,000 commercially available videotapes on every conceivable music topic from learning to play the panpipes of the Andes to a blending of music and film with instructions to turn the television on its side for proper viewing. In addition to popular music videos, there are substantial numbers of quality documentaries, opera and concert performances, historical surveys, and instructional titles that offer a new dimension and resource for library users. Although patrons who use music collections that circulate video prefer VHS format, music collections with a policy of on-site use only should opt for laserdisc versions of video materials when they are available. The better picture quality and the longer shelf-life make this an attractive medium for collections.

When building a music collection such as this for on-site use only, equipment should obviously be available for viewing. One problem with this, of course, is instructional video, which usually involves interaction with the student on an instrument. Practice rooms with video players or remote operation might be considered.

FACILITIES

Space

Special services as well as unique and unusual types of materials imply the need for greater attention to space planning in music collections. The layout must reflect the need to efficiently access distinct types of materials, usually separated from each other to a greater or lesser degree, and used by patrons with differing purposes. The special services that music collections feature, such as listening centers, tend to increase the number of service points and require larger staffing.

The larger and more diverse community that frequents public libraries, as well as the much greater ratio of users that are unfamiliar with libraries, call for greater concern for space efficiency and flexibility in comparison to academic institutions. Public music collection users range from primary to graduate school students, from record collectors and concert-goers to businesspeople, from advertising agencies to radio stations. A majority of these users have not had the advantage of a course in bibliographic instruction and require much more of a music librarian's time. In addition, a significant percentage of public library music users make inquiries by phone and expect prompt attention to their requests.

A music reference desk must be centrally located with access to circulating shelves, the reference collection, or at least a ready reference shelf and the card or online catalog. Access to a computer containing in-house indexes and modem capability for online searching is most desirable. Service points should be combined or in close proximity to allow for support and crossover assistance by all scheduled staff.

Listening/viewing facilities will produce various levels of noise, from headphones turned too loud to the student who likes to sing along with his favorite aria recording. Quiet study areas away from these rooms are preferable, although in public libraries visual monitoring is an important security issue.

Public libraries traditionally encourage the circulation of their collections. Indeed, budget and staffing can occasionally be based on usage statistics. Thus, these types of music collections should be placed within or adjacent to the major traffic flow with display racks and bins for popular materials to encourage borrowing. Also, signage is particularly important due to the varying formats that may have concurrent classifications. Overall, a concern for flexibility and modular design is important for all types of music collections. Few other subject areas are faced with such rapidly changing technology and the accompanying new formats, materials, equipment, and services.

Hours and Security

Determining factors of budget, number of staff, and geographic location will affect the hours of service in a public library. Suburban libraries are often open late on evenings and Sundays, while few people may venture into large urban centers after dark. Academic libraries naturally have extensive hours, not always professionally staffed, with late evening and weekend access to accommodate the special needs of their student population. Severe shortages may force libraries to limit the availability of special services, such as listening centers, to fewer open hours. In this way, a music manager can maintain that the department is open the posted hours, while reducing the number of staff hours.

Ideally, all of a music collection's holdings should be available to anyone during open hours. Shortages of staff, as discussed above, may limit access but so also should the nature of some materials in the collection.

As much as the music librarian may take pride in the research and reference level of the music collection, there is no getting away from the fact that a significant portion of the holdings consist of a format that represents a substantial market share of the entertainment industry, namely recordings. This situation, especially true for public and university libraries that collect popular music, presents a security problem in terms of both theft and problem patrons.

For many users, the listening/viewing center is looked upon as an entertainment center and, for some, becomes an enjoyable way to spend an entire day. Music librarians have long known that these types of facilities tend to attract more than their fair share of problem patrons.

Related to this situation is damage to and theft of phonograph needles, equipment, and headphones.

The popular interest in and the expense of recordings also make the music department's holdings a favorite target for theft. Reference collections must be made secure, as should workrooms where new materials are processed. This is also true for acquisition and cataloging departments if recordings are initially handled off-site. A limit on the number of records that may be borrowed at a time is necessary to prevent the malfeasant who will come in day after day, even hour after hour, until he or she gets caught. By that time, the recordings have either disappeared or been sold.

Other than recordings, anthologies of popular songs and books and scores assigned for classes are often mutilated by pages being ripped out. The same occurs with magazines that may feature the current hot pop star, the analysis of a standard symphonic work, or the charts from *Billboard.*

Music librarians must make their administrations aware of the need for a higher level of security than necessary for other units. Keeping the security staff aware of the ongoing problems that the music department faces will help them make more effective use of their resources.

BUDGET AND FINANCE

Ongoing Expenses

Like other subject collections, music collections never seem to have enough money. In what outsiders may think is a narrow, limited subject area, there is a remarkable amount of publishing going on, with a sometimes bewildering array of editions, arrangements, and formats. Where a social science department may have a policy of not acquiring books in Czech, no music collection would think of going without the printed music of Anton Dvorak and Bedřich Smetana and recordings of their works. The cliché that "music is a universal language" is a valid truth. Even in the case of vocal music, it is important to have both the original language and an English translation.

In recordings, having just one version of Beethoven's *Ninth Symphony* is nearly unthinkable, as each orchestra and each conductor's interpretation will be different. A good music collection must provide a broad range of performers to satisfy the differing needs of students, music lovers, and audiophiles.

On a similar level, a music collection must offer patrons various editions of printed scores. For example, the keyboard works of Johann Sebastian

Bach exist in an unedited "urtext" form, as well as several imprints by different editors reflecting differing views of performance practice. Yet, some patrons may need a facsimile edition of the manuscript. Guitarists may desire that certain of the keyboard works be offered in tablature editions, while a violinist may need a duo arrangement for a wedding. It is not simply a matter of having a title in the catalog. For music collections, it goes much further than that.

Another factor that contributes to the budgetary needs of music collections is that jobbers of recordings and scores usually offer smaller discounts on their materials than do book jobbers. Further, a significant portion of the published music that a larger library would collect is printed in Europe, and the fluctuating value of the dollar against foreign currencies is a consideration.

Owning special formats requires special equipment and storage. As stated earlier, LP recordings and scores require a larger depth of shelving than books and necessitate a greater expense. Backing and dividers further add to that cost. Sheet music needs cabinets or acid-free storage boxes and, ideally, file folders. Cassettes, reel-to-reel tapes, compact discs, and videos (both U-matic and VHS) demand specialized storage mediums. A minor but necessary cost is the need for circulation envelopes and wallets for the various recording formats.

Extraordinary Expenses

A listening center by its very nature is made up of expensive audio and video equipment. There can be a great cost difference between a music collection that provides a few hands-on phonograph, cassette, and compact disc players and one with a hands-off system. Such systems have professional-level fidelity playback and recording equipment, filters, and equalizers for improving the sound of archival 78 rpm and damaged discs and tapes, and computer-controlled remote control sound source delivery systems. Whatever the sophistication of the music facility, it is still a cost that other library units do not bear. Replacement of phonocartridges and damaged or stolen headphones as well as equipment maintenance and repair must also be budgeted as an ongoing and sometimes unplanned expense. Maintenance of pianos for those collections that feature practice facilities requires funds for regular tuning and occasional repair and overhaul.

Along with audio and video equipment, one should budget for a record cleaning machine. If practice rooms are a service, pianos and music stands are standard equipment. A photocopy machine that reduces and enlarges is necessary to handle the various sizes of music scores. Also, a copier designed to minimize damage to bindings is advisable.

Fundraising

Music collections have several avenues for successful grant applications. Perhaps among the most successful are ones that revolve around a collection, either donated or desired, that is in need of preservation and/or organization. As a discipline whose materials generally do not lose their value or usefulness over time and whose collections are built upon rather than weeded out, preservation is an important concern. Applications for outside funding using preservation as the main focus can include organization of the materials through in-house database indexing and publication of finding aids.

In addition, these types of collections often contain unique materials requiring cataloging work over and above the capacity of the holding institution to undertake. Providing access to these materials through computer-based union catalogs, such as OCLC and Research Libraries Information Network (RLIN), can be a successful argument for grant approval.

Academic libraries, as a part of the university as a whole, actively seek and benefit from the donations, bequests, and fundraising activities of their alumni. Public libraries do not have this built-in advantage and must seek funds through federal and state sources and corporate grants. The federally funded Library Services and Construction Act grants (administered on the state level and reserved for public libraries) can be used for acquiring, preserving, and improving access to collections, as well as building and construction projects. Public libraries have as their mission the purpose and capacity to provide unique and high levels of service to their communities and should also consider developing proposals over and above collection development activities. Music-related projects (such as a directory and referral service for local musicians, establishing a lending collection of instructional music video, or producing a concert series featuring local aspiring talent) can be suggested.

Corporate sponsorship of music collection activities rarely involves the acquisition of materials, centering instead on high visibility projects, such as concerts or programs. As music collections are part of, at least peripherally, the music community (from the amateur chamber group to the giant conglomerate record company), they should actively pursue support from their "colleagues." Radio stations can offer recordings, free public announcements of activities, and support of genre-based collections, such as blues or jazz. While not usually providing direct funds, the savings on expenses on the part of the music collection in accomplishing these activities can be a useful, if small, means of financial support.

Music, in combining both an artistic and commercial medium, engenders imaginative and diverse ideas for collaborative and outside funded projects with performers, music businesses, trade organizations, corporations, and concert promoters. Music librarians should continuously investigate and set up lines of communication with these related fields, not only as a means of possible financial support but as a way of letting them know of the music collection's existence and the services that it can offer. This approach can be much more interesting and rewarding than the traditional fundraising technique: the "sale" of old records and scores.

Local friends groups can be enlisted to participate in and support music collection services. Docent groups can be instructed to give tours, highlighting resources and exhibits to groups of all ages. Music collections may specifically focus on the local performing community as the basis for forming such a group. Funds they raise through concerts, programs, buttons, t-shirts, and book sales can be used to purchase the type of music that interests them, such as string quartets and chamber music. Any system that is mutually beneficial to the parties involved is more likely to be successful.

POLITICS

Internal

Throughout this discussion, the uniqueness of the music collection in so many areas—from cataloging to shelving—has been emphasized. As a music manager, one must make sure that the special needs of the music collection are addressed at any policy, budgetary, and planning sessions for the general library. Library departments that are most affected by these special needs are the cataloging and acquisition units. Maintaining good relations by keeping open communication, accommodating their requests whenever possible, and giving detailed instructions for unusual orders or cataloging are essential to a smoothly flowing operation and one that meets the music collection's needs.

Most performing arts collections exist in either public or academic settings, so there are other departments and administrators to confer with and instruct in the limitations, strengths, and special needs of the music section. Again, keeping open lines of communication and doing favors will ideally insure their support of the music collection's needs to the library's administrators.

In public libraries, more so than academic, one will find the music section linked to or integrated with an art collection into a "fine arts" department. Some administrators in public libraries do not see the need for hiring subject specialists. These situations will dilute the integrity and potential that a distinct music collection can offer. Means should be taken to keep the administration aware of the advantages, indeed the necessity, of music specialists through monthly reports of special services rendered and thank you letters from satisfied patrons.

In public libraries, budgets, staffing, and influence can be based on how "busy" one's department is. This is usually determined by usage and circulation statistics and head counts. Administrators need to realize that music reference is more time consuming than general reference, that many patrons photocopy material rather than borrow it, and that the higher level of service that music patrons need takes more staff time.

Music collections, through their association with composers, musicians, and performers, often acquire donations, memorabilia, collections, and so on of individuals with varying levels of celebrity status. While the value of some of these gifts may be cursory, nevertheless time, money, attention, and staff are committed to their acquisition, processing, organization, and maintenance primarily because of the status of the donor. Sometimes other library personnel will resent the time and effort needed to maintain these "pretty collections," which can seem to take more than their fair share of a library's resources and grant applications.

The music librarian will have to defend these items as being important to the core of the collection and may have to prove this through statistical analysis of usage. If the materials are not in great demand, then some other rationale will have to be presented to the dissenting parties as to the inherent worth of such items. One can argue that these gifts can encourage the donation of additional, perhaps more worthwhile materials from others or, depending on the situation, be used as a means to encourage grant funding for the library as a whole. Any favorable public relations that such materials generate may benefit the whole institution and bring the library to the attention of a larger population.

In academic libraries, music materials will be given by alumni and other notables who attended the institution. These materials must be treated with the same respect as any other item, no matter what their inherent worth. Good public relations must be maintained at all times with the patrons, the benefactors, and the administration—not an easy task.

External

Censorship is always a volatile issue and one that is never resolved. It is naturally more of an issue in public libraries because the library depends on tax dollars and other funds that come under the review of public groups and organizations. Music collections, at least recently, are more deeply involved in the issue than most other library departments. The focus of attention is on recordings and lyric contents.

In some ways, the recording industry's decision to label their product would seem to make it easier for music collection staff to identify possibly controversial materials. This label, however, is usually placed on the shrink wrap, which is discarded before the recording is processed and placed on the shelf. Hopefully, as long as a music collection acquires materials on both sides of an issue and purchases on the basis of reviews or chart-proven popularity, difficult situations may be avoided. If the circulation of a sensitive recording is a potential issue, perhaps buying only a reference copy will enable the collection to satisfy both its desire to represent all sides and mollify a constituency that may object to certain materials. Library administrators must be aware of the rights of the reader, as defined by the American Library Association and the law.

REFERENCES

Anglo-American Cataloguing Rules, 2nd ed., revised 1988. Prepared under the direction of the Joint Steering Committee for the Revision of AACR, a committee of the American Library Association, the Australian Committee on Cataloguing, the British Library, the Canadian Committee on Cataloguing, the Library Association, and the Library of Congress. Edited by Michael Gorman and Paul Winkler. Chicago: American Library Association.

BiblioFile A/V Access. 1991– . CD-ROM. Inwood, WV: Library Corporation.

Bielefelder Katalog. 1953– . Bielefeld, Germany: Bielefelder Verlaganstalt.

Billboard. 1894– . New York: BPI Communications.

CAT CD 450 Music Cataloging Collection. CD-ROM. Dublin, OH: Online Computer Library Center.

Fling, Robert Michael. 1981. *Shelving Capacity in the Music Library.* MLA Technical Reports no. 7. Philadelphia: Music Library Association.

Gramophone. 1923– . London: General Gramophone Publication.

The Music Index: A Subject-Author Guide to Music Periodical Literature. 1949– . Detroit: Information Coordinators.

Music Index on CD-ROM. 1991– . CD-ROM. Alexandria, VA: Chadwyck-Healey.

New York Public Library, Music Division. 1975– . *Bibliographic Guide to Music.* Boston: G. K. Hall.

Notes: The Quarterly Journal of the Music Library Association, Series 2.
1943– . Canton, MA: Music Library Association.
Phonolog Reporter. 1948– . San Diego, CA: Phonolog Publishing.
Schwann Record & Tape Guide. 1949–1990. Boston: W. Schwann.

5

Theater Collections

Romaine Ahlstrom, Brigitte J. Kueppers, and Helene G. Mochedlover

INTRODUCTION

Academic and public institutions have traditionally collected and made available a variety of materials documenting the cultural history of their city or region. Scrapbooks of playbills, photographs, clippings, and other ephemera have found homes in academic and public institutions, including historical societies. In university, college, and public libraries, the traditional books-only-oriented English and/or literature department has expanded by accepting a wide range of donated theater materials in order to build a collection of historical theater records and documents and to provide the necessary resources in the community for research in the history and development of theatrical activities.

Steady growth has warranted the establishment of separately managed theater collections in many of these institutions. In academic settings, the establishment of a theater collection has also been justified by the growing need for added instructional resources to support undergraduate and graduate level courses of expanding or newly established theater departments.

Toward the end of the 1980s, many libraries found it difficult to maintain the level of financial support allocated to the management of a separate and autonomous collection of theater materials. In recent years, due to enormous nationwide pressures, the previous movement of expansion, autonomy, and decentralization has been reversed and has resulted in mergers and consolidations in an effort to centralize and, thus, economize. Once again, theater collections are becoming part of larger administrative library units.

In the academic setting, a contributing factor to this reversal can be found in the current trend in higher education—a response to societal demand—on the growing emphasis on hard and social sciences, medicine, business, and law. Therefore, the arts, specifically theater, performance history and criticism, and theater crafts (acting, directing, designing, producing, and managing), are considered a relatively low priority and not among the growing academic fields. Naturally, current funding for programs, services, and materials is a reflection of this trend in today's society and its declared priorities.

This chapter attempts to describe the management of theater collections in academic and public libraries. It distinguishes the variety of materials and services provided, mentions problems, and offers guidelines applicable to medium or large size institutions.

PERSONNEL

Staffing Levels

Levels of staffing for a theater collection will be determined by the existing staffing patterns for departments within the public or academic institution in which theater materials are found. If the theater collection in a public library is a stand-alone department, its head will usually be a third- or fourth-level supervisor with a master's degree in library science. This staff member may be a department head and may report to the director of the library. In an academic library, the head may manage the collection in a separate branch within the library system and may report to a staff member who supervises several arts branch libraries or to one who is in charge of all humanities for the system. These patterns will vary with the institution. The importance of theater within the institution may be reflected in the level of the staff member in charge. Clearly, this will have implications for the ability of the theater arts head to define policies and effect changes in the unit.

Theater materials may be a collection within a collection, either within a performing arts unit, a fine arts unit, a literature collection, a department of special collections, or in some other configuration. Responsibility for the full range of collection development, the selection of specific titles (both monographs and serials) and, in particular, the overall policy defining the scope and depth of the collection lies with the head of the unit. Selection of titles in specific areas, such as reference tools or biographies, might be assigned to the reference staff.

Reference functions will typically be carried out by theater librarians with a master's degree who report to the head of the unit. Reference interviews for special materials, such as personal papers and manuscript holdings, will frequently be conducted by the unit head, unless the unit is able to support a staff position for a manuscripts librarian. Support services for the unit, some technical and all circulating services, will be carried out by paraprofessional and clerical staff. Acquisitions and, in particular, the cataloging of print materials will be carried out by the institution's central acquisition and cataloging divisions. Because a sizable proportion of necessary materials in the field of theater are not in print and not easily acquired through commercial publishers or vendors, their identification, acquisition, and processing are usually handled by staff in the unit rather than centrally. The proportion of professional to clerical staff will likely follow the pattern of the larger institution, and this will not be easy to alter.

Professionals

For theater librarians, a master's degree in library science is usually required. Further graduate work, represented by another master's or even a doctorate in theater or a relevant subject area, may be desirable but hardly necessary. Training, with or without an additional degree, in archival practice may be relevant. An intense and ongoing interest in theater is probably as important as advanced degrees. On-the-job training and continuing education are vital.

Paraprofessionals, Students, and Volunteers

Academic libraries, unlike public libraries, may require paraprofessionals, usually at the library assistant level, to have a bachelor's degree. However, unless stated as a requirement in a job description and approved by the personnel department, this will not be the main determining factor in selecting the final candidate from a pool of qualified applicants.

Paraprofessionals play important roles in supervising clerical staff, bibliographically checking items for ordering, preparing materials for cataloging, and doing simple reference work and many other tasks. The ratio of theater librarians to paraprofessionals may be one to several, depending on the organization of the department and institutional practice. (It can be said that library assistants together with the student work force make up the infrastructure of an institution.) It is recommended that any theater collection, however small it may be, is staffed with at least one full-time library assistant. Otherwise, the services of this unit may be seriously curtailed due to vacation time, professional assignments outside the library, or illness.

Paraprofessionals can also occupy temporary positions in the theater collection as subject specialists hired for special projects. Funding for these positions is often raised from external sources or supported by special funds from the library administration. Often, these adjuncts are hired as consultants and as such cannot take advantage of the library's benefit system, such as vacation and retirement, but they may be entitled to sick leave and health insurance.

A welcome addition to the staff of a theater collection are interns and graduate students from academic degree programs in the performing arts or library and information science. Interns differ from volunteers and from general student assistants because of their career orientation toward either library science or the performing arts. Interns bring with them a professional interest in the work and the subject matter. Although their employment is temporary (ranging from one to three academic quarters), they can make significant contributions to the theater collection. Their individual input is worthwhile, and their suggestions can often be implemented because they are well formulated and drawn from a very specific knowledge and background. Continuous supervision is required. The teaching and reviewing of processing procedures and techniques require some extra time from the supervising staff member. This may be the unit head or a qualified staff member. The reward, however, of having a project well done and in a professional manner is worth the initial input of time and attention.

The use of volunteers in a theater collection is problematic. It is time consuming to train volunteers. They may not be willing or able to come regularly. The danger is that boredom with routine tasks slows down productivity when, after a few weeks or months, a project loses its attractiveness. Supervisors have hardly any corrective measures on which to rely to help improve a deteriorating situation since volunteers are not part of the staff review system. In academic libraries, the employment of volunteers in the theater collection is rare, except in cases of retired staff members who bring a personal commitment to the collection. The ideal theater collection volunteer has experience in and/or a passion for theater and the project to which he or she is assigned. This volunteer comes to work regularly and does mundane work with enthusiasm and commitment. Each volunteer will require at least one staff member who is familiar with the volunteer's job assignment and is available to assist him or her whenever questions or problems arise.

Continuing Education, Recruitment, and Mentoring

To the greatest extent possible, theater librarians should be encouraged to attend local and national conferences of relevant organizations, like the Theater Library Association; Arts Section and Rare Books and Manuscript Section of the Association of College and Research Libraries; Modern Languages Association; Society of American Archivists (including the Performing Arts Round Table and local chapters, such as Southern California Archivists); and Special Library Association (particularly the local chapters). In academic institutions, theater staff is often permitted to attend these meetings on "library time," and reimbursement of expenses can be obtained, at least partially, when the individual participates as a panelist delivering a paper or is the coordinator of a conference session. In addition to attending conferences, theater staff may be encouraged to undertake committee work for the associations. In many academic libraries, though not in public libraries, work time is allowed for these duties.

Theater staff should also be encouraged to take academic classes from time to time, to deepen knowledge about subjects relevant to the work of the theater collection. In the academic setting, arrangements can be made with instructors to audit classes. This is an option frequently chosen by incoming new staff members, who need to familiarize themselves with the particular subject orientation of faculty members. However, many universities and colleges do not permit staff members to pursue an academic degree or take courses for degree credit on the campus by which they are employed.

In some institutions, public as well as academic, mentoring programs are a tradition. This requires from the professional (the mentor) an extra amount of time in planning, consultation, and personal attention given to the individual being mentored (the mentee). The mentor needs to be up to date with current theater collection publications and issues since a wide range of topics (beyond the immediate concerns relating to a project) should be discussed in regular session with the mentee. Some discussions might deal with and introduce the mentee to theater collection management and administrative issues concerning acquisition, processing, funding, and donor relations. Proactive versus reactive approaches to acquisitions and collection building—this being the most important management issue for theater librarians—should also be covered. Since it is voluntary and mutual, the relationship between the mentor and mentee can be, and often is, a fruitful and long-lasting one. Optimally, both parties are the beneficiaries.

COLLECTION DEVELOPMENT

Policies

A written collection development policy statement is vital to the management of a theater collection. Describing the past and present nature of the collection and its future thrust, the policy specifies the scope of the collection, its depth and breadth, as well as its strengths and weaknesses. It outlines what kinds of materials form the core of the theater collection and what are peripheral. (A common structure for a collection development policy was published in a series of guides by the Collection Management and Development Committee—now Section—of the Association for Collections and Technical Services of the American Library Association.) A further element in a theater collection policy statement is rating the level of collecting intensity for each segment of the collection, based on a breakdown of the Library of Congress or the Dewey Decimal systems of classification. Ratings may be from 0 to 5, with 0 meaning out of scope and thus not collected by the library at all and 5 meaning a comprehensive collection that seeks all materials on a subject, in all formats, published and unpublished, in all relevant languages.

In academic libraries, the format for a theater collection development policy might follow and adapt the American Library Association guidelines or be designed by the associate librarian for collection development. In public libraries, the policy is usually written by the head of the unit housing the theater collection. Thus, theater collection development policies will vary from institution to institution. In all cases, the purpose of a written theater collection development policy is to codify current practice and to explain past, present, and future collecting activity to staff old and new, administrators, faculty, funding bodies, and the public. The policy acts as a map and a guide. It should be looked upon as a living document that can, and should, be updated regularly.

Unlike collection development policies for theater collections in public libraries, those for academic libraries need to be very specific regarding programmatic information. Primary research and instructional focuses in theater, such as undergraduate concentrations and graduate degrees offered, as well as subjects emphasized and subjects excluded or of marginal interest, need to be taken into account. Attention also needs to be paid to serving research and instructional programs offered by schools and departments other than the theater department: classics, dance, English, children's literature, creative writing, humanities, world literature, musicology, and foreign languages (the latter offering courses on dramatists or on the history of a country's national theater tradition). Theater materials may also serve as resources for interdisciplinary degrees offered.

Both public and academic libraries often have cooperative agreements and other commitments, such as depository and repository responsibilities, shared purchase agreements, and understandings with professional community organizations and institutions. Statements of responsibility for these should also be part of a theater collection development statement.

The rigorous specificity of a theater collection development policy assures appropriate administrative funding (particularly in academic institutions, where a theater school or department may develop or expand its instructional program and offer additional courses in the curriculum). While it is crucial in public libraries that the theater librarian be aware of the community's needs, it is vital in academic libraries that the theater librarian be in touch with faculty, deans, and department chairs. The ideal academic situation is where a library committee has been established to bring together faculty and library staff for regular meetings. This committee can serve as a venue for positive feedback, a place to discuss issues, an opportunity to share information, and a time to present and explain policies and procedures issued by the library administration. It may also be the forum for purchase alerts due to changes in class enrollment, curriculum, or faculty and graduate research.

Subjects to be specified in a theater collection development policy may include acting, design and production (scenic, costume, lighting, production management/technology, and sound), directing, playwriting, and producing. In academic libraries, faculty advice may be helpful, not so much in acquiring new publications in these fields but in establishing policies for regularly adding the latest editions of standard texts or discarding earlier ones and in focusing on authors used most frequently in classes. However, in any theater collection development policy, a balance needs to be maintained between serving specific requests and general public and consortial requirements.

Selection Tools

Some theater materials can be selected from familiar sources, such as *Publishers Weekly*, which list books in advance of publication, or from review media that appear after publication, like *Choice*. However, the usefulness of an evaluative review may be offset by the title in question being out of print by the time it is ordered. To build and maintain a theater collection that is both in-depth and of the appropriate scope to respond to users' needs (be it faculty and students or various community groups), standard selection media for current theater materials must be supplemented by other, more fugitive sources.

A number of special publishers for theater and drama regularly issue catalogs that are useful acquisition tools. These publishers include Drama Book Publishers, New York; Samuel French Bookshops, New York and Los Angeles; Applause, New York; and Theatre Communications Group (TCG), New York. Book lists developed by theater and drama bookstores and specialty, rare book, and out-of-print dealers can also be helpful. Among the bookstores and dealers whose book lists are distributed nationally are The Theater Bookshop, Santa Cruz, California; Dramatis Personae, New York; Golden Legend, Los Angeles; Theatricana, Athens, Georgia; Bowie & Weatherford, Seattle, Washington; Backstage Books, Eugene, Oregon; M. M. Einhorn Maxwell Books, New York; Lyman Books–Theatre, East Otis, Massachusetts; and Elliot M. Katts: Books on the Performing Arts, Los Angeles.

For selection of titles in foreign languages, the major national bibliographies from England, France, Germany, and Italy are usually routed throughout a library system to all subject selectors, including theater and drama. The same routing mechanism is often used for publication announcements (primarily for English-language titles) from Latin America, India, and Asia. Several internally produced documents can also be valuable tools in the process of selecting and maintaining a theater collection, particularly in academic libraries. One example is a library's monthly or quarterly acquisitions list, which serves as an information tool but can also generate ideas for other new acquisitions. In larger library systems, these lists can be produced by the library's online computer system; in smaller libraries or institutions without a centralized bibliographic database, these lists are and have been compiled by staff. The value of these lists is indisputable, fostering trust and communication between the library and its patrons.

In academic settings, class reserve lists can also serve as purchase alerts for theater materials inadequately held by or lacking from the library's collection altogether. Since these lists are submitted to the library by faculty and teaching assistants, they indicate which items are supplied by instructors and which and how many have to be borrowed from another library unit repeatedly. These lists also indicate any changes in class size or course structure that might necessitate a review of the theater collection development profile and policy. If these changes have not previously come up in meetings of a library committee, brief interviews with faculty will often identify the situation as being temporary or permanent, and appropriate action can be agreed upon and implemented.

Circulation statistics—daily records of items checked out, number of holds put on specific titles, and recalls and renewals of items—are a third "live wire" providing important and useful data for considering corrective measures in balancing, maintaining, and developing an existing theater collection. An automated circulation system plays an important role in developing a selection tool that is without bias and free of manipulation. Manual record keeping is tedious and tends to be less accurate since it relies on human factors and qualities, such as conscientiousness, consistency, and efficiency in every member of the circulation staff.

Publishers and Vendors

Many larger institutions, both academic and public, deal primarily with vendors and dealers and secondarily with individual publishers and university presses. However, usually only well-funded, large theater libraries can afford an approval plan with one or several vendors. The approval plan assures that the library's theater collection development policy is translated into a collection profile for the dealer, and all appropriate publications in the field are shipped automatically to the institution.

An approval plan breaks down and expresses the scope and range of the collection development policy for the theater collection in as much detail as allowed by the list of subject headings provided by the dealer. Refinement of the theater collection profile is the responsibility of the theater bibliographer, selector, or the unit head. The profile assures that all pertinent theater materials arrive at the library directly from the dealer. The intent is to add all items to the theater collection, returning only a few to the dealer or forwarding them to another library unit, such as women studies, political and social studies, foreign languages, music, or photography.

The theater collection profile does not necessarily have to be tied to an approval plan. Arrangements can be made with a dealer to send only order slips for items in scope. In this case, orders are placed by returning the slips only for the items selected. Order slips can be sent either prior to the publication date by a vendor, such as Academic Book Company, or as soon as publication appears on the market, for example by dealers such as Coutts and Yankee Book Peddler. Specialized and foreign dealers include Hennessy and Harrassowitz.

Donors and Donations

Libraries always have connections to individuals and groups from the community who want to donate library materials of all kinds. Theater collections are no exception. On the contrary, theater collections depend heavily on, and can benefit greatly from, this external support. Donors can play a valuable role in two areas of theater collection maintenance and development, namely in supplying replacement copies for torn, defaced, and lost items and in acquiring nonfunded special materials and low-priority items.

The acquisition of special nonprint theater materials depends almost exclusively on donors. Most public and academic libraries are not able to allocate funds for building theater collections of special materials. Occasionally, exceptions are made for an item or a group of items that expressly serve the needs of the institution's primary clientele, such as faculty, but these require detailed justifications and often a personally stated faculty request and recommendation. (If theater materials are part of a department of special collections, the acquisition of special materials can be part of this department's written collection development policy and, therefore, will be funded regularly.)

Initiating and cultivating relationships with donors is an important responsibility of the head of the theater collection and is frequently shared with and carried out in cooperation with the development office of the institution. This might involve visiting the donor's residence or the site where the materials are being held or offering a tour of the library. Donors are especially sensitive to the future of their donations. Gift procedures and policies, particularly the disposal of duplicates or items outside the scope of the collection, need to be clearly stated in writing. The donor must be informed about how donated materials will be made available to patrons, either as integrated items in the library's theater holdings or as a separate "named" collection (with access provided by a finding aid or inventory).

Prior to accepting a donation, all gift materials should be appraised, in accordance with the theater collection development policy, by the theater librarian or professional in charge of acquisitions to determine their suitability to the theater collection. The financial appraisal of donated materials is the responsibility of the donor; the library can only provide references to established professional appraisers. (Advice on tax deductions cannot be given by library staff, except to point out general guidelines for donations of an estimated value of between $500 and $5,000.) The deed of gift, the final and official document for acceptance of the donation, must include the estimated value of the gift. Most institutions also prepare a letter of acknowledgment for the donor that is signed by the head of the library. Ideally, a successful donor transaction might also result in obtaining funds from the donor for the processing of the materials. Although this occurs relatively seldom, most donors do want their materials used by the public, and this is the only way to ensure that the materials will be made available to researchers within a specified time frame.

The gift agreement should state that rights to the physical property have been transferred to the institution. Literary rights and the right to reproduce any part of the donated material for use in a production or publication remain with the copyright holder, which can be a photographer, studio, theater company, writer, composer, designer, performer or other creator of the materials, or, in the case of personal documents and records, the donor or the executor of the estate. Researchers need to obtain written permission from the copyright holder to use these unpublished, original, and/or manuscripts materials. In cases of programs, playbills, brochures, newspaper clippings, and other press and publicity materials that have previously appeared in print, the question of literary rights does not apply. It is sufficient to credit the holding institution and cite the "named" special collection.

TECHNICAL SERVICES

Cataloging

Bibliographic access to monographs and serial titles held by a theater collection within a multilibrary or branch system is in most institutions provided by a centralized, integrated online system linking major library functions, such as cataloging, acquisitions, and circulation. Most academic libraries went online years, even decades, ago with Research Libraries Information Network (RLIN) or Online Computer Library Center (OCLC) or developed their own systems, with or without linkage to the aforementioned two major national cataloging utilities. Many public libraries have only in recent years been able to install automated systems, again with or without linkage to OCLC or RLIN.

Online records for theater materials, other than print media, present a number of questions. Decisions depend on the flexibility of the system, staffing, condition of materials, and patron use. In the case of audio-visual theater materials, the general thinking in public libraries is to fully catalog commercial releases of audio and video formats and include them in the system or plan for their inclusion at a future date. Audio recordings, like recorded interviews with important personalities, tapings of special events and award ceremonies, and videocassettes of a personal nature are considered research or personal material and do not, in most cases, receive online cataloging.

If a library splits its theater holdings and resources (as many do) between departments for literature, fiction, arts, recreation, and music, the centralized catalog will indicate which library section or unit holds published titles, monographs, serials, and special collections for stage design, costume, lighting, makeup, musical theater, performance art, mime, playscripts, theater history, biography, acting, writing, producing, and directing. The location of current issues of theater periodicals depends on the organizational structure of the library and available space for display of its serials. To house theater journals in a periodicals or serials department is the least satisfactory solution. The display of current issues within the theater unit is not only convenient for library users but also necessary for librarians responding to telephone reference questions and offering information services in the unit.

Holdings of special theater materials and collections of other nonprint theater materials, such as manuscript collections, personal papers, and archival records, are only entered online as collection level records in Machine Readable Cataloging (MARC) format. The second edition of the OCLC manual *Archives and Manuscript Control Format* describes the format for MARC records for single manuscripts and archival and manuscript collections. The second edition of *Archives, Personal Papers, and Manuscripts*, compiled by Steven L. Hensen and published by the Society of American Archivists (SAA) in 1989, offers helpful suggestions.

Some fields are very important to theater researchers. The author field (<100>) will give the name of the creator of the materials, which is often the same as the donor, the donating company or another corporate entity having created the records. The title of the collection (<200>) is usually set within brackets, indicating that the title and dates for the holdings have been supplied by the processor or cataloger. MARC fields of greatest value to the theater researcher who wants to call up records relating to all existing materials on a specific topic or person are the note field (<520>) and the fields for subject and added entries (<700> and <600>). The note field renders the scope and content of the collection as concise and as inclusive as possible. The fields for subject and added entries provide access to parts of the collections under a number of subject headings and added entries, in accordance with Library of Congress subject headings.

What is commonly and frequently called theater ephemera—programs, playbills, photographs, posters, clipping files, scrapbooks, and playscripts (unpublished but at least produced once)—is naturally not made accessible on the item level and on the library online system. However, these materials may be cataloged and can be accessed at the collection level in the online catalog. This means that the theater library or the department holding theater materials has processed its ephemera collections, and an index, inventory, or finding aid has been created that describes and locates all items in the collection. These finding aids may be prepared manually in a card catalog or on any data management system, such as dBase, or software program, like In-Magic and Pro-Cite among others, on the department's microcomputer. These inventories cannot be consulted centrally unless lists and printouts are made available at the general reference areas or in proximity to the systemwide terminals.

The sorting and arranging of special theater materials are guided by two principles, the state of the organization (or chaos) the materials arrive in and the anticipated use of the collection, as a whole or in parts. One principle relies on the method deemed most conducive to use and the other is the observance of the original order. The latter applies most frequently to personal papers and records of theater companies. File arrangement (alphabetical, chronological, or by subject) and categories for series of files often reflect functional and operational structures, which can be of historical and informational value for researchers and should not be disturbed under any circumstances. If the collection is in such a disorganized state and a structure for arranging the materials has to be applied, sorting should be done to provide access by title of production (preferably with date and city), by name of performer or other artists, and, if possible, by an array of subject headings. These are the most essential approaches taken by researchers and should be used consistently and uniformly to facilitate merging holdings into a database or online system.

Processing, Binding, and Shelving

Theater research materials consist of clippings, scrapbooks, personal papers and records, playbills, posters, window cards, and designs and drawings for costume and stage sets. Most academic and public libraries do not collect three-dimensional items, although some have wandered into theater collections and have come in handy for purposes of exhibition. Large collections of phonorecords and audiotapes are usually transferred to a music library or an archival facility, which is set up with an array of storage containers and listening, records transfer, and playback equipment. All paper materials should be stored in acid-free folders, envelopes, sleeves, and boxes.

Since many theater collections have materials that were processed prior to the availability of acid-free and archivally sound materials, decisions need to be made regarding which ones deserve priority reprocessing. Considerations should include frequency of use, rareness, and brittleness. Reboxing and refoldering materials into archival boxes and containers may be sufficient, but situations are often discovered that require special preservation techniques for unique, important, or rare items. Whenever possible, large items with paperfolds and creases created by longtime and inappropriate storage should be unfolded and stored in appropriate size, flat storage boxes.

The majority of materials found in a theater collection can usually fit into standard letter- and legal-size document boxes available from manufacturers of archival supplies, such as Conservation Resources, Hollinger Corporation, or Light Impressions. Scrapbooks should be carefully unbound and put into a series of standard acid-free folders in either flat or upright storage boxes, depending on size and condition. Smaller items can be put into acid-free phase boxes, which can be used for either upright or flat storage on shelves.

Conservation and Preservation

Most academic and public libraries with theater collections have developed a disaster preparedness plan, an emergency response program for plant and people. To raise the level of competence, understanding, and cooperation among all theater staff (not just new employees), who may need to respond immediately and efficiently to fire, water, and earthquake disasters, requires repeated training. Moreover, a disaster emergency plan for theater collections must be specific in listing in priority order the materials that deserve first attention in case of an emergency. (This might be one book, one box, a file cabinet, or items stored on a specified number of shelves.)

Fire prevention is a major issue for theater collections. Unfortunately, sprinkler systems are not always present in old buildings but are a feature in new and renovated buildings. Experience has shown that most wet theater books, if flash frozen promptly, can be recovered for use with virtually no visible damage, while burned books are gone forever.

Cooperative library systems or networks often offer workshops and seminars on all aspects of preservation and disaster planning and recovery. Theater staff should attend these meetings and training sessions, as often as possible and on a rotating basis, to ensure that everyone is aware of the basics in response and action. The Los Angeles Preservation Network has gone one step further in publishing (on disc and in paper) a list of vendors of disaster supplies that can be customized by each institution. The level of expertise and the quality of advice in this group is very high, mainly because of all it had to learn during and after the recent Los Angeles Public Library fire in 1986. One shared priority is that each institution stands ready to come to the aid of the others should the need arise.

Not all academic and public libraries are centrally air-conditioned. Many old buildings housing library collections are without air-conditioning, except for a few limited areas containing archival, rare, and special materials. Renovation and expansion of buildings, as a rule, include plans for air-conditioning and sometimes even up-to-date systems of environmental control for relative temperature and humidity levels. Air-conditioning is extremely important for theater collections in closed areas. Standards for temperature and relative humidity have been set by the archival professional community. Up-to-date guidelines can be found in SAA publications.

Major conservation and preservation concerns include the condition of certain types of theater materials—scrapbooks, clippings, playbills, programs, posters, and designs. As time and money permit, scrapbooks of clippings and loose clippings in folders can be copied onto acid-free paper. These and photographs, playbills, and programs should be stored in acid-free folders. For negatives, polyester sleeves are recommended, one sleeve per negative. These archival supplies are expensive, and funds need to be allocated in the annual budget of the unit responsible for the care of these materials. Encapsulation in mylar, which can be done by trained staff, is often feasible and appropriate for late-nineteenth- and early-twentieth-century playbills, programs, and clippings. Before encapsulation, deacidification is desirable, but because of the expense of this procedure, which usually has to be done by an outside commercial business, this step in the conservation of materials is often omitted. To do more of this level of preservation will likely require funds raised by a friends group or by one or several grants. Mylar-encapsulated items can be stored in archival document and storage boxes or can be rebound. Rebinding recreates the original format of the scrapbook and should be done for items deemed unique or of special value.

Stage settings, costume sketches and theater plans compose another group of materials that require special processing and consideration for permanent storage. Flat storage in either specially designed boxes, also available from archival supply houses, or metal map drawers is recommended. Interleaving individual items with Japanese tissue paper is particularly important for charcoal and pencil sketches and drawings executed in color. This interleaving will prevent the transfer of the artwork to the verso of the piece lying on top and avoid permanent smudge damage on the surface of the drawing. If possible, color slides should be made for materials in high demand. Reformatting originals minimizes repeated use, which can damage materials even if handled carefully.

Many academic institutions since the 1980s have created the position of preservation officer and, depending on institutional resources, a support staff. The importance of such a position has only recently been recognized. Preservation priorities are being established, actions are being planned and implemented, time frames for reaching immediate and long-term goals are being set, campus- or systemwide disaster plans are being developed, and preservation projects and activities are being coordinated with local and regional institutions. It is this office to which everyone turns with preservation questions and concerns. Some units seek immediate solutions; others ask for advice on preservation and conservation techniques, options, and costs, including reformatting procedures, preservation micro-filming, copying nitrate negatives to archival safety copies, and transferring ¼″ tapes to easy-to-use cassettes. (These are the major reformatting procedures for archival preservation of materials frequently used and in dangerously fragile condition.) In this context, it is important to note, as an example, the accomplishments of a California State Library cooperative grant, which funded a survey of a number of selected titles and collections held by several regional libraries in the state in order to identify micro-filming costs, including prefilming conservation costs, and the costs for long-term preservation of the collections.

PUBLIC SERVICES

Reference and Information Services

The strength of a theater collection lies not only in its holdings of dramatic literature and its monographs and periodicals on world theater history and criticism but also in its files, indexes, clippings, and scrapbooks that cover decades of local theater activities. Theater collection staff answer questions received from readers and researchers in person, by telephone, by letter, and by fax. Practices of handling theater reference questions vary greatly among institutions, and the difference is not so much in being a public or academic library but more in the size and expertise of the reference staff. If questions cannot be answered quickly, a call-back might be the solution, at least for local calls. Referrals to other libraries and repositories are frequently made. If information cannot be found within an hour (the time usually allotted by a library's printed reference policy), the question might be referred to a library reference and information network (such as SCAN, the State of California Answering Network, a federally funded third-level reference service for all the public libraries in the state). Each network staff member specializes in a subject area and often knows things about collections that subject department librarians do not. Network staff also have the resources to go beyond the local and regional level and make referrals to a wide variety of libraries all over the country and the world.

Theater librarians use the full range of materials and tools available to them to help patrons. They guide patrons in the use of the online catalog and CD-ROMs for information on cataloged books and serials. However, the field of theater lacks indexes to its periodical literature. *NewsBank*'s *Review of the Arts: Performing Arts* is the only tool available. This information service has been in existence since 1976 and provides coverage of live entertainment and recordings, as reported in newspapers from over 450 U.S. cities. It includes reviews of performances accessible by name and production title, interviews with personalities, and news stories dealing with all aspects of the performing arts. Full text is available on microfiche, and printed indexes are issued four times a year with annual cumulations. *NewsBank* is available on CD-ROM, but only by subscribing to the entire set of reviews. Other indexes, such as the *Art Index*, *Humanities Index*, and the *MLA International Bibliography of Books and Articles on the Modern Languages and Literature*, can provide supplementary, sometimes more marginal, but interesting references to a topic or event and are all available on CD-ROM and in printed format.

In the case of drama materials, it is advisable to acquire both trade and acting editions of plays. The acting editions are often bought in multiple copies for the use of actors trying out for roles. These editions can be kept in vertical files in the reading room or in a section of shelves reserved for them and clearly marked. Other theater materials may need to be retrieved for patrons. These include the special indexes and inventories for collections, file folders and envelopes of clippings and reviews, and photographs and scrapbooks and boxes for materials that are rare and fragile.

Reference files are also prepared by theater staff. One file often maintained is an index to reviews of current productions—a "Play Reviews File." Reviews of plays produced in major cities in the United States, Canada, Great Britain, and Australia are culled from all the periodicals received in the department. Citations are noted on cards filed by the name of the play.

Another file is an "Unpublished Play File." All new productions need to be checked by the theater staff to see if the play has been published. If

so, copies have to be ordered. If not, cards are either marked or placed in
a separate file, the "Unpublished Play File," together with an author card
for each play. This practice, if performed consistently and over a period
of time, can prove to be one of the most useful in-house files developed
by the theater unit because many plays, even successful ones, are never
published in book form, surprising as that may seem to patrons. This file
becomes even more valuable, useful, and unique if production rights and
reading copies are available from the owner; this new information can be
added to the card. Recently, Los Angeles Public Library was awarded a
grant by a local foundation to fund a project to acquire, catalog, and make
available to the public all unpublished manuscripts for plays produced in
the Southern California area. This collection will provide access to theater
materials never before available. Due to their nature, these plays will not
circulate but are for study use in the library only.

The maintenance of an "Obituary File," for prominent people in the
performance arts and entertainment industry, has also been a long-standing
policy in many libraries. Since the publishing advent of the *Variety
Obituaries*, current files need only be maintained until the next volume of
this series becomes available. A file like this is relatively easy to maintain
on a computerized database. If so desired, it can be linked to names in a
theater clipping file.

Access, Circulation, and Interlibrary Loan

Circulation policies for theater collections in public libraries differ from
those followed by academic institutions. The overriding aim of public
libraries is to keep all theater materials of lasting value. Some public
libraries have adopted the following policy: if only one copy of a theater
monograph is to be kept, it is made reference. When new theater monographs are acquired, one copy is made reference and one or more copies
are made circulating, depending on the nature, importance, and expected
use of the title. Reference copies may circulate as special loans if they meet
printed policy guidelines. Theater periodicals, serials, and reference sets
do not circulate, nor do rare theater items. There is a constant tension
between the desire to make theater materials available for home use and
the need to assure that such items will be available for current reference
queries by phone and in person and for future users. As funds for
acquisitions dwindle, this tension will become more acute. Another factor
is that the theft rate of theater materials is very high, even though all books
and recordings are protected with electronic targets. It is all too easy for
patrons simply to check theater materials out and not return them.

In academic libraries, published theater materials do circulate. However, recent patron policy changes (due primarily to economic reasons) are limiting circulation on more and more campuses to an institution's primary clientele—faculty, students, and staff. These changes are, in turn, affecting the circulation of theater materials. In order to borrow theater materials, off-campus users must now purchase a library card in a tiered price range, each range allowing for greater privileges (longer loan periods and increased number of items on loan at a given time). Telephone renewals, a long-time and very frequent practice, are no longer accepted. Overdue notices, produced automatically by the online circulation system, are now sent to patrons two weeks ahead of their due date. Academic libraries have always had—and will probably keep—their very effective rule for students: until all items are returned and bills paid for outstanding items, students are prevented from registering for the next term.

For use of the general theater book collections of public and academic libraries, letters of introduction and appointments for visits are not required. However, units housing rare theater materials usually ask readers to sign a log and to hand over a piece of identification, such as a driver's license, while rare items are being used. Rare books and special collection departments have adopted rather strict rules for patrons using theater and other materials. In many places, the researcher has to leave his or her personal belongings in a locker and may enter the reading room only with a writing tablet and a pencil. Photographs need to be handled with thin cotton gloves. The theater librarian needs to instruct and, if possible, supervise the reader in the careful handling of brittle clippings and in turning of pages in scrapbooks and pamphlets in fragile condition, as well as be available for answering questions and directing the researcher to further, additional resources at the library. The need for personal attention to the researcher makes advance notice for a visit a prerequisite.

Most academic and public libraries loan circulating theater books with no restrictions. Reference copies are not loaned. Exceptions can be made in accordance with an institution's overall circulation policy. (Some theater titles may be loaned only on the condition that they are used only in the borrowing library and not circulated for home use.) Individual volumes of sets are usually not loaned. The same rule applies for bound theater periodicals and serials. However, rare theater books and manuscripts may be loaned for exhibitions if the borrowing institution agrees to the following requirements: guarantees the full insurance value established by the holding institution, supplies proof of adequate security measures, assumes responsibility for the shipment of the materials, and maintains exhibition standards regarding temperature and exposure to light. Lacking compliance with these conditions, exhibit loan requests for unique theater items should be and often are denied.

Occasionally, performing arts libraries, including theater collections, form consortia to share information and resources. In Southern California, there is an informal consortium called the Performing Arts Library Network of Greater Los Angeles. This group (founded in 1985 and currently consisting of thirty-five public, academic, and special libraries) was formed to "encourage the use and improve the scope of library resources in the performing arts, and to facilitate cooperation among libraries in the greater Los Angeles area having collections of performing arts materials" (*Operational Guidelines* 1991: 38). The first project completed by the network is a directory in which each member library is described, indicating name, location, hours and other details of access and collection strengths. Future projects include the possibility of more formal coordination of collecting, producing, and sharing information files in computerized form, addressing preservation needs, and preparing grant and other funding proposals. (The network cooperates with another area consortium, the Los Angeles Preservation Network.)

Copyright Issues

Copying machines (coin-operated or equipped for debit cards) are usually provided for public use in academic and public libraries. All public machines must display the notice of the copyright law, which gives the public the responsibility for obeying the copyright law, while an institutional copy service or reproduction department automatically follows copyright guidelines. Information on copyright law and on intellectual property in general, a complex subject, can be obtained at most reference points.

Copying of unpublished play scripts, even copying only a few pages of an unpublished play script, presents special problems. Copyright of these scripts remains with the authors. In most cases, researchers will be able to use them under staff supervision, but no copying of any kind will be allowed, except with the express permission of the copyright holder, the donor, or creator of the material. Herein arises a dilemma or contradiction of sorts. Since note-taking from special and manuscript materials is generally allowed, readers are often permitted to hand copy, dictate into a tape recorder, or use a typewriter or computer for transcribing an original text. A recommended procedure to follow when deciding whether or not to make theater materials of such a special nature available is to conduct a reference interview in order to be fully informed—if this is possible—

about the research purpose and future use of the materials requested for study. The distinction lies mainly between commercial publication and academic research. After clarification of this issue, the manuscript material, which may include typescripts in archival collections and personal papers, can either be granted or denied until permission is obtained.

Special Programs and Services

Unlike academic libraries, there is usually no formal program of bibliographic instruction or user education in public libraries. Instruction in finding theater materials and handling them is much more individualized, and public library practice emphasizes a level of helpfulness not found in the academic library.

In an academic library, the theater collection serves a relatively small number of academic clientele and offers formal bibliographic instruction in response to requests by instructors or students. However, good and often excellent service can be offered when a group of students is seated around the reference terminal, and a theater librarian goes over all command options, searching techniques, and possibilities available on the library online catalog and assists them in choosing specific and relevant theater research topics.

NEW TECHNOLOGIES

Software

As mentioned in the Technical Services section, data management systems on personal computers are used in increasing numbers in theater collections. InMagic, ProCite, and dBase programs are adapted to store and retrieve data contained in collections and print reports, inventories, and finding aids in a variety of formats. CD-ROM databases are in use in most public and academic libraries but in a limited fashion at present. Some very large CD-ROM databases might be available at only one reference desk—for example, the full text edition of *The Los Angeles Times*. The reference desk must, of course, have access to *Books in Print* or any similar online catalog. ProQuest, also best stationed at reference desks, is another reference tool with access to indexes and abstracts to a broad range of recent newspapers and periodicals, including information on theater. Most libraries are experimenting with interactive online databases, a field that is continually changing and offers new and better products all the time.

Media and Hardware

Upgrading existing systems might be a necessity, but it is costly and needs to be calculated and provided for in the budget or paid for from special funds. It is becoming more and more common that every workstation for every theater staff member be equipped with a terminal or personal computer, often with dialup or hardwire access to the mainframe.

Library, archive, and museum applications of digital or analog imaging of objects, text of any length, and illustrations (photographs, drawings, slides, posters) are currently being discussed at meetings of professional organizations and are of special interest to theater librarians. Sessions present pilot and pioneer projects and discuss advantages and insufficiencies of the present state of this technology. Most theater librarians take the conservative position vis-à-vis the many unanswered questions about these new developments. Among the questions being asked are ones related to the permanency of this new reformatting medium, the availability of a suitable data management system for retrieval and manipulation of data, the costs not only of the purchase and installation of the equipment but also of maintenance and support services from the vendor, the memory space required in the mainframe computer, the expense of training staff to work effectively with this technology, and, last but not least, the issue of networking and national access to such specialized and unique data files.

Since 1988, the Library of the National Geographic Society has used the Stokes Imaging Services, a videodisc system linked to a database. Master negatives (35mm) have been created for improved video quality of the original. If video imaging technology improves or changes, a new video image can be produced directly from the master without having to handle the original again. Eleven million photographs and illustrations are stored in analog format on discs, permitting faster retrieval than the digital format. This is an important factor since the image database is heavily used for a variety of in-house Society productions (publications, educational filmstrips, audio-visual productions books and exhibits).

The Library of Congress is testing the presentation of various types of materials in electronic format with its optical disc project for the American History Project Series, which would make the Library of Congress's unique special collections available on modest and widely used equipment. The University of California at Berkeley has developed a system and program called ImageQuery, an image-oriented database access system that runs on networked workstations and can be used with a variety of commercial database management packages. This project demonstrates the feasibility of multimedia online access to digital images of maps, slides, paintings, photographs, rare manuscripts, museum artifacts, botanical specimens, and other visual materials. The project addresses issues of fast networking, distributed data and processing, massive storage requirements, color display and printing, software portability, and non-traditional uses of computers.

Several museums (e.g., Henry Ford Museum in Michigan and Southwest Museum in Los Angeles) have selected the Argus collection management system developed by Questar Systems to automate acquisition, cataloging, research, and other object-related functions. The combination of creating a data file for large collections of any type of material, including unprocessed ones, and being able to call up groups of items by subject for viewing on a multi-image screen with the possibility of printing the selected items for reference/research purposes is fascinating and greatly desirable for many large, unsorted theater collections. Designing the program most suited to theater materials that will also serve the needs of patrons is the most important factor in achieving satisfactory results from this technology.

FACILITIES

Space

In libraries where the theater collection is not a separate library unit or subunit, the major collections of monographs and bound serials are housed in the general stacks with all of the library's holdings. Stacks are usually open to the public. The core collection of theater texts dealing with history, criticism, biographies, development of stage practices, makeup, costumes, stage design, and historical and critical studies of directing and acting styles and techniques are shelved together with dramatic world literature, textual analysis, and drama criticism.

A separate space, not accessible to the public, is required for special theater materials: files or boxes of clippings, photographs, and programs; shelves to hold scrapbooks; and large cabinets for posters and designs. All special collections, such as early playbills (pre-1900 and early twentieth century), personal papers of theater professionals (including scrapbooks, photographs, playbills, and designs), and—in universities—theatrical production books and accompanying production information files, are housed in closed stacks and require paging by staff.

If separate, the theater reference area (with a desk for the librarian on duty) houses directories, guides, indexes, yearbooks, and so on and is used frequently for answering reference queries in person or over the phone.

This area should include a reference terminal for accessing the online catalog, a CD-ROM catalog of monograph and serials holdings, an array of special in-house indexes and inventories, microfilm reader-printers, a copy machine, and tables for readers. The reference area is best situated in close proximity to or as part of the area often called the "electronic island."

Most of the library's periodicals will be stored centrally, but theater units have legitimate reason to insist on having the current issues of their subject periodicals displayed in their unit. A browsing area for current theater literature should be included in all libraries as part of the services offered to clientele. Proximity and access to recent periodical literature is vital to the task of the theater reference librarian.

Work spaces for staff are of great importance for any theater collection. Large tables are needed to sort and gradually organize collections. Shelves or library trucks can accommodate boxes in which material can temporarily be stored until overall organization and structure have been established.

In spite of decentralized management of theater collections, space problems are a universally shared concern in libraries, both academic and public. The University of California has found a unique and very successful solution to these problems. Several years ago, two regional library facilities were built (SRLF and NRLF for the southern and northern campuses, respectively), which were designed to house materials deposits from the campuses of each region. Library units transfer a vast number of titles annually to this shared facility. Transfers include monographs of low use, duplicate copies, earlier editions of standard works from both reference and general collections, and runs of serials for years specified by the depositing library unit. Materials can circulate to all campuses, and requests are placed online at all public terminals by patrons with a valid library card. Turn-around delivery occurs within twenty-four hours, and patrons can specify the location of the library where they want the item delivered. These library facilities also store all special collections materials that are fully processed and boxed into archival storage containers. Access is provided by a collection inventory or finding aid available at the special collections unit of the depositing library. Paging of these materials can only be done by the depositing library, and materials have to be used in the library that deposited the collection.

Hours and Security

Access to standard theater materials in a public library is available at any time during "hours open." In these times of economic retrenchment, however, as theater staff are lost and not replaced, it may be necessary to limit the hours during which rare theater books are made available or to require appointments for viewing.

Appointments to view theater materials in special collections departments are the rule in academic libraries because these specialized libraries operate on a different, reduced schedule compared to general or main libraries. Opening and closing time might be, respectively, as late as 10:00 A.M. or as early as 5:00 P.M., and these units usually remain closed on weekends and all legal holidays. In some cases, the theater collection might be open only on certain days during the week. Letters of introduction are seldom needed, but theater researchers are well advised to write or call in advance of their visit so that special theater materials can be made ready for them before their visit to the library. This will eliminate unnecessary time pressure and allow theater staff to respond fully to the request at a time convenient for them. It also helps to minimize "surprise" situations, where taking care of special requests might interfere with the demands made by scheduled visitors and casual library users, the "drop ins."

The presence of an on-site, around-the-clock security staff is almost a rule in public and academic libraries. In academic libraries, guards from the campus security office make regular rounds through all public and staff areas. Most special collections storage spaces, stacks, and staff workrooms are accessible only by off-master keys, keypad locks, or security systems with codes known only to authorized personnel. Theater staff may have to wear picture identifications at all times and be required to challenge any persons in staff-only areas who are not wearing such badges. Many libraries monitor activities through security cameras installed throughout the building. All theater items, if circulating or not, should be treated upon arrival in the unit with a magnetic security tape that, if not deactivated at one of the circulation checkout points, will set off an alarm when exiting the building.

BUDGET AND FINANCE

Ongoing Expenses

In both public and academic libraries, the annual budget for materials is divided into appropriate amounts for monographs and for serials, and occasionally for special projects. The theater collection manager makes recommendations for the budget. Increases often require a written justification and can only be granted if submitted with a revised and updated collection development policy. Ordinary costs for a theater collection include commercial theater and drama titles, which comprise about one-third of the collection. This proportion will vary with the level of the institution's collecting intensity in this subject area. Budgetary restrictions in recent years have limited the number of theater titles that are bought in both circulating and reference copies. When a choice must be made, usually a reference copy only is bought, so that there is always a copy in the library for consultation. In public and academic libraries, which have traditionally served and supplied materials in support of activities of community theater groups and acting, directing, and producing programs of the school or department, it is often the practice to buy circulating and reference copies of play scripts, in both trade and acting editions, to satisfy the needs of students and professional actors.

Theater collections annually require substantial budget allocations for supplies, not for office materials but for archival storage boxes, folders, envelopes, negatives sleeves, tissue paper for interleaving, acid-free labels, and the basic tools and supplies for in-house conservation work. Most often, however, institutions, public and academic, can hardly afford these expenditures. (Historical societies and private libraries are in a comparatively better situation.) Lacking adequate financial support for the purchase of the above long list of archival supplies, theater staff learn to handle special materials with loving care and concern when processing, storing, and making them available to researchers and to look outside the library for funds for processing and preservation.

Extraordinary Expenses

Fund allocations specifically for retrospective theater purchases are rare and, most often, treated as an extraordinary cost. It is, therefore, advisable to reserve a certain percentage, perhaps 10 percent or up to 15 percent, of the annual budget for the purchase of out-of-print monographs or periodical runs needed either as replacements or completion of sets of historical importance to the theater collection. Since this must usually be the responsibility of the theater department, it is often not done as systematically as it should be.

As the technology of information retrieval has advanced, it has proved difficult for many theater collections to keep pace. Computer equipment is expensive, and only well-justified projects can be supported. In old buildings, it is often impossible to bring in enough electrical capability to support more than a few computers and provide online access from homes and businesses. While annual book budgets for library book materials have been relatively constant and dependable (because this portion of the budget is being determined in direct correlation with public services), funds for computer equipment are handled differently, on a more *ad hoc* basis. Allocations allow for only a small number of purchases. Careful selection of a tested product and a clear definition of need might allow the theater manager to purchase new, up-to-date electronic equipment. A number of questions must be explored before submitting a request for funds: Will it serve the collection's needs for years to come, or is it a temporary convenience? Is the product tested? What are the reports concerning performance, costs of maintenance, and compatibility with other equipment to be developed in the future?

Fundraising

Marketing—a function of public relations aimed at the community and at fundraising sources to advertise library collections and services—will most likely be an official activity in public libraries. Theater collections can be part of this outreach strategy and benefit from it in a planned or often unexpected manner. The library's public information office produces flyers and press releases of public programs held in the library. This office also publishes brochures on the holdings and services of the departments and selected special collections within them, as requested by the department staff. Professional staff are also encouraged to reach out to the community and make contacts with appropriate groups and organizations, both to inform people about the library's collections and services and to get input about how well these are meeting people's needs.

Fundraising in public libraries will, as a rule, also be handled centrally within the library system. A principal librarian working under the direction of the assistant city librarian might be charged with exclusive responsibility for writing grant proposals for the system. The granting agencies usually approached by this high administrative level are governmental, although foundations and corporations are also solicited.

From time to time, individuals, companies, organizations, or foundations will approach the library with projects they wish to fund. One such instance that helped spur interest in a public library's theater collection occurred shortly after the Los Angeles Public Library arson fires in 1986. The Skirball-Kenis Foundation offered to support a project to acquire unpublished, locally produced plays. In this case, the theater department sent out letters to various community agencies expressing its desire to build such a collection, and the foundation responded by giving a grant to support the project.

This form of proactive fundraising from extramural sources is an absolute must for most libraries maintaining and building theater collections. Recent widespread budget cuts have made it mandatory for any theater librarian to view his or her position as a dual one of librarian and fundraiser. The primary goal of these activities is to build a support community for financing projects and acquisitions that are out of budget scope and cannot be funded by the institution. Personal efforts are needed to attract donations of archival records, personal papers, and special collections dealing with the history of the entertainment industry and performing arts activities. Their proper management, processing, preservation, and access require the theater librarian to take an aggressive stance and to allot a certain amount of time to explore a wide range of means to secure necessary support funds.

Whenever possible, donors of theater collections must be asked to remain involved with the institution. This can result in an additional financial contribution designated for the processing of theater materials, including the preparation of a finding aid or inventory. The theater unit head needs to work together with the development office on drafting proposals. Theater collections are also encouraged to form friends groups. Such groups supporting one small subject area can be extremely successful. Not only can the group raise funds and solicit gift collections for the department, but it can also help publicize the theater collection.

In universities and colleges, it is more usual to find one organization know as the "Friends of the Library." Most of these groups have a long-standing history of funding special acquisition opportunities for the humanities, arts, and social sciences. Funding proposals for special and high-priced materials for theater collections are submitted to the board. The Friends can also, on occasion, finance an event or reception in honor of a donor.

POLITICS

Internal

It goes without saying that the theater collection exists within a larger matrix of collections in any institution and must vie, overtly or covertly, with competing collections for all necessary resources, from funds for acquisition and staffing to space and even a position on the organization chart. The arts do not seem to be a vital priority now, in the academic as well as in the public library, even though lip service is often given to their importance. In academic institutions, the sciences and the professional schools that bring in dollars have the primary attention of administrators when resources are allocated. In the public library, business and technical areas are being examined for the revenue they can return through fees for services that have formerly been provided free or for enhanced services that have never been offered before. A field like theater cannot be brokered in this way.

The head or principal librarian in charge of a theater collection must assume the responsibility of explaining and presenting the role that the arts play in society and in communities all over the country. The arts do feed the soul and constitute an important factor in social education and personal development, besides their commercial, recreational, and leisure aspects. It seems to be a wise policy for the manager of a theater collection to play on this theme without at the same time inflating the importance of the field in an unrealistic manner. Within the institution, it is important to maintain cordial working relationships with all other units and divisions. One can never know, particularly within a large institution, with whom one may suddenly be working closely, rather than at a distance as before. It is particularly important to be available—and to make all levels of staff available—for work on library committees that may have little or nothing to do with the daily work of the theater department and to participate fully with the good of the larger institution in mind. Otherwise, the theater collection may be viewed as an ivory tower section not pulling its weight. If the theater collection begins to seem irrelevant, it is easier to justify reduction of resources, and support may begin to dwindle.

Exhibits are an excellent means to draw attention to the theater collection in a subtle and aesthetically pleasing way. If related to a community event or activity, a current theme or regional issue, even a small display of selected items can serve to highlight the theater collection. Simultaneously, and most important, such exhibits publicize and point out the relevancy of the theater collection by contributing unique and singularly informative, descriptive, or pictorial documents of the commonly shared past and present. Thus, an exhibit, intelligently and cleverly staged, can by implication state the need for continuing, if not increasing, financial support for the theater collection.

On the other hand, a theater collection can contain many items that are delightful to exhibit and to view, like posters, playbills, programs, photographs, and renderings of costumes and stage sets. Exhibits of this kind can spark interest in the theater collection, but there is the danger that they will also insinuate that the collection is frivolous in nature on the one hand and that the more "serious" or "research" materials (printed, published materials, papers, and archives) are not sought or are not included. To guard against this possibility, exhibits can be designed to include the full range of types of materials in the theater collection, and printed brochures can give more weight to the less glamorous items.

External

It is as important to maintain good working relationships outside the library as well. For academic libraries, relations with departments of theater and literature are vital. For both academic and public libraries, relations with the local theater community are also very important. This can take a mutually beneficial form, whereby the library will help a theater company with information and background materials needed for their productions, while the company, in return, might deposit its archival files and current materials in the theater collection. (Properly arranged and inventoried, current materials can be retrieved for the company's use almost immediately.) An interesting example of extramural cooperation is demonstrated by the Mark Taper Forum in Los Angeles. The company uses the resources of the literature and fiction department of the Los Angeles Public Library and invariably acknowledges the source of its information in the theater's published programs.

Censorship is an issue that waxes and wanes in society and in libraries. At the present time, performance art is on the cutting edge of the limits of "taste" in the area of theater. Academic libraries are more insulated than public libraries in this matter, perhaps because the traditional climate of intellectual freedom on the campus is more secure than in society at large. Conservative or vigilante traditions or temporary periods of censorship activities in a community are difficult to deal with and are best handled with the explicit agreement on issues from the library administration. The ideal situation, of course, is a local government and city officials with a certain sophistication or a live-and-let-live attitude, in addition to a board of library commissioners that firmly supports the concept of intellectual freedom. Sometimes, theater staff members who agonize about putting a certain controversial theater title on the open shelf can be surprised to find that when they do no one protests. Library-sponsored theater events and exhibits must be planned and managed with sensitivity and consideration for the status and needs of community members. The mandate of a public library, which governs administrators and staff, is to preserve documents of human knowledge, activity, and experience and to provide access to this information in order to effect a balanced education for everyone. The best defense against the censor, besides a theater staff committed to the freedom of access to ideas, is a collection development policy that clearly supports this concept.

REFERENCES

Archives and Manuscript Control Format, 2nd ed. 1986. Dublin, OH: Online Computer Library Center.

Art Index. 1929– . New York: H. W. Wilson.

Art Index. 1984– . CD-ROM. New York: H. W. Wilson.

Books in Print. 1948– . New York: Bowker.

Choice. 1963– . Middletown, CT: Association of College and Research Libraries.

Collection Management and Development Guides. 1987– . Chicago: American Library Association.

Hensen, Steven L. 1989. *Archives, Personal Papers, and Manuscripts*, 2nd ed. Chicago: Society of American Archivists.

Humanities Index. 1974– . New York: H. W. Wilson.

Humanities Index. 1984– . CD-ROM. New York: H. W. Wilson.

MLA International Bibliography. 1981– . CD-ROM. New York: H. W. Wilson.

MLA International Bibliography of Books and Articles on the Modern Languages and Literature. 1922– . New York: Modern Languages Association.

NewsBank: Review of the Arts: Performing Arts. 1976– . Microfiche and CD-ROM. New Canaan, CT: NewsBank.

Operational Guidelines. 1991. Los Angeles: Performing Arts Library Network of Greater Los Angeles.

Publishers Weekly. 1872– . New York: Bowker.

Variety Obituaries 1905–1988. 1991. New York: Garland.

6

Selected Annotated Bibliography

Carolyn A. Sheehy

INTRODUCTION

The primary goal of this annotated bibliography is to assist nonspecialist librarians and students of librarianship in understanding the management of performing arts collections in academic and public libraries. The works listed include background sources intended to acquaint nonspecialists with the performing arts, and management tools directed toward helping nonspecialists face the unique challenges confronting managers of performing arts collections. The bibliography incorporates the editor's recommendations and chapter authors' suggestions (which complement or reiterate works cited in their chapters). Only works published in English since 1980 are annotated.

Selected titles are divided into five major sections: General, Dance, Film Studies, Music, and Theater. "General" includes a broad range of works that cover a number of performing arts disciplines. The other four sections deal primarily with one performing art discipline. Each section is further subdivided into Background Sources and Management Tools. The works noted are usually comprehensive, rather than reflective of a particular institution. The bibliography offers only a glimpse of materials available; it does not purport to be all inclusive or exhaustive.

GENERAL

Background Sources

Couch, Nena, and Nancy Allen. 1993. "Performing Arts." In *The Humanities and the Library*, 2nd ed., edited by Nena Couch and Nancy Allen, pp. 173–

211. Chicago: American Library Association (ALA). Any librarian working in a performing arts collection in a public or academic library could benefit from reading this chapter. As defined by the chapter authors (also the editors of the book), performing arts includes dance, film, and theater. (Music is covered in a separate chapter.) The authors provide an excellent overview or profile of the performing arts and examine the special considerations performing arts collections pose and the users they attract. The authors also profile performing arts librarianship, including education, professional associations, and continuing education. Special attention is given to the literature of the performing arts, both primary and secondary sources, and the cataloging, classification, and housing of these materials.

Entertainment, Publishing and the Arts Handbook. 1982– . New York: Clark Boardman Callaghan. The purpose of this journal is "to provide articles on the latest developments in the expanding field of entertainment, publishing and the arts" (xi). Although written primarily for practitioners by legal experts, librarians new to performing arts collections will want to be exposed to current legal thinking on issues in the performing arts, such as copyright implications of digital audiotape, performing rights to music, or conflicts between motion picture licenses and home video rights.

Handel's National Directory for the Performing Arts, 5th ed. 1992. New York: Bowker. For any librarian unfamiliar with contemporary performing arts activity in the United States, *Handel's National Directory for the Performing Arts* will acquaint him or her with more than 900 performing arts organizations and facilities and over 300 educational institutions offering courses in the performing arts. Dance, instrumental music, vocal music, theater, and performing series are covered in the two-volume work. First published in 1973 by Bea Handel, "who perceived that the explosive growth of the performing arts in all sections of the United States required an authoritative directory to document and encourage that development" (vii), the entries are arranged alphabetically by state, city within each state, and arts area.

Journal of Arts Management and Law (formerly *Performing Arts Review*). 1969– . Washington, DC: Heldref. Librarians seeking a broader understanding of the role of the performing arts in society and wanting to keep abreast of specific public policy and legal issues related to the performing arts will want to peruse this journal. Offering in-depth articles on such topics as marketing, advocacy, funding sources, labor relations, and technology in the arts, the journal includes a book review section. In addition to lawyers, arts administrators, and public policy makers, contributors have included James Billington, Librarian of Congress, and Ellsworth H. Brown, former president and director of the Chicago Historical Society.

Mapp, Edward. 1990. *Directory of Blacks in the Performing Arts*, 2nd ed. Metuchen, NJ: Scarecrow. The first edition of Mapp's *Directory of Blacks in the Performing Arts* was selected by the American Library Association as one of the outstanding reference books of 1978. For librarians desiring more information on the contributions of blacks to the performing arts, the second edition contains over 1,100 entries on black performers in film, television, radio, theater, dance, and musical performance. Arranged alphabetically by last name of artist, each entry provides personal and career facts, including information on all of an artist's creative work. For example, under Katherine Dunham, specific productions or titles are given for her "Musical Compositions," "Publications," "Films," "Theater," and "Television." A "Directory of Organizations" at the end of the book includes archives and film centers.

McNeil, Barbara, and Miranda C. Herbert. 1981. *Performing Arts Biography Master Index*, 2nd ed. Detroit: Gale. For the librarian unfamiliar with individuals connected with the performing arts, this index gives 270,000 citations to biographical sketches of individuals, living and dead, representing a broad spectrum of performing arts. The citations are to over 100 principal biographical dictionaries available in most library reference collections. The items cited provide at least a moderate amount of biographical, critical, or career-related information. Among the personalities indexed in the work are performing arts librarians (for example, Genevieve Oswald and Louis Rachow).

Performing Arts Journal. 1976– . Baltimore: Johns Hopkins University Press. From interviews with Rainer Werner Fassbinder, Herbert Blau, and Mac Wellman to articles on Meredith Monk's "Atlas" and Nam June Paik's video sculptures, this journal provides essays, plays, and book reviews on contemporary dance, film, music, and theater. For the librarian who wants to learn more about the avant-garde performing arts scene, this journal contributes critical insights and observations.

Performing Arts Resources. 1974– . New York: Theatre Library Association. This annual publication of the Theatre Library Association is designed to gather and disseminate scholarly articles dealing with the location of resources in the performing arts; descriptions, listings, or evaluations of such collections; monographs of previously unpublished original source materials; and recent discoveries. Articles on theater, film, broadcasting, and popular entertainments are among the topics that have been featured. For librarians seriously interested in learning about other performing arts collections and research sources, this series should be regularly consulted.

Slide, Anthony, Patricia King Hanson, and Stephen L. Hanson, comps. 1988. *Sourcebook for the Performing Arts: A Directory of Collections, Resources, Scholars, and Critics in Theatre, Film, and Television.* Westport, CT: Greenwood Press. This unique sourcebook offers information on both collections and individuals in the performing arts; "A listing such as the latter has never before been attempted" (vii). Performing arts defined by the author include theater, film, radio, and television; music and dance are covered only when those fields "overlap into these areas, as in film scores" (vii). The book remains a tremendous boon to librarians new to the field who need biographical information on performing arts scholars, critics, archivists, and librarians.

Management Tools

Audiovisual Policies in ARL Libraries. 1990. Compiled by Kristine Brancolini, Spec. Kit no. 162. Washington, DC: Association of Research Libraries. Noting a growing number of academic research libraries collecting audio-visual materials, the author surveyed all members of the Association of Research Libraries (ARL) in the spring of 1990. This kit includes not only the results of that survey but also documents produced by ARL libraries to deal with audio-visual materials— brochures, fact sheets, circulation and fine policies, collection development and selection policies, and reserve policies and procedures. For any librarian in a performing arts collection struggling to write a policy or procedures for the first time, copies of collection development guidelines from libraries such as the Avery Fisher Center for Music and Media at New York University or the Phonograph Record Library at Princeton University are invaluable.

AV Market Place 1993: The Complete Business Directory of: Audio, Audio Visual, Computer Systems, Film, Video, Programming with Industry Yellow Pages. 1993. New York: Bowker. Librarians in performing arts collections who are looking for companies that transfer slides to video or distribute digital audiotapes will find this comprehensive directory of over 1,400 products and 11,952 companies in the United States and Canada extremely useful. As managing editor Richard Lanam states in the "Preface," "*AV Market Place*, now in its 21st edition, continues to be the one-stop guide to the everchanging AV industry" (viii). In addition to sources for audio-visual equipment and new technology, the directory offers sections on "Associations" (including library groups with an AV interest), "Periodicals" (media-oriented publications), "Reference Books" (major audio-visual reference materials), and "Awards and Festivals."

Blazek, Ron, and Elizabeth Aversa. 1988. "Accessing Information in the Performing Arts" and "Principal Information Sources in the Performing Arts." In *The Humanities: A Selective Guide to Information Sources*, 3rd ed., pp. 166–261. Englewood, CO: Libraries Unlimited. This guide to the humanities offers librarians working in either public or academic performing arts collections a wealth of superbly organized reference information and an indispensable collection development tool. Two chapters, totaling over 100 pages, cover issues of access in the performing arts (major divisions of the field, users, computers, organizations, publishers, and special collections) and sources (in the performing arts in general and specifically in music, theater and drama, dance, and film, radio, television, and video). The authors, who both teach advanced-level reference courses in graduate library schools, offer thorough annotations for all reference tools. Titles of periodicals are excluded, unless they have reference value. Computerized databases are integrated with books.

Cohen-Stratyner, Barbara Naomi, ed. 1990. *Arts and Access: Management Issues for Performing Arts Collections*. Performing Arts Resources vol. 15. New York: Theatre Library Association. In this volume of the Theatre Library Association's annual *Performing Arts Resources*, "issues of accessibility for collections and their staffs are presented by librarians, archivists and curators" (viii). Intended as a companion volume to *Preserving America's Performing Arts*, the work is divided into three sections: "Creating the Collection," "Managing the Collection," and "Interpreting the Collection." The contributed essays by experts in the field range from documenting an oral tradition and collecting ephemera to putting performance online. This volume is a rich resource both for those new to managing performing arts collections and for those who are experienced practitioners.

Cohen-Stratyner, Barbara, and Brigitte Kueppers, eds. 1985. *Preserving America's Performing Arts: Papers from the Conference on Preservation Management for Performing Arts Collection, April 28–May 1, 1982, Washington, D.C.* New York: Theatre Library Association. This work is essential reading for any librarian interested in the preservation of performing arts collections. The contributed essays are written by well-recognized authorities in the field. The authors address preservation problems unique to performing arts collections. Some articles describe preservation problems in general (such as Jean Geil's "Preservation Problems in Music Libraries"), while others are specific how-to texts (for example, Dorothy L. Swerdlove's "Clippings: Practical Problems of Preservation"). Performing arts librarians will be particularly interested in two management-oriented articles: Lawrence J. McCrank's "Collection Management and Preservation" and Marilyn Kemp Weidner's "Management of Collections—Preservation Programs."

DePew, John N. 1991. *A Library, Media, and Archival Preservation Handbook*. Santa Barbara, CA: ABC-CLIO. Designed for "those who have little knowledge of the preservation of library materials" (xxiii), the book clearly describes preservation procedures that are widely used in archives but not normally in libraries or media centers. Helpful references and a glossary are included. Performing arts librarians will be interested in the clear guidelines offered for the basic preservation of photographs, film, slides, phonograph recordings, magnetic tape media, computer disks, and compact discs. The separate chapter on disaster preparedness is an especially important contribution.

Ellison, John W., ed. 1985. *Media Librarianship*. New York: Neal-Schuman. The author (an associate professor of information and library studies) discusses media librarianship without regard to type of library. Two of the most helpful sections of the book for librarians in performing arts collections are Nancy Allen's chapter on "Mass Media Information Sources," which includes film, and the author's chapter on "Non-Book Storage and Care Self Evaluation Form." The author developed a checklist for a storage and care program for active collections (rather than for collections in long-term archival storage), which was field tested in twenty different institutions that represented various types of libraries. The simple, clearly defined checklist works for seven different formats, including those found in performing arts collections.

Ellison, John W., and Patricia Ann Cootie, eds. 1987. *Nonbook Media: Collection Management and User Services*. Chicago: American Library Association. *Nonbook Media* is a compilation of twenty-two separately authored chapters on nonbook formats, such as audiotapes, films, music scores, phonograph records, videodiscs, and videotapes. Of particular interest to librarians in performing arts collections are the sections on "Management Problems and Solutions" offered for each format. These two- to eight-page sections offer succinct looks at problems to be encountered with each format and ways of resolving those problems.

Fothergill, Richard, and Ian Butchart. 1990. *Non-book Materials in Libraries: A Practical Guide*, 3rd ed. London: Clive Bingley. Although this book has a decidedly British orientation, the technical information that it contributes on materials, formats, and equipment is easily understood and useful to any librarian working in a performing arts collection with nonbook materials. The book covers the practical changes in management methods that new formats—such as magnetic tape, vinyl discs, optical storage systems (videodiscs, CD-ROMs), and interactive video—require.

Frost, Carolyn O. 1989. *Media Access and Organization: A Cataloging and Reference Sources Guide for Nonbook Materials*. Englewood, CO: Libraries Unlimited. The focus of this book is "to offer a comprehensive approach to the organization and access of nonbook materials" (xvii). The work serves as an aid to librarians in performing arts collections engaged in the descriptive cataloging of nonbook materials or in locating information in nonbook formats. The author's approach is clear and concise and includes not only discussions of key rules from the 1988 revision of the *Anglo-American Cataloguing Rules* but also cataloging examples. An added feature are the lists of reference tools at the end of each chapter, "which complement the cataloging process, and which assist the reference librarian in finding information contained in nonbook formats" (xvii).

Intner, Sheila, and Richard Smiraglia, eds. 1987. *Policy and Practice in Bibliographic Control of Nonbook Media*. Chicago: American Library Association. Any librarian managing a performing arts collection will be dealing with nonbook media. The nine essays in the first part of this book, "Background, Theory, and Management Concerns," will be of particular interest to library managers. The second part, "Cataloging Individual Media," is more technical and relates to cataloging specific formats. "Developing

Nonbook Collections" by Sheila S. Intner and "Using Policy Statements to Define and Manage the Nonbook Collection" by Hugh A. Durbin are brief, helpful introductions to management concerns. This work grew out of a series of regional institutes on nonbook materials sponsored by the Resources and Technical Services Division (RTSD) (now Association for Library Collections & Technical Services [ALCTS]) of the ALA and the RTSD Council on Regional Groups.

Lesk, Michael. 1990. *Image Formats for Preservation and Access: A Report of the Technology Assessment Advisory Committee to the Commission on Preservation and Access*. Washington, DC: Commission on Preservation and Access. No librarian can be immune to issues of conservation and preservation. For the performing arts librarian dealing with a variety of formats, resolving these issues is essential. This report discusses the effect of digital technology on preservation concerns regarding paper-based materials, comparing digital and microfilm imagery. Various possibilities for digital storage are explored: magnetic disk; optical disk; digital video-tape; digital audiotape; conventional nine-track, ½" magnetic tape; CD-ROMs; and "digital paper." ASCII conversion is also considered. Whichever method is appropriate, the author urges librarians to begin dealing today with deteriorating collections rather than to wait until those collections are gone.

Mason, Sally, and James Scholtz. 1988. *Video for Libraries: Special Interest Video for Small and Medium-Sized Public Libraries*. Chicago: American Library Association. Librarians in small and medium-sized public libraries who are attempting to build performing arts video collections will want to consult this bibliography. Videos listed were selected by experts in the field, using the following criteria to determine inclusion: authenticity, utilization, content, and technical qualities. Over 100 performing arts videos are included in the book. For example, the chapter on "The Arts" suggests 39 videos for music, 21 videos for opera, 18 for dance, and 21 for film and television; the chapter on "Literature" offers 18 video titles for "Theater." Producers and distributors and video wholesalers and retailers are provided in appendices. The titles are arranged by Dewey Decimal Classification numbers with Library of Congress subject headings.

Performing Arts Books 1876–1981: Including an International Index of Current Serial Publications. 1981. New York: Bowker. For retrospective collection development, this comprehensive work is essential. Its nearly 50,000 titles, published in or distributed in the United States, represent over 100 years of performing arts publishing. (Performing arts is defined very broadly.) The subject index includes some 12,000 Library of Congress subject headings. Works are arranged by main entry and, in addition to full bibliographic descriptions, Library of Congress Classification number, Dewey Decimal Classification number, and Library of Congress card number and tracings are indicated.

Wasserman, Steven R., and Jacqueline Wasserman O'Brien, eds. 1985. *The Lively Arts Information Directory*, 2nd ed. Detroit: Gale. Subtitled "A Guide to the Fields of Music, Dance, Theater, Film, Radio, and Television in the United States and Canada . . . ," the book contains 9,000 listings (2,300 more than in the first edition) in a variety of areas. Of the book's 13 sections, the ones of most interest to librarians in the performing arts include "National and International Organizations" (which encompasses library organizations), "Journals and Periodicals," "Special Libraries" (libraries that concentrate in one or more of the following subject areas— music, dance, theater, film, and broadcasting), "Research and Information Centers" (university-related and independently operated research institutes and information centers in the lively arts), and "Books and Media Publishers."

DANCE

Background Sources

Adshead, Janet, ed. 1988. *Dance Analysis: Theory and Practice*. London: Dance Books. Understanding how a dance is put together and understanding its meaning or significance are challenges for any librarian. Janet Adshead (research fellow in Dance at the University of Surrey) compiled a series of contributed essays to help unlock the mysteries of dance analysis. The first part of the book raises theoretical concerns, while the second part describes dance analysis in practice. Adshead's chapter on "Describing the Components of the Dance" is especially helpful in delineating a framework for understanding dance works. Essays, such as Valerie Briginshaw's analysis of variation in choreography and performance of the Act II Pas de Deux of *Swan Lake*, offer examples of interpretation.

Adshead, Janet, and June Layson, eds. 1983. *Dance History: A Methodology for Study*. London: Dance Books. Librarians will appreciate this unique approach to dance history, which clearly connects the study of dance to the study of primary and secondary sources—from photographs, newspapers, video and film, periodicals, manuscripts, and books to street directories. (The editors developed the work after teaching graduate courses in dance history at the University of Leeds.) Although the text focuses on dance in the Western world and, in particular, on dance in the United Kingdom, the editors' system could be adapted to other areas and periods of dance. Highly informative is Janet Adshead's excellent treatment of monographs in "Studies in Dance History." Rather than a simple chronological or alphabetical arrangement, titles are grouped by subject area.

Cohen-Stratyner, Barbara Naomi. 1982. *Biographical Dictionary of Dance*. New York: Schirmer. For librarians unfamiliar with those who have contributed significantly to the world of dance over the last 4 centuries, this dictionary profiles more than 2,900 known and unknown individuals. Performers, choreographers, impresarios, and historians, as well as composers and artists connected to the dance, are included in the work. Short biographies (arranged alphabetically by professional name) are followed by listings of works presented at live performances on or before December 31, 1980, or works created for filmed or taped media and released in 1980 or 1981. Some entries include a bibliography.

Copeland, Roger, and Marshall Cohen. 1983. *What Is Dance? Readings in Theory and Criticism*. New York: Oxford University Press. Roger Copeland (assistant professor of Theater and Dance at Oberlin College) and Marshall Cohen (professor of Philosophy at The College of Staten Island) compiled this series of sixty essays on dance. The contributors—from Jean-Georges Noverre to Yvonne Rainer—represent different historical periods (from the eighteenth to the twentieth centuries) and different backgrounds (critics, choreographers, historians, and philosophers). The essays are grouped into seven topics, and a bibliography and index are provided. For the librarian wanting to explore dance theory and criticism, this book provides a comprehensive and sophisticated introduction to the field.

Emery, Lynne Fauley. 1988. *Black Dance: From 1619 to Today*. 2nd rev. ed. Princeton, NJ: Princeton Book Company. Emery's work serves as a welcome source for librarians interested in studying the history of dance performed by African Americans from the beginning of the slave trade to the twentieth century. As noted choreographer Katherine Dunham states in her "Foreword" to Emery's first edition, "Until the publication of Lynne Emery's fascinating book, *Black Dance in the United States*, there has been in this country no comprehensive study of the dance forms of people of African origin" (vii). Previously unknown African American dance pioneers are revealed for the first time by Emery, a social scientist and historian. The author's extensive research is reflected in her bibliography, which includes published and unpublished material.

Guest, Ann Hutchinson. 1989. *Choreo-Graphics: A Comparison of Dance Notation Systems from the Fifteenth Century to the Present*. New York: Gordon and Breach. Dances may be preserved through a variety of dance notation systems that describe movement using stick figures, music notes, or abstract symbols. A librarian working with dance materials will benefit from a brief acquaintance with these systems. Ann Hutchinson Guest, a pioneer in the field of labanotation, introduces the reader to thirteen historical and contemporary dance notation systems (from Feuillet and Saint-Léon to Loring and Benesh). Advantages and disadvantages of each complex system are clearly noted, and a survey of the main systems is included. For those who want to pursue the subject further, a bibliography is provided.

Robertson, Allen, and Donald Hutera. 1990. *The Dance Handbook*. G. K. Hall Performing Arts Series. Boston: G. K. Hall. Allen Robertson (dance critic for London's *Time Out*) and Donald Hutera (a free-lance writer and radio broadcaster on the arts) have organized—in chronological sequence—

data on 200 major dancers, dance companies, choreographers, and dancers (interspersed with their comments and opinions). For the librarian looking for a quick introduction to Western theatrical dance, this handbook provides sections like "Lineage," historical links between dancers and dance companies and works; "Follow-up," data on the various stagings of a choreographic piece; and "Databank," a glossary of dance terms, a bibliography of dance books, and information on dance companies, magazines, festivals, and organizations.

Management Tools

Adamczyk, Alice J. 1989. *Black Dance: An Annotated Bibliography.* Garland Reference Library of the Humanities, vol. 558. New York: Garland. As the author notes in her "Introduction," this work is "the first attempt to compile published material documenting black dance in all of its forms" (ix). For the librarian wanting to develop a collection of materials on black dance, this bibliography will be of great service since it lists almost 1,400 items (mainly printed works in English published in the western hemisphere). Works are arranged alphabetically by author, and most entries are briefly annotated. A subject index, which includes entries for general topics as well as for specific dances and ceremonies, is provided.

Braun, Susan. 1986. *Modern Dance & Ballet on Film & Video: A Catalog.* New York: Dance Films Association. Braun's work offers easy access to information on dance films and videotapes for the librarian interested in retrospective collection development. Arranged alphabetically by title of film or video, the work describes classic dance films and videos available at the time for distribution and offers eight indexes and guides. The catalog was edited from information contained in the *Dance Film and Video Database,* "A computer depository of facts and statistics describing more than 1,600 films and videos, concerning all types and many aspects of the dance" (i). Descriptions include running time, medium and format, date of release, performers, production credits, and contents.

Dance Film and Video Guide. 1991. Compiled by Deirdre Towers for the Dance Films Association. Princeton, NJ: Princeton Book Company. *Dance Film and Video Guide* is an updated and revised edition of the Susan Braun's catalog published by the Dance Films Association in 1986, *Modern Dance & Ballet on Film & Video: A Catalog.* This guide lists over 2,000 films and videos available for rent or sale. No evaluation is made of the titles. To be listed, films and videotapes only have to have distributors for noncommercial use in the United States. (A directory of distributors is included at the end of the book.) Titles are presented in alphabetical order. Entries include a brief description, a list of personnel, and pertinent performance data. Indexes are offered for subject, choreographers,

composers, dance companies, dancers, and directors. For those wanting
to build a dance film or video collection, this guide is a place to start—but
not to finish, since it contains no reviews or evaluations.

Forbes, Fred R., Jr. 1986. *Dance: An Annotated Bibliography 1965–1982.*
Garland Reference Library of the Humanities, vol. 606. New York: Garland.
Modeled on Paul Magriel's *Dance: An Annotated Bibliography* (New
York: Blom, 1936), Forbes's bibliography of over 1,000 entries contains
references to dance in 8 specific subject areas: aesthetics, anthropology,
education, history, literature, physiology, psychology, and sociology.
Works are arranged alphabetically by last name of author, and materials
annotated include books, articles, book chapters, dissertations, and theses
published in English from 1965 to 1982. For the librarian creating a dance
collection that is broad in scope, this work presents a unique, multidisci-
plinary approach to dance information sources.

Leslie, Serge, ann. 1981. *A Bibliography of the Dance Collection of Doris Niles
and Serge Leslie,* reprint of 1966 ed. London: Dance Books. For developing
a historical dance collection, this bibliography is essential. Although the
work consists of approximately 2,000 items from a private collection
(mainly twentieth-century publications), entries include many heretofore
unknown items, such as obscure ballet librettos. Since the collector was a
dancer, teacher, and producer, his evaluative notes are helpful to the dance
librarian attempting to understand the importance of such historical
dance works. The titles are arranged alphabetically by author, and a subject
index is included at the end of each volume.

National Dance Association. 1990. *Dance Resource Guide.* Reston, VA: National
Dance Association. This resource directory emerged from a project funded
jointly by the National Endowment for the Arts and the U.S. Department
of Education. Although geared for those teaching dance in kindergarten
through grade twelve, it contains collection development information that
any librarian starting a dance collection might find useful (particularly the
chapters on "Multicultural Resources" and "Resources Currently Being
Developed"). Using a broad definition of dance, the directory includes
data on dance organizations, books, journals, newsletters, videos, slides,
films, recordings, distributors, and publishers.

Pease, Edward. 1982. *Researching Theatrical Dance: A Guide to Basic
Collections, Bibliographies, Reference Books, Serials, Historical Surveys,
Manuals, Special Studies, Films, Addresses, and Other Essentials;
Primarily as Related to Theatrical Dance.* Washington, DC: Educational
Resources Information Center (ERIC). There is not a surfeit of bibliographies
for dance. As Edward Pease (a faculty member at Western Kentucky
University) laments, "At present, nearly all dance history bibliographies
are either quite specialized or out of date" (vii). He seeks to remedy that
situation by creating extensive lists of theatrical dance materials. Materials

are arranged in twenty sections, including "United States Prior to 1900" and "20th-Century Scandinavia." For a librarian wanting to do retrospective collection development in dance, Pease's work is one place to begin.

Robinson, Doris. 1989. *Music and Dance Periodicals: An International Directory & Guidebook*. Voorheesville, NY: Peri Press. Although the majority of the 1,867 periodicals annotated in this guide are music related (only 150 are dance related), the directory's importance to a librarian building a performing arts collection may be greater as a selection tool for dance than for music. Historically, information on music periodicals (which far outnumber dance periodicals) has been easier to obtain. The author has conveniently divided the titles into 19 sections. For example, music periodicals can be found under "Composers and Song Writers" and "Music Industry." The author includes a number of helpful indexes: title, publisher and organization, subject, country of publication, and International Standard Serial Number (ISSN).

FILM STUDIES

Background Sources

Allen, Robert C., and Douglas Gomery. 1985. *Film History: Theory and Practice*. New York: Alfred A. Knopf. *Film History* is not a history of film but rather a reflection by two teachers of film history on the historical study of film. Divided into three parts, the goal of the book is to "enable the student of film history to become a more sensitive and discriminating reader of film historical works and to enable him or her to conduct and write film history" (iv). Of particular interest to librarians new to film studies are the chapter on researching film history, which discusses filmic and nonfilmic evidence, and the chapter on writing film history, which includes possible resources for local history. A useful selective guide for further reading concludes the work.

Ellis, Jack C. 1990. *A History of Film*, 3rd ed. Englewood Cliffs, NJ: Prentice-Hall. One of the appealing aspects of *A History of Film* for librarians is that it is international in scope. It covers not only film in the United States and Western Europe but also in Asia, Eastern Europe, and the Third World. Ellis (who teaches at Northwestern University) concentrates on narrative fiction film but also deals in part with avant-garde, documentary, and animated film. This edition attempts to incorporate recent historical research on film, especially on American film, while maintaining the organization and structure of the previous editions. The work interprets major films, the culture surrounding them, and their creators. Following each chapter are helpful lists of "Films of the Period" and "Books on the Period."

Kawin, Bruce F. 1987. *How Movies Work*. New York: Macmillan. How a film is put together is both a technical and a creative achievement. Although from the title one might suspect that this work would cover only the technical aspects, in reality it covers both. For the author, "This is a book of film appreciation" (vii). The book is divided into three parts—"Film and the Physical World," "From Shot to Sequence," and "The Film Artist and the Movie Business." Using numerous illustrations, the author elucidates the technology of film construction and film production. For librarians new to the field, this book will unlock the mysteries of film-making. At the end of the book, the author also offers suggestions for further reading and viewing and a glossary.

Mast, Gerald. 1992. *A Short History of the Movies*, 5th ed., revised by Bruce F. Kawin. New York: Macmillan. Gerald Mast's work, widely used in college courses on film history, discusses film not only as an art but also as a business and a commodity. Revised after his death by Bruce F. Kawin (a teacher of film history at the University of Colorado), the book points out significant trends in film history, particularly—though not exclusively—those in American film history, and concentrates on fiction film. This edition, as contrasted to previous editions, provides more information on women and African-American filmmakers. In addition to being richly illustrated and easy to read, this edition also offers—for the first time—a glossary. An extensive reading and viewing list is included in the appendix, as well as a list of distributors.

Management Tools

Armour, Robert A. 1980. *Film: A Reference Guide.* American Popular Culture Series. Westport, CT: Greenwood Press. Robert A. Armour (who has taught film courses and written a book on *Fritz Lang*) wrote this book "to provide a reference guide to film for the person beginning the serious study of the medium or for a viewer wanting to pursue in depth what has been a casual interest" (xi). Although titled a "reference guide," materials are not organized into traditional reference categories. Instead, the book is in the form of a bibliographic essay. Works are organized by subject and evaluated in relation to other materials on the subject. The guide describes approximately 1,500 items and, for the librarian starting a film studies collection, can serve as an important tool in building a quality collection.

Blum, Eleanor, and Frances Goins Wilhoit. 1990. *Mass Media Bibliography: An Annotated Guide to Books and Journals for Research and Reference*, 3rd ed. Urbana: University of Illinois Press. Containing almost 2,000 entries of print materials published before 1987, this bibliography updates previous editions of Eleanor Blum's *Basic Books in the Mass Media* (Urbana: University of Illinois Press, 1972; 1980). As the authors point out, "It is worth noting the growth of the broadcasting and film sections in this edition, reflecting the increasing importance of and interest in these areas" (vii). The chapter on "Film" includes 400 entries arranged alphabetically by author or title. The annotations for each title give a concise assessment of the work reviewed. Important film studies resources are also listed under "Bibliographies," "Directories and Handbooks," and "Indexes to Mass Communication Literature."

Calmes, Alan. 1990. "New Preservation Concern: Video Recordings." *Newsletter*, Commission on Preservation and Access, 22 (April): 5–6. For film studies librarians faced with a medium that is short-lived and requires equipment that is quickly becoming obsolete, Alan Calmes's article contains important information. He offers clear guidelines for storing, handling, and preserving video recordings. He also recommends copying video images to black and white motion picture film in order to guarantee longevity (100+ years).

Dewing, Martha, ed. 1988. *Home Video in Libraries: How Libraries Buy and Circulate Prerecorded Home Video.* White Plains, NY: Knowledge Industry. In the first part of *Home Video in Libraries*, Martha Dewing (publisher and editor of *Children's Video Report*) has compiled perspectives on video in libraries from a librarian, a large video publisher, a small video publisher, and a video distributor. The chapter by Randy Pitman (publisher and editor of *The Video Librarian*) offers librarians a brief overview of video in libraries and may serve as an introduction to problems librarians face in collecting video. The remainder of the book reflects the results of a 1987 survey of more than 840 public libraries with video collections and includes 12 library case studies, which discuss philosophy, selection policy, cataloging, patron access, budget, hardware, and software.

Fisher, Kim N. 1986. *On the Screen: A Film, Television, and Video Research Guide.* Littleton, CO: Libraries Unlimited. Kim N. Fisher (former chair of the Arts Section of the Association of College and Research Libraries) has designed a very accessible research guide "to acquaint the student, researcher, librarian, and anyone interested in motion pictures and television with the important English-language reference works in these fields" (xii). Academic and public librarians alike will benefit from Fisher's selections (publications from the early 1960s through 1985). Special sections on core periodicals, research centers and archives, and computer-assisted databases are particularly beneficial to the librarian new to the field.

Gordon, Paul L., ed. 1983. *The Book of Film Care.* Rochester, NY: Eastman Kodak. Written for a variety of audiences (from film buff to film lab technician and projectionist), this comprehensive work assists its readers by delineating for each group which chapters should be consulted. Chapters suggested for the film archivist and the librarian with a film collection include "Storage and Preservation of Film," "Handling and Maintenance of Processed Film," "Rejuvenation/Film Treatment," and

"Restoration/Duplication." Appendices include a bibliography and a "Film-handlers' Checklist." Practical information is clearly written and well organized. Even librarians new to film studies collections will be able to understand the technical data presented with easy-to-follow explanations.

Jones, Craig A. 1983. *16mm Motion Picture Film Maintenance Manual.* Consortium of University Film Centers, Monograph Series no. 1. Dubuque, IA: Kendall/Hunt. Craig Jones (Audio Visual Services, Utah State University) clearly describes four critical areas of film maintenance over which a librarian has some control—storage, handling, inspection, and cleaning and lubrication—and an area—damage—over which a librarian has very little control but is responsible for correcting. Types of damage are characterized, and common ways to repair film are discussed. Step-by-step instructions and clear illustrations make the section on repair work easy to follow. The author includes samples of film damage evaluation forms and a point system for determining film damage limitations. An eight-page glossary will also help librarians unacquainted with the field to understand complex terminology.

Julien, Don, and Beverly Owen. 1986. "Watching Movies: A Guide to Video Review Sources." *Collection Building* 7.3: 10–13. According to Don Julien (a head librarian) and Beverly Owen (a media specialist), "[t]raditional library review sources have not ignored the videocassette. They have, however, been rather selective in what gets reviewed. The videos selected tend to be similar to the special-interest, educational, or cultural films traditionally reviewed over the last twenty years" (13). To counteract this, the authors offer credible sources for video reviews. For the librarian wanting to build a video collection, the authors also offer resources on the feature film industry, since a careful monitoring of these tools can guide future video selections.

Loughney, Katharine. 1991. *Film, Television, and Video Periodicals: A Comprehensive Annotated List.* Garland Reference Library of the Humanities, vol. 1032. New York: Garland. Katharine Loughney (a former librarian at the Library of Congress's Motion Picture, Broadcasting, and Recorded Sound Division) has arranged alphabetically by title over 1,100 serial publications devoted to moving image materials. Scholarly and non-scholarly periodicals are listed. Each entry includes country of publication; title changes or variations; publisher's name, address, and telephone number; frequency of publication; ISSN number and, when available, Online Computer Library Center (OCLC) information; publication span; short description of scope; and Library of Congress and Dewey Classification numbers. Eight special indexes provide in-depth access to the titles. This work could serve as both a comprehensive reference source and a collection development guide.

Lunde, Erik S., and Douglas A. Noverr, eds. 1989. *Film History.* New York:

Markus Wiener. Edited by two Michigan State University faculty members who teach courses in film studies, the book consists of thirty-one course syllabi contributed by twenty-nine U.S. scholars who represent twenty-three institutions. The syllabi are divided into three categories (film history, film genres, and European and world film) and include the titles of films, basic texts, and supplementary readings used in the courses. As the authors state in their "Introduction and Overview," "[w]hat is instantly impressive about these syllabi are the length and breadth of the reading and screening lists" (3). For a librarian establishing a film studies collection, these lists can be unique collection development tools.

Maillet, Lucienne. 1991. *Subject Control of Film and Video: A Comparison of Three Methods*. Chicago: American Library Association. A professor of library and information scene, Lucienne Maillet analyzes the headings assigned to 100 educational films under 3 different systems: PREserved Context Index System (PRECIS), the *Library of Congress Subject Headings* (eighth edition), and the subject index to *The NICEM Index to 16mm Educational Films* (seventh edition). After a detailed report, the author offers her findings and recommendations. Librarians interested in this topic may also want to consult Sheila Intner and William E. Studwell's *Subject Access to Films and Videos* (Lake Crystal, MN: Soldier Creek Press, 1992).

Manchel, Frank. 1990. *Film Study: An Analytical Bibliography*. Rutherford, NJ: Fairleigh Dickinson University Press. This monumental, encyclopedic four-volume work is, as Howard Suber states in his "Foreword," "a far more ambitious, far more detailed, and far more comprehensive work than Dr. Manchel's earlier publication" (23), *Film Study: A Reference Guide* (Rutherford, NJ: Fairleigh Dickinson University Press, 1973). The fourth volume exemplifies the scope of the project with nine appendices and seven indexes. The entire work discusses in depth 500 books, annotates 2,000, and references almost 4,000. The author's introductions to each chapter serve as a history of film. The chapter "Approaching Film History" and the appendices, including a glossary and selected lists of periodicals, publishers, and video distributors, offer the librarian launching a film studies collection a wealth of information.

Miller, Jerome K. 1987. *Using Copyrighted Videocassettes in Classrooms, Libraries, and Training Centers*, 2nd ed. Copyright Information Bulletin no. 3. Friday Harbor, WA: Copyright Information Services. Jerome K. Miller, a librarian with a doctorate in educational media, opens his book with a disclaimer: "The opinions contained herein reflect the author's informed opinion, but do not constitute legal advice" (v). Nevertheless, this short work clearly and succinctly explains copyright regulations for video performances in libraries in light of *Columbia Pictures. v. Redd Horne* and *Columbia Pictures v. Aveco*. The chapter on "Librarians' Rights" will be especially important to librarians who manage film and video collections and who deal with copyright issues on a regular basis. Miller makes the seemingly incomprehensible comprehensible.

Pitman, Randy, and Elliott Swanson. 1990. *Video Movies: A Core Collection for Libraries*. Santa Barbara, CA: ABC-CLIO. This useful annotated bibliography of 500 video movie titles (selected by the editor and publisher of *Video Librarian* and the head of branch services at a regional library) could serve as a starting point for librarians interested in developing a diverse and balanced video movie collection. The list reflects an overall history of cinema, a sampling of the best of the major genres in film, a representation of the work of the best directors, and a popular collection. (Only made-for-TV movies and foreign films available only in English-dubbed versions were excluded.) Each entry includes key data about the film and a critical synopsis. Lists of video movies by genre, year of release, and director, as well as closed-captioned video movies, conclude the work.

Rehrauer, George. 1982. *The Macmillan Film Bibliography: A Critical Guide to the Literature of the Motion Picture*. New York: Macmillan. George Rehrauer, author of *Cinema Booklist* (Metuchen, NJ: Scarecrow, 1972) and *The Film User's Handbook: A Basic Manual for Managing Library Film Services* (New York: Bowker, 1975), compiled this monumental two-volume film bibliography. This comprehensive work of 7,000 annotated citations (all English language) will be of benefit to almost all librarians and researchers in film studies. Extensive indexes provide access by subject, author, and script. Although the main focus of the bibliography is books, periodicals are briefly covered.

Scholtz, James C. 1989. *Developing and Maintaining Video Collections in Libraries*. Santa Barbara, CA: ABC-CLIO. Although the author focuses primarily on public libraries, "[t]he purpose of this book is to provide librarians with a how-to manual concerning video collection and service development that will give them all the basic tools necessary for establishing a new collection or redirecting an existing one" (xvii). Information on all major aspects of managing a video collection is clearly presented, easy to follow, and very pragmatic. Diagrams for workplace design and display units, a guide to selecting and maintaining video equipment, a sample collection development policy, and an example of guidelines for the use of copyrighted video programs are illustrative of the book's practical orientation.

Scholtz, James C. 1991. *Video Policies and Procedures for Libraries*. Santa Barbara, CA: ABC-CLIO. An outgrowth of James C. Scholtz's *Developing and Maintaining Video Collections in Libraries* (Santa Barbara, CA: ABC-CLIO, 1989), the purpose of this text is "to provide public and school librarians with a sampling of video policies and procedures that present alternative methods, operations, and applications for video service" (xiv). The author presents elements of collection and selection policy statements, circulation and use policies and procedures, and copyright

issues and policies and offers samples of each from various libraries.
He also discusses intellectual freedom issues and policies. For any public
or school librarian—as well as any academic librarian—trying to create
and manage a video collection, Scholtz's book will be a worthwhile aid.

MUSIC

Background Sources

Bradley, Carol June. 1990. *American Music Librarianship: A Biographical
and Historical Survey*. Westport, CT: Greenwood Press. Carol June
Bradley's work is a significant contribution to the study of music librarianship in the United States. The survey is filled with vivid biographies not
only of early pioneers but also of lesser known but equally important
figures in the history of the profession. Based on extensive interviews
and research of published and unpublished documents, Bradley's text is
divided into five sections. For any American music librarian, this work is
an essential history of the field.

Cary, Tristram. 1992. *Dictionary of Musical Technology*. Westport, CT:
Greenwood Press. A composer and teacher, Tristram Cary breaks down
the complexities of modern music technology, since "[t]here is no doubt
at all that the future of music lies largely with electronics" (xxxi). For
librarians unfamiliar with "envelope shapers" or "analogue synthesis
techniques," this one-volume work can act as a decoder.

Mann, Alfred, ed. 1989. *Modern Music Librarianship: Essays in Honor of Ruth
Watanabe*. Festschrift Series no. 8. New York: Pendragon. This *festschrift*
honors Ruth Watanabe's forty years of service to the Eastman School of
Music's Sibley Music Library of the University of Rochester and her
contribution to modern music librarianship. It consists of a series of
scholarly essays on music library administration and organization. Experts
in the field write on topics such as conservation and preservation, new
technology, collection development, and technical services. The work
incorporates old and new approaches to music administration and
management and reflects the complexities of modern music librarianship.
For anyone seeking to gain perspective on the field, it holds a cache of
information.

Rebman, Elizabeth. 1993. "Music." In *The Humanities and the Library*, 2nd ed.,
edited by Nena Couch and Nancy Allen, pp. 132–172. Chicago: American
Library Association. Elizabeth Rebman (reference librarian in the Music
Library and lecturer in cataloging in the School of Library and Information
Studies at the University of California, Berkeley) has produced a very
thorough and detailed introduction to music, music collections, and music
librarianship. For any librarian unacquainted with the field, this chapter
would be an excellent place to begin gathering information. The author
clearly and simply defines terminology that might be new to the reader,

yet offers sophisticated insights and observations on the field. Electronic formats are included in the section on music literature.

Sadie, Stanley, ed. 1980. *The New Grove Dictionary of Music and Musicians.* Washington, DC: Grove's Dictionaries of Music. Although a bit daunting for a newcomer to the field, this work is an essential resource for the study of music. First published in 1879–1889, this 1980 twenty-volume dictionary is comprehensive, containing signed entries on music history, theory, practice, and terms. Biographical entries for individuals include their "Works" and "Writings," as well as "Bibliography" of materials about them. The section on music libraries includes an introduction to and history of music libraries, as well as a survey of music libraries throughout the world.

Thorin, Suzanne E., and Carole Franklin Vidali, comps. 1984. *The Acquisition and Cataloging of Music and Sound Recordings: A Glossary.* MLA Technical Reports no. 11. Canton, MA: Music Library Association. This work is divided into two parts—definitions for terms used in the bibliographic description of music (primarily printed and manuscript material) and definitions for terms specific to sound recordings. The text may be useful not only for accomplished music librarians but also for librarians lacking a music education who are responsible for managing all or part of a music collection. Only two types of terms are excluded from the work: those that can be found in standard music dictionaries and those abbreviations for many thematic indexes and catalogs used by the Library of Congress in cataloging an individual composer's works.

Management Tools

Bryant, Eric Thomas, with the assistance of Guy A. Marco. 1985. *Music Librarianship: A Practical Guide*, 2nd ed. Metuchen, NJ: Scarecrow. The first edition of Eric Thomas Bryant's *Music Librarianship: A Practical Guide* was published in London in 1959 and intended primarily for British public librarians. As noted music librarian Ruth Watanabe states in her "Foreword" to this second edition, this book, too, is addressed primarily to British public librarians, but "discusses broad topics of universal concern from which public and academic librarians in both Canada and the United States may also profit" (ix). The chapter on "Music Library Administration" may prove especially helpful to new managers of music collections since it offers practical and realistic guidelines on matters from staffing to stationery. An extensive bibliography is included.

Byrne, Frank P., Jr. 1987. *A Practical Guide to the Music Library: Its Function, Organization, & Maintenance.* Cleveland: Ludwig Music. The title description of this book as a *practical* guide to the music library is accurate. However, this hands-on account is geared toward one type of music library, the performing music library, which exists to serve a regularly performing ensemble (for example, a band or orchestra) rather than to support reference and research activities. Questions unique to performing music libraries, in areas such as cataloging, storage, and control, are dealt with in a straightforward manner. Whether writing on breaking down concert folders, choosing and using a photocopier, or software recommendations, the author's style is both informal and informative and may prove helpful to music librarians serving other types of clientele.

Cassaro, James P., ed. 1989. *Planning and Caring for Library Audio Facilities.* MLA Technical Report no. 17. Canton,MA: Music Library Association. This valuable report consists of five essays that deal with the four basic components of planning an audio facility renovation or building: space, equipment, preservation,and new technology. Since the essays are written in clear, concise prose, even those librarians usually intimidated by technical issues will find this report easy to follow and helpful in demythologizing the complexities of new audio technology. Of particular interest to managers are essays addressing an ongoing music library issue, hands-on versus hands-off designs; the preservation of audio hardware; and types of equipment used in hands-on situations.

Duckles, Vincent H., and Michael A. Keller. 1988. *Music Reference and Research Materials: An Annotated Bibliography*, 4th ed. New York: Schirmer. As the introduction to the fourth edition states, "Music librarians and general reference librarians should find this classified bibliography helpful in pursuing their dual responsibilities of building and interpreting library collections" (vii). The late Vincent H. Duckles (president of the Music Library Association from 1960 to 1962) and Michael A. Keller (who succeeded Duckles as head of the University of California at Berkeley's Music Library) amassed over 3,200 entries arranged by category (for example, dictionaries, encyclopedia, histories, etc.), making this an invaluable reference source. Author, subject, and titles indexes are given.

Fling, Roger Michael. 1981. *Shelving Capacity in the Music Library.* MLA Technical Reports no. 7. Philadelphia: Music Library Association. This short (thirty-six pages) report provides essential information on shelving requirements for materials typically found in music libraries. The author gives statistics and formulas for the shelving of music books, scores, and sound recordings. Since music libraries have different storage needs than other libraries, this monograph offers data that does not usually appear in library space planning documents. For the librarian looking for information on shelving music materials, this is the place to turn.

Fling, Robert Michael, ed. 1983. *A Basic Music Library: Essential Scores and Books.* Compiled by the Music Library Association Committee on Basic Music Collection under the direction of Pauline S. Bayne. Chicago: American Library Association. This work is designed "to serve as a buying guide or selection tool for those who have the responsibility for collecting music library materials in small and medium-sized libraries, whether public or academic" (v). Recommendations for a basic music library are arranged in six categories: score anthologies, performing editions, vocal scores, instrumental methods and studies, and musical literature. Only English-language works are included. An index of sixty-eight pages makes access to titles very easy. For a librarian new to music selection, this is a good place to start.

Robinson, Doris. 1989. *Music and Dance Periodicals: An International Directory & Guidebook*. Voorheesville, NY: Peri Press. See entry under "Dance."

Rosenberg, Kenyon C. 1990. *A Basic Classical and Operatic Recordings Collection on Compact Discs for Libraries: A Buying Guide*. Metuchen, NJ: Scarecrow. The author of *A Basic Classical and Operatic Recordings Collection for Libraries* (Metuchen, NJ: Scarecrow, 1987) provides public and academic librarians with useful suggestions for forming the nucleus of a classical music and opera collection on compact discs. The selections are arranged alphabetically by last name of the composer. Works are denoted as "useful in medium and large public and academic libraries" or "recommended only for large and academic libraries" (xii). Codes are given to indicate whether a recording was made from an analog or digital master and whether the remastering was analog or digital. Short descriptions are humorously offered by the author for "Performers: The Good, the Bad, and the Boring."

Shaw, Sarah Jean, and Lauralee Shiere. 1984. *Sheet Music Cataloging and Processing: A Manual*. MLA Technical Reports no. 15. Canton, MA: Music Library Association. This short technical manual is intended for music catalogers and support staff. Prepared for the Brown University Library Title II-C Sheet Music Cataloging Project, the text describes cataloging sheet music as rare books, according to *Anglo-American Cataloguing Rules* second edition (AACR2), using Library of Congress subject headings and classification, and the Machine Readable Cataloging (MARC) scores format for input to the Research Libraries Information Network (RLIN) scores database. The cataloging detailed is extremely complex (forty-two data elements and seventeen access points), but librarians can still benefit from learning about this approach to the MARC scores format, even if they choose not to treat sheet music as special collections materials. (The MARC coding procedures used are transferable to the OCLC system.)

Smiraglia, Richard P. 1989. *Music Cataloging: The Bibliographic Control of Printed and Recorded Music in Libraries*. Englewood, CO: Libraries Unlimited. The author designed this work as a textbook "to introduce the field of music cataloging to students of music librarianship, students of cataloging, and/or music librarians or general catalogers who find themselves in need of a basic explanation of the prevalent practices in the bibliographic control of music materials" (xi). The author has limited his coverage of music materials to scores and musical sound recordings and his audience to those with a basic musical background. Most chapters include suggested readings. A glossary and selected bibliography complete the work. The author's approach is clear and easy to follow.

Wursten, Richard B., comp. 1990. *In Celebration of Revised 780: Music in the Dewey Decimal Classification, Edition 20.* MLA Technical Report no. 19. Canton, MA: Music Library Association. Constant dissatisfaction with the Dewey Decimal Classification for music has led to numerous revisions of the scheme. The most successful appears to be the latest edition (1989). This report contains "the first published collection of writings on the revised schedule for Music in *DDC* 20" (20). The book's six contributed essays consider five aspects of the revised 780: its history and development, physical characteristics and practical applications, use in online music subject retrieval, effect on shelf arrangement in a large university, and implications for public libraries. Since, as Richard B. Wursten reports, over 85 percent of all libraries in the United States and Canada use the Dewey scheme, this report is an essential resource for those managing music collections.

THEATER

Background Sources

Boulanger, Norman C., and Warren C. Lounsbury. 1992. *Theatre Lighting from A to Z.* Seattle: University of Washington Press. The world of theater lighting is filled with terms unknown to many librarians. In addition to providing definitions and historical background, the book offers explanations that will help the librarian understand the practical application and use of the terms. Written by two emeritus theater professors, this encyclopedia of nearly 1,200 entries expands on the treatment of lighting technology covered in Warren C. Lounsbury and Norman C. Boulanger's *Theatre Backstage from A to Z* (Seattle: University of Washington Press, 1989). For example, the section on "Lighting Practice," which covers aesthetics, properties and classifications of lighting, as well as instrument positions, can serve as a primer on the subject.

Hartnoll, Phyllis, ed. 1985. *The Oxford Companion to the Theatre*, 4th ed., reprinted with corrections. New York: Oxford University Press. Phyllis Hartnoll (editor of *The Oxford Companion to the Theatre* since the first edition was published in 1951) has amassed detailed information on all aspects of theater, from theater buildings, actors and actresses, writers, directors, and companies to makeup. Individuals instrumental in the development of theater collections in the United States, such as Rosamond Gilder and George Freedley, have also been included in the work. Given the work's historical perspective, a librarian can use this tool to easily obtain an education in almost 2,000 years of theater history. An extensive bibliography is included.

Herbert, Ian, ed. 1981. *Who's Who in the Theatre: A Biographical Record of the*

Contemporary Stage, 17th ed. Detroit, MI: Gale. *Who's Who in the Theatre* offers a capsule look at prominent figures in contemporary British and American theater. The work is divided into two volumes. One volume consists of casting information from playbills for all major London and New York productions during the period from 1976 to 1979. The other volume includes about 2,400 biographies, consisting of revisions of entries for individuals included in the previous edition and additional new names. For librarians unfamiliar with British and American actors, actresses, directors, playwrights, and producers, the biographical volume will be especially important.

Lounsbury, Warren C., and Norman Boulanger. 1989. *Theatre Backstage from A to Z*, 3rd ed., revised and expanded. Seattle: University of Washington Press. Understanding the technical elements behind a theatrical production is often a difficult undertaking. This reference work compiles information on staging and theatrical technology, clarifying terminology for the uninitiated librarian as well as the initiated. A brief introductory survey of stage scenery and lighting practices in the United States is offered, followed by definitions and explanations of historical as well as contemporary components of theatrical sound, lighting, and scenery. For, as the authors state in the case of the wind machine, "yesterday's answers to the same problems are still valid" (201).

Trapido, Joel, ed. 1985. *An International Dictionary of Theatre Language.* Westport, CT: Greenwood Press. Theater has a language of its own. With assistance from numerous contributors, Joel Trapido (Emeritus Professor of Drama at the University of Hawaii at Manoa) has compiled theater terms from throughout the world. "More specifically, the *Dictionary* enters some 10,000 English terms, as well as 5,000 from more than 60 foreign languages. The aim has been to find and define any theatre term which has been used by readers or speakers of English" (xxv). In addition to the breadth of entries, librarians will also be interested in "A Brief History of Theatre Glossaries and Dictionaries" at the beginning of the book and a forty-six-page bibliography at the end.

Management Tools

Bailey, Claudia Jean. 1983. *A Guide to Reference and Bibliography for Theatre Research*, 2nd ed. Columbus: Ohio State University Libraries. Claudia Jean Bailey (librarian and associate professor at the Community College of Rhode Island) compiled this guide "to provide the students and researchers in the theatre arts with a basic list of both general and specialized sources of reference and bibliographical information" (ix). The book's 654 titles are divided into 2 parts—general reference, and theater and drama (the second part is subdivided into theater arts, drama, and literature). Although the selections included were published through the fall of 1979, many titles are useful for retrospective collection development. Continuing the work pioneered by Bailey is Irene Shaland's *American Theater and Drama Research: An Annotated Guide to Information Sources, 1945–1990* (Jefferson, NC: McFarland, 1991). Shaland's guide is a useful resource for post–World War II research.

Bolton, Helen K. 1989. "Development and Use of Theatre Databases." In *Advances in Library Administration and Organization: A Research Annual*, vol. 8, edited by Gerard B. McCabe and Bernard Kreissman, pp. 131–144. Greenwich, CT: JAI Press. The author explores the state of computer-assisted theater research. Specialized databases for theater research are described, examined, and evaluated. The essay is particularly helpful to those new to the field since it covers both privately and commercially developed theater databases. The author gives a historical perspective on the development of databases in the field. She offers reasons for the slower growth of databases in theater and other performing arts, as contrasted to their swifter development in other fields. "Observations, Discussion, and Conclusions" is well written and informative.

Hitchcock, Leonard A. 1989. "The Play's the Thing . . . If You Can Find It! An Assessment of Play Indexes." *RQ* 29.2 (Winter): 248–259. Leonard A. Hitchcock (humanities librarian at Idaho State University), frustrated after years of using play indexes ineffectively to find copies of plays for patrons, took on the task of evaluating the various indexes and developing a strategy for play index use that "will provide some assurance of efficiency and effectiveness" (248). After conducting his study of the major play indexes, he succeeded in devising two very simple rules for searching play indexes. These rules can instantly relieve any librarian "sallying forth to tangle with these indexes . . . not an enterprise that fills the average reference librarian's heart with glee" (248).

Howard, John T., Jr. 1982. *A Bibliography of Theatre Technology: Acoustics and Sound, Lighting, Properties, and Scenery*. Westport, CT: Greenwood Press. The four technical components of theater covered in this bibliography—acoustics and sound, lighting, properties, and scenery—are essential ingredients of any production. The author (an assistant professor of Theatre Studies at Mount Holyoke College) lists, alphabetically by title, over 5,700 references in these four areas, as well as a fifth—"Research Materials and Collections." A subject index of each of the four sections and an author index complete the work. For the librarian developing a theater collection, this work fills a vacuum in theater bibliographies.

Karp, Rashelle S., and Bernard S. Schlessinger. 1989. "A Core Reference Theatre Arts Collection for Research." In *Advances in Library Administration and Organization: A Research Annual*, vol. 8, edited by Gerard B. McCabe and Bernard Kreissman, pp. 215–240. Greenwich, CT: JAI Press. The authors used an interesting and exacting methodology to identify a valuable core research collection of English-language reference materials and periodicals on traditional stage drama. After compiling a list of nearly 500 sources from 5 standard selection tools, they compared these works to those in theater arts research collections at 2 public libraries and 2 academic libraries. The items that were listed in at least 4 of the standard selection tools and held in each of the 4 selected libraries were identified as potentials for the core collection. This pared-down list was then submitted for review to a group of 5 subject specialists. The specialists deemed 54 titles on the list "necessary" or "indispensable" and added 6 new sources, forming a final count of 60 titles.

Miletich, Leo N. 1991. "The Play's the Thing: 72 Years of Award-Winning Modern Dramas for Your Collection." *Collection Management* 14.3/4: 149–161. For those librarians "who desire a guide to the most honored of modern dramatic works, the following lists will serve as a roadmap" (150). Leo N. Miletich (a free-lance writer who is an administrative assistant at the University of Texas at El Paso Library) has compiled a core collection of modern dramas that have won one of Broadway's three major drama awards: the Pulitzer Prize, the Antoinette Perry or Tony Award, and the New York Drama Critics Circle Award. From the very first award through those given in 1990, the original publisher is cited for most winners, while anthologies are also listed for some of the older and perhaps out-of-print works.

Nemchek, Lee R. 1981. "Problems of Cataloging and Classification in Theater Librarianship." *Library Resources & Technical Services* 25 (October/December): 374–385. There is very little literature on the cataloging of theater materials. Anyone new to the field will welcome Lee R. Nemchek's article. Her goal is to examine "the limitations of existing classification systems for use with theater collections, past attempts to develop special systems, patterns in cataloging nonbook theatrical memorabilia, and current trends toward standardization" (375). Although the findings of her survey are not encouraging, the role of library associations and of increased computerization do present hope.

Snow, Marina. 1990. "Theatre Arts Collection Assessment." *Collection Management* 12.3/4: 69–89. Marina Snow (Theatre Arts Subject Specialist at California State University at Sacramento) did an assessment of the theater arts collection at her university in 1987. Her report is important since theater librarianship lacks "professional standards and guidelines for theatre arts collections" (70). Snow's work may serve as a model for other institutions that want to evaluate their theater collections. The author used "collection-centered" measurements (such as the *National Shelflist Count*, checklists for periodicals and reference books, and approval plans) and "client-centered" measurements (such as a faculty survey).

Woods, Alan. 1983. "The McDowell Research Classification System for the Cataloguing of Scene and Costume Designs." In *Performing Arts Resources,* vol. 8, edited by Ginnine Cocuzza and Barbara Naomi Cohen-Stratyner, pp. 30–35. New York: Theatre Library Association. Alan Woods describes a classification system devised by Dr. John H. McDowell at the Ohio State University Theatre Research Institute in the 1950s. McDowell's Research Classification System is based on an iconographic approach, especially applicable to scene and costume designs, theater plans, and technical drawings. Although the system displays the idiosyncrasies of its author (for example, personal biases in the geography category), it groups together like materials and includes various cross-reference catalogs that provide valuable links to materials in the collection. While the system, according to the author, works "extremely well for pictorial material, it does not work at all for the textual" (34).

Index

About the Editor
and Contributors

CAROLYN A. SHEEHY is Clare and Lucy Oesterle Director of Library Services at North Central College. Formerly, she was assistant professor/reference librarian (head of department) at the University of Illinois, Chicago, and prior to that, administrative curator of special collections at The Newberry Library, where she helped launch the Chicago Dance Collection. She holds an undergraduate degree from Scripps College and master's degrees in dance from Mills College and in library and information studies from Northern Illinois University. Her publications include works on the performing arts, archives and manuscripts, and reference and information services (including "Reference and Information Service" in *Academic Libraries in Urban and Metropolitan Areas: A Management Handbook*, edited by Gerard B. McCabe, 1992). She served as secretary of the Arts Section of the Association of College and Research Libraries and on the Dance Advisory Panel of the Illinois Arts Council and the Board of Directors of the Chicago Dance Coalition. She currently holds several positions of responsibility in local, state, and national library associations.

ROMAINE AHLSTROM is manager of the Arts and Recreation Department at the Los Angeles Public Library, where she has worked for many years, first as a children's librarian and then as senior librarian in the Literature and Philology Department and as collection development manager. She received an undergraduate degree in English literature from Brown University and an M.S. in L.S. from the University of Washington.

KRISTINE R. BRANCOLINI is head of Media and Reserve Services and film studies librarian at Indiana University. She holds a B.A. in English from Scripps College and an M.L.S. from Indiana University. She completed her coursework for a Ph.D. in instructional systems technology at Indiana University. Her most recent publication is "Video Collections in Academic Libraries" in *Video Collection Management and Development: A Multi-type Library Perspective*, edited by Gary Handman (Greenwood Press, forthcoming).

NENA COUCH is the curator of the library of the Jerome Lawrence and Robert E. Lee Theatre Research Institute, The Ohio State University. She was formerly project archivist for the Francis Robinson Collection at Vanderbilt University. She holds B.A. and M.M. degrees in music from George Peabody College and an M.L.S. degree from Vanderbilt University. Her publications include works on the humanities and the performing arts. A member of the board of the Theatre Library Association, she is a dancer and dance historian.

ROSALINDA I. HACK is division chief of the Visual and Performing Arts Division of the Chicago Public Library.

BRIGITTE J. KUEPPERS is special collections librarian and archivist at the Arts Library, University of California, Los Angeles, where she has collection development responsibility for twentieth-century American theater. She worked as a theater librarian and archivist at the Billy Rose Theatre Collection at the New York Public Library from 1970 to 1977 and at the Shubert Archive, New York, from 1976 to 1986. She has an M.L.S. and an M.A. in Theater from New York University.

HELENE G. MOCHEDLOVER is head of the Literature and Fiction Department of the Los Angeles Public Library. She has written on indexing plays appearing in collections published between 1900 and 1985.

RICHARD SCHWEGEL is head of the Music Information Center of the Chicago Public Library. He has a master's degree in music history from Northwestern University and has been chair of the Public Libraries Committee of the Music Library Association.

BEVERLY L. TEACH is associate director for media resources at the Center for Media and Teaching Resources, Indiana University, where she has worked since 1970. Her responsibilities include the video/film library and media equipment services. She holds M.L.S. and Ph.D. degrees in Library and Information Science from Indiana University. She has served as president and member of the boards of directors of the Consortium of College and University Media Centers (CCUMC) and the American Film and Video Association (AFVA) and as editor for two editions of the *Educational Film/Video Locator*. She sits on several advisory boards and regularly serves as a juror for film/video festivals.